THE MISSING MATISSE

THE
MISSING
MATISSE

Pierre H. Matisse

**TYNDALE®
MOMENTUM**

An Imprint of
Tyndale House Publishers, Inc.

Visit Tyndale online at www.tyndale.com.

Visit Tyndale Momentum online at www.tyndalemomentum.com.

Tyndale Momentum and the Tyndale Momentum logo are registered trademarks of Tyndale House Publishers, Inc. Tyndale Momentum is an imprint of Tyndale House Publishers, Inc.

The Missing Matisse

Copyright © 2016 by Pierre H. Matisse. All rights reserved.

Cover artwork and interior illustrations copyright © 2016 by Pierre H. Matisse. All rights reserved.

Interior photographs of the author with Si Robertson and the Robertson family copyright © Korie Robertson. Used with permission.

Interior photograph of Henri Matisse in his studio copyright © Michel Sima/Rue des Archives/Granger, NYC. All rights reserved.

Interior photograph of the author's baptism copyright © John Howard. Used with permission.

Unless otherwise noted, all interior images are from the personal collection of the author and are used with permission.

Author photograph copyright © John B. Olivo. All rights reserved.

Designed by Pierre H. Matisse and Dean H. Renninger

Edited by Bonne Steffen

Published in association with the literary agency of The John Howard Agency, 102 Yellowood Drive, West Monroe, LA 71291.

Unless otherwise indicated, all Scripture quotations are taken from the *Holy Bible*, New Living Translation, copyright © 1996, 2004, 2015 by Tyndale House Foundation. Used by permission of Tyndale House Publishers, Inc., Carol Stream, Illinois 60188. All rights reserved.

Scripture quotations marked KJV are taken from the *Holy Bible*, King James Version.

The stories in this book are about real people and real events, but some names have been omitted or changed for the privacy of the individuals involved. Dialogue has been recreated to the author's best recollection. In addition, culturally offensive language as well as some profanity is used occasionally in these pages, contrary to the normal editorial standards of Tyndale House Publishers. In order to accurately reflect the dialect of the wartime period depicted, we have permitted such instances to stand.

Library of Congress Cataloging-in-Publication Data
Names: Matisse, Pierre H., date, author.
Title: The missing Matisse : a memoir / Pierre H. Matisse.
Description: Carol Stream, IL : Tyndale House Publishers, Inc., 2016. |
    Includes bibliographical references.
Identifiers: LCCN 2016031504 | ISBN 9781496413833 (hc)
Subjects: LCSH: Matisse, Pierre H., date. | Matisse, Henri,
    1869-1954—Family. | Artists—United States—Biography. | French
    Americans—Biography. | Christian biography—United States.
Classification: LCC N6537.M3945 A2 2016 | DDC 759.4 [B] —dc23 LC record available at
    https://lccn.loc.gov/2016031504

Printed in the United States of America

22   21   20   19   18   17   16
7   6   5   4   3   2   1

First and foremost, I would like to thank God and dedicate this book to Him. Now I've come to the realization that He has always been there for me, and He's always had my back.

This book is further dedicated to Tata, Papa, Maman, all my grandfathers, my dear wife Jeanne, and all our children, grandchildren, and great-grandchildren. Also to the numerous good people who have helped me in difficult times, to survive and prosper along the way.

Last but not least, this book is dedicated to all the children in the world who suffer and should not.

Contents

Introduction

I AM RENÉ PIERRE LOUIS HENRI MATISSE.

When I was a young child, my mother and father would often tell me the story of my names before I went to sleep. The first decades of my life were a journey with many surprising twists and turns—through the happy early years growing up with my artistic family to the harrowing years of living in Nazi-occupied France. When I was twelve years old, everything changed—my most prized name, the one that held family, history, and promise for the future, was torn from me in a single abrupt moment amid the surrounding destruction and chaos of World War II. For most of the rest of my life I felt alone, until I discovered an astonishing truth that allowed me to see my life in a new light. My quest was over. And, in the end, I knew I had never really been alone.

My story is complex, but I tell it simply. This is how it happened.

Prologue

FOUR COLORS, TRAGEDY, AND ADVENTURES

*If it makes you laugh, if it makes you cry, if it rips
your heart out, that's a good picture.*

EDDIE ADAMS

IT IS JULY 1939, and I am a budding artist at eleven years old. It's not surprising, since both of my parents are French artists. My father, Jean Matisse, is a sculptor, and my mother, Louise Milhau Matisse, is a talented painter and ceramist.

For a month, my mother has been trying to teach me the theory of colors. She graduated from the prestigious École Nationale Supérieure des Beaux-Arts in Paris, but her lessons with me fall on deaf ears. I can't make sense of the color wheel she keeps referring to, and in my expert opinion, her explanations of chromatic what-have-you and primary and secondary somethings get in the way of my artistic creativity.

I have my own ideas. For me, the more tubes of colors, the greater the artist. If an artist has ten tubes, he is only a ten-bit painter.

Whenever I am sent to the art merchant on errands for my parents, I buy another glorious tube of paint for my carefully selected collection, all purchased with my savings.

With my box of thirty-plus paint tubes, I am obviously a more dedicated and talented artist than others.

If only I could afford all the Sennelier colors displayed on the shelves, then imagine what I could paint!

I can't wait to show all the colors to my grandfather Henri Matisse— the master of color. When we are in Nice, I will be getting a lesson from him.

THE SUMMER BEGINS with the promise of a very special vacation for our family of four—my father, my mother, my eight-year-old brother, Gérard, and me. My parents have planned this vacation for months. It will turn out to be the only family vacation we ever take.

During our two-month-long trip to visit all of my grandparents, we will first drive from our home in Paris to Grandfather Henri's on the French Riviera. I'm excited that we'll be in Nice on July 14, Bastille Day, to watch the spectacular fireworks for which the city is so famous.

While we travel, I will paint a few pieces to hang in the Louvre, side by side with the great masters, as nothing less will do. Like Grandfather Henri, I am an artist on my way to fame and a life of adventure.

It is a beautiful sunny day in paradise when we arrive on the French Riviera. I understand why Grandfather lives here. Everything is perfect. When I stand on the beach, I see countless boats, swimmers, and sunbathers, some enjoying French bread, cheese, and sardines. I love the smell of the sea and the fresh air with a taste of saltiness. And the light seems to shimmer off everything. I will have time to explore this later. For now, I have to prepare for my art lesson.

Gaining private access to Grandfather in his studio is like getting an audience with the pope. He is a busy man, and I am well aware it is a great favor to be granted some of his precious artistic time. So I arrive right on time, proudly carrying a box packed solid with paint tubes in every color imaginable. I have memorized some of the convoluted names of the color tubes, ready to speak the art lingo to Grandfather Henri like a pro.

His studio is on the top floor of a hotel, and I am excited to work there with him, maybe forever. Large windows overlook the Mediterranean, and easels and paintings fill the room. I find Grandfather Henri with his back to me, busy tracing a few charcoal lines on a big canvas. A model reclines on a couch, bathed in the summer light.

Grandfather turns away from the canvas when he hears my footsteps.

"Ha! So here you are, Pierre . . . the artist, hum!" he greets me, motioning to put my box on the table. Still holding his charcoal stick, he walks over and forages inside my precious box of paint tubes.

"Hum! One, French ultramarine blue; two, chrome yellow; three, vermilion; and white—this makes four colors."

He points his charcoal stick at each color, repeating, "*Bleu, jaune, rouge, et blanc. C'est tout ce que tu as besoin.*"

Wait! What did he say? Only four? That's all I'll need?

He pauses, then smiles. "I'm confiscating this box. Hum! Now you go paint with those four colors. Furthermore, I forbid you ever to buy anything else than those four colors. C'est tout."

He returns to his canvas. "End of the color lesson. Tell your mother, father, and brother that I send my love." This is the last time I will see Grandfather during this visit.

I can't believe this! My superb collection of carefully selected colors did not impress him at all. *Grand-père is getting old and losing his mind, I think.*

As I make my way down the stairs, I mutter to myself, "How can a talented artist like me paint something serious with only four miserable colors? Unheard of! This is crazy!"

Eventually I calm down and realize that this is a challenge. Because I am a man of action I will show Grandfather Henri what an artist like me can do with only four colors.

To my surprise, using only four colors has its merits. There are two definite advantages—painting becomes much less complicated, and I don't have to carry around a cumbersome box of paints. My artistic endeavors improve dramatically. How about that! I have to admit that my grandfather is not as crazy as I thought.

For the rest of the time in Nice, our family enjoys the festivities of Bastille Day and the natural beauty surrounding us.

SOON IT'S TIME to leave for Beauzelle near Toulouse to visit Grandmother Amélie Matisse, whom I have heard has recently separated from Grandfather Henri. I'm not looking forward to this part of the trip, since Grandmother Amélie rarely smiles and, for whatever reason, doesn't seem to like me. Nevertheless, I look forward to roaming the grounds of her magnificent country estate, which is surrounded by sheep pastures and cornfields. The estate itself is enclosed by high stone walls, and within the walls is a spectacular garden as well as a large wooded area at one end, where I spend most of my time.

I am disappointed that there is no sea, no beaches, no lake, no rivers, not even a small pond in Beauzelle. I am drawn to water, although it's often where I get into the most trouble.

However, the country scenery at Grandmother Amélie's is very inspiring, so I immerse myself in my painting. Thanks to Grandfather Henri's four-colors-only strategy, I have turned out a couple of small landscapes in a short period of time that I believe are pretty good.

The last week of August, we pack up the car to head for Saint-Georges-de-Didonne, where Grandfather Milhau, my mother's father, has a fantastic estate on the Atlantic Ocean. I'm tired but in good spirits. My great-aunt Tata, who is like a grandmother to me, will be there too.

Grandfather's sprawling property is just five hundred feet from the beach, with two houses, a shop where he makes navigation instruments, and a beautiful garden with flowers and vegetables.

I enjoy spending time with Grandfather Milhau because he is mechanically minded, and I take after him in that way. On one of his visits to Paris when I was about nine, I confided to my grandfather that I was working on a new project—color photography.

A few days later, Grandfather took me with him to meet the inventors Auguste and Louis Lumière, who had built an early motion-picture camera and projector called the Cinématographe. I remember one of them projecting a single photographic slide on a screen that featured his granddaughter in a *yellow* dress jumping over a *red* rosebush. Her leap had been caught in midair, the image crisp, not blurred. Grandfather marveled that the Lumières had successfully captured colorized movement in the photo.

Rats! I couldn't believe they had already achieved what I set out to do—color photography. I was both impressed and depressed. From that point going forward, I decided all my future projects would remain hush-hush until completed.

A WEEK LATER, in the late afternoon, Grandfather Milhau, with tears in his eyes, gives us the bad news. "France has declared war on Germany. This war is going to be a nasty one, a lot worse than the one in 1914," he says. It is September 3, 1939. England and France have declared war on Nazi Germany. Our wonderful world as we know it is gone forever.

Early the next day, my father and I go for a walk alone on the deserted beach. Suddenly Papa stops and looks out over the ocean as I stand beside him. For a while he says nothing. We take solace in the sound of the surf soothing our heavy hearts.

Then I hear Papa's voice, in a low tone just a decibel above the surf's relentless song. "Tomorrow I am going to war." He clears his throat. "Some soldiers will never return. I might be among the ones who never come back. Today you are not a child anymore, Pierre. War is making you a man. For you, the childhood games are over. From now on you will have to look after your mother and your brother."

Papa lights a Gauloises cigarette, takes a puff, and puts his arm around my shoulder. He keeps his eyes on the ocean, looking far off in the distance. "The time has come to be brave. Do you understand, Pierre?"

"I do, Papa."

I get my father's message, indeed I do. I've grown up with a visual history lesson around me—the Paris streets are full of crippled survivors of World War I, many missing limbs or with faces scarred from shrapnel. They are part of everyday society, and I never stare at them because it is impolite. Now I will be part of history, part of the war against the Nazis.

On this day I am proud to have been declared a man by my father at eleven years old.

What I don't know is how long this war will rage on and how many millions will suffer and die. The women, in tears, will pray to God to save their men. The men, as they leave for war, will pray to God for their loved ones and for courage. There is much that will change for me and my family. If only I could have been warned.

Pierre H. Matisse

1

FATHER AND SON

Even a minor event in the life of a child is an event
of that child's world and thus a world event.

GASTON BACHELARD

HOW FAR BACK can you remember in your childhood?

My first memory at about three and a half comes to me in exact details. This day is alive with vivid colors, the aroma of warm café au lait, and the sounds of a household in action. The golden rays of the sun stream through a large window, casting a warm light in the big dining room. It is July 4, 1931.

We are at our home in Sèvres, a place famous for its porcelain, in the southwest part of Paris.

It is breakfast time and, strangely, I am eating alone at the large antique Spanish table that is Maman's prized possession, with my brown cocker spaniel, Bouboule, at my feet. He is my best friend and an inseparable

1

companion. But usually Maman, Papa, Bouboule, and I eat breakfast together.

The maid serves me my breakfast, an *oeuf à la coque* (soft-boiled egg), toast with butter and jam, and café au lait. She is in a wild hurry as if her apron were on fire. Today nobody is paying attention to Bouboule and me. Even more unusual, Maman is nowhere to be seen.

As the maid scurries by, I ask for my mother. She abruptly tells me, "Shhh! Keep quiet."

Within minutes, the staircase at the end of the dining room becomes crowded with people going up and down. An older man with a black leather bag races up the stairs. Then this large bossy woman whom I've never seen before starts giving orders to everybody. I see Papa! He looks sick as he runs up and down the staircase carrying basins of hot water, taking the steps two at a time. With all the excitement going on, I have barely eaten. The bossy woman comes into the dining room and tells me to go outside and play in the garden with Bouboule.

Following commands has never been my strong point, or Bouboule's either. We must find out what this commotion is all about, so I slide under the table, and Bouboule quickly joins me. From our vantage point, we watch undetected as the scene unfolds. We feel the tension mounting higher and higher from moment to moment.

The large woman who has taken over the whole household is now telling my father to get out of the way. She is surely in big trouble for that! I wait breathlessly to see what happens, and I'm stunned that Papa does what she says.

Suddenly the scenario changes. People stream down the stairs and start hugging one another. There is a lot of excited talk, punctuated by laughter. My father opens a bottle that makes a loud pop, and I hear more laughing. Then somebody accidentally steps on Bouboule's paw, which is sticking out from our hideaway, and he lets out a plaintive howl. I freeze. *Our cover is blown.* Faces peer at us beneath the table, and I am coaxed out. Now everybody hugs and kisses me.

"Pierre!" Papa scoops me up in his arms and carries me straight up the stairs to my parents' bedroom. My mother is on the bed, comfortably propped up with many pillows. She is lying on her side, smiling. And wrapped in a blanket beside her is a tiny baby.

"C'est Gérard. He is your brother," Papa says.

I stare at the infant who is just minutes old. We are now a cozy family of four—Papa, Maman, Gérard, and me. My new brother is not what I expected; he is too small to play with, and I lose interest in him quickly. At least I still have Bouboule.

A FEW YEARS LATER, our family moves to Spain. We arrive on the cusp of the Spanish Revolution and reside in a home in the charming fishing village of Tossa de Mar, not far from Barcelona. Here, as a seven-year-old, my adventurous life takes off at full speed.

One night, I hear my father and two of his friends leave the house, and a few minutes later I follow. They walk along a country road, and as I trod behind, I am certain that I've concealed myself well.

Suddenly, someone grabs my arm in the dark. "What is this!" Papa says. I've been discovered.

He tells me to stay where I am. After a short discussion with his comrades, they decide to keep me with them. We are too far from home to turn back.

It is pitch dark. Then a minute or two later, the moon comes out on the other side of a cloud, and I can see the shimmering bay almost as if it were daylight. Bathed by the mysterious moonlight, the Mediterranean takes on a bright silvery color.

"Watch out," Papa says in a hushed tone. We crouch down beside the road. Soon I hear footsteps coming in our direction.

"Let's hide here. Kneel down in the ditch, behind this big rock. Be silent. Not a sound."

Papa is leading this adventure. His friends furtively hide behind other large boulders while my father holds me tightly in his arms. First, we hear only guttural Spanish voices. Judging by the sounds, there are two of them. One is laughing. These are two *guardias civiles*, Spanish policemen.

The two men walk so close to us that I can clearly see the texture and patina of their black cocked hats shining in the full moonlight. I even smell the pungent garlic sausage mixed with cheap red wine on the fatter policeman's breath when he burps loudly a couple of times. Papa holds me close up against him and puts his hand over my mouth to keep me quiet. For a while we hear their heavy footsteps crushing the gravel in the road leading down to the bay. The sounds fade away as the two men disappear into the night. Then everything is silent again.

One of Papa's comrades lets out an expletive. "That was close."

We walk for what seems like hours along the road. I keep my fear pressed deep down inside, and when I catch Papa glancing at me, I push my weary legs faster and raise my chin higher. I don't know our mission, but I follow our leader without question.

We arrive home as morning touches the horizon. Maman is waiting for us. When she sees us, Maman goes from anxious to relieved to furious.

"What were you thinking, Jean? Are you insane?" Maman stands straight as a rod with her hands clenched behind her back.

"I didn't take him; he followed me incognito. When I found him, there were two gendarmes close by, leaving me no other option than to continue my mission with him." My mother has not moved, but I can see that her eyes are flashing with both anger and relief.

"What about a spanking for the delinquent, Jean?"

My parents look at me slumped in a chair, tired and hungry. Papa shrugs his shoulders and takes pity on me. "Look, he is exhausted. The long march in the night is punishment enough. He is not going to follow me again anytime soon."

Maman nods in agreement, and she sends me off to clean up. As the crisis appears to be over, Papa can't help himself. "But, Louise, you should have seen him; he was a real trooper. He is good. You can be proud of him. I am!"

"Good at what, Jean?"

"Good at being bad . . . and that takes lots of guts," Papa says.

"Oh yes, a future revolutionary who will end up executed by a firing squad or hung for subversive activities against the government."

I fall asleep to my parents' voices discussing whether or not I should be punished. I never learn the purpose of the secret nocturnal expedition with Papa. Knowing my father, my guess is they were smuggling illegal firearms, ammunition, or perhaps some vital secret information. Papa has an irresistible taste for freedom and welcomes any daring opportunity passing his way. My favorite part of this adventure was my father holding me tightly while the two gendarmes were walking nearby.

My mother has told my father many times, "Pierre is constantly getting into mischief! He is impossible. You need to take this little troublemaker firmly in hand."

Papa often defends me. "He is at a difficult age. It will pass."

I am always involved in some kind of "funny trouble," as my mother calls it. When I get in a fight with a bully, Papa explains to my angry mother, "Louise, he was defending his brother from a bully who was at least two years older than he is!"

"He didn't have to break his nose," Maman says. "Maybe you should give Monsieur 'Pierre Extraordinaire' a medal. But don't spend too much money on it; remember, we have to pay the doctor for that kid's broken nose."

"Well, maybe now the local bullies will leave the French kids alone."

My mother does not understand me as Papa does. I am an adventurer at seven years of age. And I am in love.

HER NAME IS AURORA, and she is our new Spanish maid. The first time we meet, she asks me with a charming smile, "What is your name, little boy?"

"Pierre, mademoiselle," I tell her, staring into her deep brown eyes.

"Ha! Pedro, eh? But you aren't Spanish. Let's see . . . I'll call you Tatiou. It suits you perfectly." She seems very satisfied with me and my new name.

"What does Tatiou mean, mademoiselle?"

"We are friends, so you call me Aurora. Tatiou means 'little clown boy' in Arabic."

Later, Papa shares my new nickname with my grandfather, who laughingly agrees that it is fitting for me.

One day, as soon as Aurora leaves the kitchen, I am in like a flash. There is only a short time to get to the bottle of wine under the sink, pull the cork out, take a good sip, and put everything back in order before she returns.

However, I move too quickly and do not realize what I have gulped down is detergent, not wine.

Aurora finds me lying on the cold ceramic tiles, writhing in agony. She takes me straight to the doctor to get my stomach pumped. When I return home, she nurses me back to health.

When I am lying in bed, I overhear Papa and Maman talking about my escapade.

"He got a good lesson here," Papa says.

"He doesn't learn," Maman replies. "The only one getting ahead here is the doctor. You don't mind paying him because he's one of your drinking buddies. Our son could have died, you know."

"What do you mean, my drinking buddies? Are you accusing me of being a drunkard?"

"Sorry, Jean. Not at all, of course not. It's just that Pierre is like a monkey, impossible to catch. The only way that I can get some control when he misbehaves is to throw a full bucket of cold water at him and hope that my aim is good."

"What he needs is some real adventure. I'll take him fishing with me. That should calm him down a bit."

Maman shakes her head. "Rewarding the young scoundrel? What a policy."

Week in and week out, my love deepens for Aurora. I finally let her know my intentions. "When I am all grown up, Aurora," I say, "I plan to marry you." She smiles and accepts my proposal, so now we are engaged.

After being rescued by Aurora, my commitment to her is total. I must marry Aurora now. My honor is at stake. Besides, she is so good-looking!

THESE EARLY YEARS in Spain for me are alive with adventure. My father loves the bullfights, and he will go with a family friend Monsieur Pablo Picasso, but I like it when he takes me instead. When we go, he selects a place on the hard wooden bench close by the gate from where the bulls enter the arena. He always carries his little German 35 mm camera to take photos to use as references for future sculpture projects.

I am fascinated with that camera and get my first taste of photography through it. Each time Papa clicks a photo, it feels imprinted upon my memory at the same time. Those bulls are so huge; how can they fit in my father's small camera? Then I reason, if they can fit in my mind, why not in Papa's camera? Bingo! I solve that mystery.

While Papa clicks his camera, I sit on the edge of that hard bench and watch the scene unfolding in the ring below. The crowd roars as the matador turns and steps aside with a whoosh of his red cape, avoiding the sharp points of the bull's horns. *Olé!* The spectators rise to their feet cheering and Papa clicks the camera, but my excitement fades when the bull is defeated and dragged away by two horses in a blur of sweat, blood, and dust.

IN CATALONIA, the region of Spain where we live, just like in France, *Le Père Fouettard* (Father Whipper) comes with Saint Nicolas. He is like the bad Santa Claus, delivering mandatory spankings on Christmas night to the children who have misbehaved too often.

Le Père Fouettard pays me a visit in the middle of Christmas night. I cry out at the spanking I receive, but I am more upset that I receive no gifts from Santa Claus the next morning.

Gérard gets some very nice gifts, and I watch him with envy. Only Aurora can comfort me. She takes it upon herself to write to Santa on my behalf.

A week later I receive a big package from the North Pole. Inside is a Meccano construction set, the European version of the American Erector set. How does Santa know that I am going to be an inventor? I have told this secret only to Aurora in strictest confidence.

Included with the gift is a letter from Santa. It reads: "There was a small mix-up because you are a borderline bad boy. Not that bad . . . but you'll have to watch it and do a lot better from now on."

I resolve to get in less trouble, although I continue to be an adventurer and to love Aurora. But in the summer of 1936, revolution breaks out in Spain.

My parents quickly prepare to leave Tossa de Mar for Collioure, a little fishing village in France just on the other side of the Spanish border. But then I make an awful discovery. Aurora is not packing up her belongings, only ours. I race to my mother to get to the bottom of this.

"Pierrot, we cannot take Aurora with us to France." Pierrot is one of my nicknames.

I am defiant and determined.

"If you won't take her, I will!" I stand with my hands on my hips as if ready for battle, but I don't have a plan. I hold back the pain inside my chest, but hot tears erupt from my eyes and roll down my cheeks.

Maman's expression softens, and she comes toward me. "Listen, my darling Tatiou. We all love Aurora, but she is Spanish, and right now she wants to stay in Spain."

"Why? I don't understand. We are engaged. Why won't she come with me?"

"Because she has a father and two brothers who are at war against General Franco, and she wants to stay close to them."

"Okay. I will stay in Spain and fight Franco too. Where is he?" No general is going to mess up my life.

My mother explains that I am a boy still and that I must go to France with her, Papa, and Gérard until the war in Spain is over.

AS SOON as we are settled in Collioure, Papa joins sculptor Aristide Maillol, a longtime friend of our family, working in his studio. Whenever I am looking for Papa, I know where to go first—next door.

One day, as I stand at the studio entrance, Maillol looks up from the sculpture he is molding and invites me inside. Unlike Grandfather Matisse, who disappears into his art and often cannot be disturbed, Maillol is always aware that I'm there and he welcomes me. I know never to wear out my welcome.

The spacious studio is filled with light that comes in through large windows like in a church. It is a place of infinite order where one can almost feel the hand of God creating things of ultimate beauty. For me, I feel closest to God when I am outside, aware that it is His place that He created.

A model is in the studio, motionless, holding her pose. The clay has a fresh smell, and in Maillol's magic hands, it is taking shape.

I catch Papa frowning at me, concerned that I will distract Maillol, but I disregard his look. I have been invited here, and I know how to behave around an artist who is working.

Maillol motions me closer. "Look very carefully, Pierre. Here, under our eyes, is the most profoundly beautiful thing on earth—a woman."

I watch him and wonder how he can manipulate all this clay without getting any of it into his long gray beard. He continues the lesson.

"Always treat women with respect. They can give you a lot of trouble."

The model seems to smile just a little. This woman is beautiful, but she is no match for Aurora.

"Aurora is no trouble at all. When she comes here after the Spanish Revolution, I want you to make a statue of her."

Maillol looks at me. "Who is Aurora, Pierre?"

"My fiancée in Spain."

Maillol listens as I tell him about Aurora. He continues to work, and I am mesmerized by the way he beautifully creates the figure of a woman out of the clay.

Maillol turns and says, "I have a gift for you." He hands me a little watercolor paint set that has a folding ring beneath the palette for one hand to slide into, freeing up the other hand to hold the brush. I thank him and hurry out of the studio.

From this day, I consider myself a serious and genuine artist and must get started.

Later at dinner, I tell my parents that I have decided to be an artist as well as a writer who will illustrate my own books. I'm sure that my parents were expecting me to follow in my father's footsteps and become a sculptor. But my mind is made up, and I give my reasons with authority: "Being a sculptor is too complicated and takes too much space."

I stay out of mischief for a while, spending most of my time gathering flat stones on the beach. The beaches on this part of the Mediterranean coast are covered with stones instead of sand, stones of all sizes that have been polished by the surf. The flat stones are perfect canvases for painting masterpieces. Using my watercolors, I paint nautical scenes.

My first love is Aurora, then art, and then boats.

Pierre H. Matisse

2

CONTRABAND, PIRATES, SARDINES, AND STARS

I am not an adventurer by choice but by fate.

VINCENT VAN GOGH

BOATS, FISHING, AND THE SEA are such wonderful things to get me into trouble, as well as a perfect place to recharge my artistic, creative juices. My father often takes me fishing for sardines with him, and when I disappear from the house, my parents know that they'll find me at the harbor.

One late afternoon when I've escaped to the docks, I climb aboard Papa's boat. The boat is about twenty to twenty-five feet long, with a tiny hold that also serves somewhat as a cabin, although it really is more like a locker. Lately, Papa has been sleeping all day and going somewhere at night. Even more unusual, he has not taken me fishing for a while.

I miss our time together, but at this moment, I care for nothing, because now I am a pirate sailing the stormy seas. I fight off other pirates to save my treasures. But piracy is a tiring business. As the sun falls behind me and the sea takes on a silvery glow, I climb beneath a pile of dirty tarpaulins in the cabin. *I will hide here, waiting to make a surprise attack when the next battle begins. I will just rest for a moment.* Soon, I fall soundly asleep.

Tug . . . tug . . . tug. The sound of the engine wakes me. The boat moves through the water, rolling and pitching in the swell. The small hatch to the cabin is closed, but through a crack between the planks, I see the stars shining in the night. We are at sea. Then I hear voices.

"Those rifles are Lebels from the last war, rusted and worn out. Not nearly as good as the last German Mausers shipment." I recognize Papa's voice.

"Some are using pitchforks and knives to fight with now. These guns are better than nothing!" another voice replies, one I cannot place. "As long as the firing pins aren't worn and the loading bolt is not too loose, they'll work."

I hop out of the hold and join the men on deck. I see two men with Papa. I am now a *contra bandito,* a bandit fighting against the government, and I am delighted to be here. I understand now why it was so uncomfortable sleeping on the tarpaulin. The guns were hidden underneath layers of tarpaulins beneath mine.

When Papa sees me, his eyes widen, and he's furious, though not that surprised to see me appearing by magic out of the tiny hold.

"Louise is going to hear about this, and she will keep that kid locked up," he says to his compatriots. "Or even better, ship him one way to his great aunt in Paris."

Fortunately, my two other partners, who are gunrunners extraordinaire, take my side.

"The kid has to learn about a man's world someday. This day is as good as another," says the skinny one. He has a face like a weasel, with a strange-looking crooked pipe firmly set between his teeth.

The other one, with a huge mustache that makes him look like an authentic pirate, adds in a baritone voice, "If you want him to be good at anything, you have to start him young, Jean."

"I don't want him to be a good smuggler or a gangster, Marius, and neither does his mother. Besides, how do we keep his mouth shut?"

"Let's make the best of it. He's one more set of hands to pass on the guns and ammo at the rendezvous point," answers Marius, my number one supporter.

I am frozen, waiting for Papa to make a final decision about me.

"Tatiou will be all right after I tell him a story," promises Marius. Marius pauses and then suddenly he says, "I'm hungry. It's time to eat. Alberto, pass the bread and sausage. The onions and the wine are in the port basket with the nets."

"Monsieur Marius," I say respectfully, "you said you were going to tell me a story."

"Oh! Yes. What you see while you are on this trip must be kept secret. You understand?"

"Yes, Monsieur Marius."

The pirate is speaking to me. I am all ears.

"Because if you speak to anyone—" he leans closer to me—"the gendarmes will arrest you and cut off your ears." He shifts his eyes in that frightening pirate fashion that one comes to expect from such a cutthroat character.

"Did the gendarmes cut off Papa's friend Monsieur Bouliers's leg?"

"No! It was the German gendarmes in the last war who did that because he didn't keep his mouth shut," Alberto cuts in with a low mysterious tone as he theatrically mimics the cutting of ears and a leg. A shiver goes down my spine. Instinctively, I check my ears and my left leg, too, to make sure they are still attached.

"The kid won't say a word," declares Marius.

I now feel accepted in the smuggler fraternity. They all pull out their *couteaux à cran d'arrêt* to slice pieces of sausage. I reach in my pocket for my knife too.

"Pierrot, where did you get that knife?" Papa asks me with narrowed eyes.

"From your desk drawer. You never use it." I shrug just like Papa. What good is it to him if he doesn't use it? This line of reasoning seems logical to me.

"I've repeatedly told you not to take it!" I can hear the exasperation in my father's voice.

"I'm sorry," I reply, "but I will need it if I meet up with one of Franco's spies."

Doesn't Papa know that they have been hot on my trail ever since I declared war on General Franco?

"Besides," I add, "surely I am not expected to walk around half-naked in these dangerous days, am I?"

The men burst out laughing, and Marius sprays us with wine and sausage bits from under his long mustache.

"What's so funny?" I demand to know.

This brings more laughter.

"Stop the engine, Alberto," my father orders, clearly in command.

The boat, now silent, drifts in the light swell. In the west, on the horizon, we can see the dark outline of the coast. A few faint lights are visible here and there.

"That's the place," my father points out, after taking a couple of bearings with the compass.

"Do you think they will come?" asks Marius.

"They will," my father says confidently. "They are desperate for guns."

The boat rocks on the waves, and all of us settle in to wait.

"This wine from Banyuls is perfect," Alberto says as he holds up the canteen.

Monsieur Marius begins to tell his pirate story again, but my father interrupts him and looks at me. "Pierrot, some of your grandmother Matisse's ancestors were genuine buccaneers."

My eyes widen. Whoa! Now I understand. This explains everything about my father's character and mine. We are pirates by blood.

Marius continues his story, and I sit on the edge of the bench and listen as the boat rocks and the stars twinkle above us. Marius's deep voice is like the lulling of the rocking boat, and I scoot back, fighting a strong urge to fall asleep. Eventually I lose the Battle of Sleep.

"It's going to be a long night" are the last words I hear before drifting away into slumber.

I FALL out of the bunk in the hold. Daylight is streaming through the cracks in the trapdoor. It's morning. As I get up and sit down on the bunk, I am unexpectedly thrown hard to starboard. The waves roll us up and down. Then I vomit . . . everywhere. I am seasick for the first time in my life. From the deck, I hear voices coming and going.

"Keep her steady at forty-five degrees."

The wind is howling through the short rigging.

"As soon as we pass the cape, it will calm down."

"With this weather, how are we going to fish for sardines?"

"It will be calm in the bay. I know a good spot. There are plenty of places on the rock bar."

"*If* that wretched wind doesn't chase the sardines away."

"Pass the wine and shut up. You're always complaining!"

Eventually the wind dies down, and despite my queasiness, I fall back to sleep.

When I wake up later, I'm feeling much better. I look around. Something's amiss. I pull up the tarpaulin. The guns are gone! Where are the guns? Have I slept through the whole contraband deal and missed all the action?

I scramble up on deck and find my father and Marius taking a nap. Alberto is seated by the tiller, cleaning his crooked pipe.

"Bonjour, Monsieur Pirate. What's up?" he asks me with a broad smile.

"You didn't wake me to help with the guns! I thought we were in this together."

"You were only a reserve." Alberto's answer has saved my pride, yet I'm still disappointed. But being in the fresh air has settled my stomach.

"I'm hungry and thirsty," I say sullenly.

"We can't risk mutiny," he says with an indulgent smile. "Here is water mixed with wine, and a piece of bread with a few dried figs. There is nothing else left to eat, but soon we will have plenty of sardines." Alberto passes me a canteen and the food.

The bread and figs taste great, but the water and wine taste like the aluminum canteen. Yuck! Soon I curl up on deck and fall asleep again, and when I wake, the three men are pulling the net from the sea. It seems as though a million or more shiny sardines are jumping into the woven baskets and onto the slippery deck. We return to the harbor late in the afternoon.

I see Maman waiting on the docks with a few friends, watching us closely.

"Uh-oh," Papa says.

When I leap from the boat onto the dock, Maman takes me in her arms. She is crying. "Are you okay, Bunny Rabbit?" she asks. I'm stunned by this emotional display of her relief that I am alive. I thought for certain that she was going to be very upset with me. On top of that, usually my mother lives in her own world. Her focus is on her art, Papa, and Gérard. My younger brother requires more attention than me because he is a small boy. Though I understand that she loves me, I often feel like a spectator in her life.

I savor this moment in her arms. Then she looks at Papa, who is still on the boat. She still holds me, but her body goes rigid, and her tone changes.

"Jean, you are totally irresponsible. How could you take him on such an outing? This is it! All you can think of is boats and sardines, but what about how I feel?"

Papa drops a net onto the deck. "It was not my idea to take Tatiou. He was under a tarpaulin."

My parents quarrel for a while, but with my safe return and buckets full of fish, Maman's anger fades, and soon the two of them kiss and make up.

I lucked out on this adventure. Gunrunning, pirates, fishing—and I'm not even in trouble with Maman!

Papa builds a bonfire on the beach, and he grills the fresh sardines on charcoal right there in the sand. The sun falls into the sea as I sit happily on a dry net next to Papa. I hold a sardine by the head in one hand and the tail in the other and eat everything in between, leaving only the backbone, a method Monsieur Picasso has taught me. It is divinely delicious. A pirate never eats sardines from cans.

With stomachs full, our friends leave to go home. I lean back and contemplate the sky and sea. The oil lamp hanging from a pole behind us makes the flecks of sardine scales stuck in my father's beard shine like diamonds. Slowly he extends his right arm, holding a sardine in his hand and pointing it toward the sky.

"Look, Tatiou. By the tail of the sardine, you'll see the constellation of Orion. Orion is the most magnificent constellation in the whole sky. It is the constellation of the hunters. In Greek mythology, Orion was a giant hunter slain by Artemis."

I take note. I have to see to this Artemis for slaying the great Orion. I stare into the sky at the magnificent Orion shining with a glorious mystery and feel goose bumps prickle all over my skin.

This is what I like most about Papa. He doesn't just tell me about ordinary things. He gives me history lessons and tells me fascinating and important things concerning life to stimulate my curiosity.

Then nature calls and I trek off into the dark. When I return, the lantern has been turned off, and Papa and Maman are in each other's arms, tenderly kissing. Such moments make me pause with wonder at my parents, who are so happy and in love.

PAPA OFTEN TAKES Maman, Gérard, and me on picnics in the Pyrenees. We travel in his Mathis car, a brand that sounds like our name, Matisse. In fact, I believe we own the car factory, and I brag about it to anybody who will listen.

Papa drives on rough roads, almost trails, way out in the wilderness, and we bounce all over in the car like dice in a gambling tumbler. Even so, I'm able to enjoy the view. Grassy slopes undulate in the wind, creating a range of color I have never seen anywhere else. Some fields are covered with jonquils of a yellow so beautiful that I could not possibly paint them or capture their vibrancy. I take this all in as I grip the seat for safety.

"Be careful, Jean! Slow down. This road is terrible," Maman complains on a particularly bouncy excursion.

"This is not a road," Papa says. "It's a pathway to a Roman marble quarry that was abandoned long ago."

Maman appears as intrigued as I am. She must realize what a privilege it is to experience such magnificent beauty and history because her attitude changes. "Next time I shall take a cushion to put under my bottom," she says with a smile.

The days in Collioure are rich with memories for me. It is a time in paradise, the calm before the storm.

Then, abruptly, everything changes.

Perhaps it is my mischief that causes my parents to follow through with their threats to send me away, or maybe it's some influence of this new regime in Germany led by some newly appointed man with a strange little mustache. I overhear my parents and their artist friends discussing and debating about this in the bistros and cafés.

Whatever precipitates it, one day in 1936, when I am eight years old, Tata arrives at our house. When she sees me, this small woman takes me in her arms and hugs me so tightly that it surprises me, even as a boy of eight.

She has come to take me to live with her in Paris.

ORION

Pierre H. Matisse

3

TATA

Only divine love bestows the keys of knowledge.

ARTHUR RIMBAUD

PARIS AND TATA ARE SYNONYMOUS.

Her legal name is Henriette Escousse, but if I could have a say, it would be changed to Saint Henriette. This adorable lady, in her mid-sixties, is a teacher by profession and a recognized scholar in Paris. She was born in the City of Light and has lived here all her life. This fact makes her a true Parisienne.

Tata's whole personality radiates kindness and love toward me. She quickly becomes my favorite person in all the world. However, under her small and frail physical appearance resides a will of tempered steel and the courage of a lion. I have been told stories of Tata all my life, particularly how she was decorated with the prestigious *Légion d'honneur* for organizing the evacuation of her students under fire from the monstrous German howitzer, Big Bertha, a gun used by the German army to bombard Paris during World War I.

I have mixed emotions as I say good-bye to Papa, Maman, and Gérard. I'm sad that I am being sent away, but these feelings are quickly replaced by the excitement of this new adventure on the horizon.

We are traveling to Paris by train, powered by a steam locomotive. I try to get a good look at it from the platform before we depart. The locomotive fascinates me, and I want to study how it works. But it's time to board so Tata hurries me along. On the train, I settle into my seat by the window. On this route from the south of France to the north, the scenery is mesmerizing. We go through ancient-looking villages, past ruins of castles on hillsides, over green rolling countryside, and beside vineyards as far as the eye can see. Mountain ranges rise from the horizon, and valleys stretch from farm to farm. I'm in awe of the beauty of my homeland and bombard Tata with questions.

"What color of cheese would that cow make? Would a spotted cow make spotted cheese? Who lived in that castle over there?" and on and on for nearly the entire twelve-hour journey.

Finally we arrive in Paris! Although I was born here, this is really my first time being aware of it all.

What an extreme contrast this city is compared to tranquil Collioure. When we arrive at the Paris railway terminal, Tata is tired. The long trip, along with my nonstop bombardment of questions, has gotten the best of her. Yet what patience she has with me—she hasn't even lost her smile.

"Porter! Here, please," signals Tata as we get off the train.

"Madame, this steamer trunk is very heavy," the porter remarks, puffing heavily as he loads it into the trunk of the cab. "It's unusually heavy for a regular tourist."

Before we left Collioure, I threw a whale of a tantrum to get a special package inside the big trunk of the taxi. I was so insistent and the theatrics of my scene were so outrageous that finally the big people gave in.

"Tatiou, I would like to know why this package that you have insisted on taking is the heaviest of all our luggage?" Tata asks as she dips regally into the cab.

"It's a gift for you, Tata," I say as I settle into the seat beside her. The taxi driver quickly merges into the lane, zigzagging in the heavy traffic.

"And what is it, dear?"

Excitedly I reply, "It is a surprise, Tata. I made it myself, especially for you."

On our drive from the railway terminal to Tata's apartment, my face is pressed against the window, taking in the buildings and the people on the streets. The traffic is congested, with horse carts, cars going in all directions, and buses with back balconies. People are rushing everywhere. I want to see everything and understand what I'm seeing.

I WILL FORGET most of the addresses where I have lived during my life, except for two: one on the French Riviera with my family and Tata's address: 23 rue Morère, on the fourth floor of an apartment building in the fourteenth *arrondissement* (district) of Paris. It is located not far from Montparnasse in *le quartier des artistes*, the artists' district. Now I am an artist living in the mecca of the arts. With my mini watercolor paint set from Monsieur Maillol, I am quite certain that my artistic abilities will grow by leaps and bounds.

There is no elevator in Tata's building, so the taxi driver has to wrestle with the luggage all the way up the stairs. When he starts to complain, Tata says, "Elevators are bad for your heart."

"Not if you drive a taxi all day, Madame," he replies, completely out of breath.

"I'll give you a good tip," she says. When he hears this, his face lights up.

When all of the luggage has been brought up and the taxi driver is on his way with Tata's generous tip, I am ready to give my aunt her gift. I watch her unwrap the colorful paper, and I hear a gasp. *She must be pleased*, I think.

Inside is a large beach stone with a special name: a *galet*. This galet is well polished by the surf of the Mediterranean and still has the salty pungent odor of the sea. Its large, flat surface was the perfect canvas for me to paint my first masterpiece: a nautical scene with blue sky and white clouds above the sea, where a sailing ship is being carried by the wind, its sails full and billowing. In the right corner of the painting is the signature of the famous artist himself: Tatiou.

"What a wonderful boat, Pierre!" Tata says, her eyes clouded with tears. She is touched by my gift.

"It's not just a boat, Tata. It's a pirate ship—the *Orion.*"

Even though it has already been a long day, Tata listens to my wildly exaggerated version of Marius's pirate tales.

Finally, she says, "I have a gift for you, too, Pierre," and leads me to the guest bedroom where I will be staying. In the corner on the floor, sitting on its own stand, is a magnificent model sloop, decorated with a red ribbon. A beautiful card is attached that reads: "To Pierre, Welcome to Paris. With love, Tata."

It is the first toy I have ever been given.

"We shall sail her in the Tuileries pond," Tata promises.

"Yes! But before her maiden voyage, she needs an anchor, and I have to paint her name on the bow," I reply.

"And what will that be, Pierre?"

"*Orion,* Tata."

"But of course," she muses with a grin.

DAY TWO IN PARIS. I pick up Tata's newspaper on the dining room table and can't believe what I see. It's a jumble of words that I cannot read. Frustrated, I start to panic, profusely swearing in Spanish as I pace back and forth. Tata calmly and firmly demands an apology and an explanation for my outburst. I deliver both immediately. As she takes the offensive paper from me, she smiles and places her arm around my shoulder.

"I know how to solve this problem," she says with confidence. That morning we go to the bookstore, and she buys me a thick red volume entitled *Le Petit Larousse Illustré,* a French-language encyclopedic dictionary. This is my lifeline. I carry it everywhere with me and sleep with it by my pillow at night. Tata has given me the key to knowledge.

I fall in love with Paris, enticed by her promises of wonderful opportunities for an innovative and adventurous spirit like me. At every opportunity, Tata takes me out to explore the streets of Paris.

Everywhere I look there is an extraordinary spectacle. Merchants with wooden carts overflowing with an abundance of fresh vegetables and colorful fragrant flowers. I am taken with the street musicians: violinists, a singer accompanied by an accordionist, and a cappella singers who pass their hats for a few francs after their performances. There are discreet businessmen selling contraband on the sly out of their suitcases, keeping their eyes open for the *flics* with their white batons. The cops' uniforms have black capes that take dramatic shapes on windy days.

This amazing show never stops.

There are gypsies in colorful clothing, with golden earrings, who have large black bears with rings in their noses that are tied to a rope. The bears go up on their hind legs, which makes them very tall, and they dance to the sound of tambourines while the gypsy women pester passersby, offering palm readings guaranteed to fulfill their dreams.

Sometimes we see the Auvergnat shepherds, dressed in blue overalls, guiding their flocks of goats with long canes through the streets of Paris while peddling their goat cheese wrapped up in a big plane tree leaf.

I look around at people from many countries of the world. Black Africans and Arabs in their traditional clothing sell oriental rugs and various wares. Crowding the streets are horses pulling heavy carts loaded with huge wine barrels. Everywhere I look there is something that catches my eye—the spectacular statues, the majestic monuments, the Eiffel Tower, the fabulous fountains shooting their water high into the sky. All this is Paris.

The stylish men and the chic women are dressed in the latest fashions of the season and are out for a stroll on the promenade. I smell their perfume a mile away. Oh, and then there are the magicians, the jugglers, and the organ-grinders cranking their music boxes while a monkey holds and shakes a tin can, entertaining the audience for a tip. Then I spy the entrepreneurs who demonstrate their mechanical toys on the sidewalk. My senses are overloaded with sights, smells, and sounds. I can't believe what I see; I am filled with wonder at this extraordinary city. This is 1936, when Paris is still Paris.

TATA ENROLLS ME in grammar school. I must learn some manners, including not using the Spanish profanities I learned from Monsieur

Picasso, whom Maman had chased out of the house with a broom when she heard him giving me lessons.

Tata polishes my French, which was all mixed up with Spanish. She improves my reading skills in record time and in the process passes on to me her love for literature. I can't get enough to read—Victor Hugo, Voltaire, Antoine de Saint-Exupéry, and Mark Twain. For Tata, teaching is not a job; it is a calling, a crusade against ignorance, a sacred mission. She is more than a teacher; she is an educator who loves her students.

Early in her teaching career, her exceptional abilities were recognized by her superiors. She was promoted to director of the rue d'Alésia School for girls. Dedicating her entire life to her career, she never married, but she raised my mother when my grandmother Milhau died giving birth to Maman. It wasn't a good way to start her life, but fortunately Tata was there for Maman and thus became my surrogate grandmother.

I have three women in my life: Aurora, Maman, and Tata. Someday, Aurora and I will have our life together. While I adore my mother, she has too many things to do, and I am too much of a pain in the neck for her. Maman has always shown me motherly attention and concern, but according to her, Tata spoils me rotten.

Tata is very smart. I believe she knows everything. If I mess up, she knows, and what is more important, she understands why. Often, she even knows before I get into trouble and catches me just in time. I watch her with interest, wondering about her special powers.

My first day of school, when I come home for my two-hour lunch, there on the table is a plate with beautifully cut radishes—it looks like a still life arranged for someone to paint. It is one more way that Tata shows her love to me in small but meaningful ways.

On Thursdays and Sundays, my days off from school, Tata gives me my real education in the museums of Paris. We visit them often, and I never grow tired of these excursions.

Tata is my personal guide, offering fascinating stories or interesting comments. She tells me about our family history dating back to Charlemagne. When we explore the military museums, Tata tells me stories about her father, who served seven years in a Zouave regiment under Napoleon III. There is a painting of her father, Louis Escousse, in his spectacular Zouave uniform hanging prominently above the living room mantelpiece. He was a sergeant who fought in the campaigns of Mexico, Italy, and North Africa. Behind Tata's desk in her study is a golden frame protected by glass that holds all her father's medals earned on the battlefields of Napoleon III's war campaign.

Tata and I explore the Louvre, the Trocadéro, le Petit and le Grand Palais, Versailles, le Musée de l'Homme, and les Invalides, which contains Napoleon's tomb and artifacts detailing French military history. We rarely miss any art exhibit of the most famous painters, and I am surprised to see some of the work of my parents' closest artist friends—Salvador Dali, Picasso, Georges Braque, Marc Chagall, and, of course, Grandfather Matisse. We attend lectures at la Salle Pleyel, where explorers and scientists show slides or movies of their voyages and discoveries.

In the evenings, we go to the theater to see plays and attend concerts featuring all kinds of music, from symphonies to jazz performances in cabarets. Tata takes me to see the movie *Snow White and the Seven Dwarfs*, which I am crazy about. The animation is fascinating to me, and for some time afterward, when I paint something, my artwork moves in my dreams.

We are always so busy with something interesting to do or see that I seldom get into trouble anymore. I love every minute of it.

I have the best of both worlds. I have Paris, full of wonder and intrigue, and Tata, who could not love me better and takes me on small vacations, and I have my longer summer vacation with Papa, Maman, and Gérard. I am blessed.

Papa, a man of action, is my bigger-than-life hero. Whenever I return to Paris with Tata, I constantly wonder what he's up to. Is he still leading late-night gunrunning or going on forbidden moonlit hikes?

Papa has taught me to be my own man and to make logical deductions based on my own reasoning, and he has taught me responsibility so that I can learn from my mistakes. In Paris, Tata introduces me to intellectual knowledge, which is the perfect counterpoint to Papa's lessons about a man's world of adventures. Both were giving me precious gifts, the kind that couldn't be bought at any price or taken away, even with all that was to come. The ideal world would have been to live life to the fullest with Maman, Papa, Gérard, and Tata at the same time, all together.

IN FEBRUARY, Tata and I take the long journey on the train to the fabulous winter carnival in Nice. While in Nice, we visit Grandfather Matisse in his studio.

Le Carnaval de Nice is a grand event, one Grandfather Matisse seems to enjoy as much as I do. There are parades with giant floats coming down the street, flooding the square. Bands fill the air with music, and confetti rains down on the crowd, thrown by people leaning from the balconies above the street. Grandfather Matisse leaves his studio and joins Tata and me for the festivities. I notice that his eyes are shimmering as he takes everything in. He and I seem to share a secret world at the carnival, one full of vibrant colors, music, and gaiety that only we know about or can enjoy. He expresses such a childlike excitement that I run and jump beside him, feeling a close kinship with him.

When summer vacation arrives, Tata takes me to visit France's castles. We visit all of them; les Châteaux de la Loire, Fontainebleau, and others in different provinces. Then we travel to Grandfather Milhau's home. As soon as we come close to the ocean, I begin pestering every adult in sight to get me into a boat on the water.

If I am introduced to someone who has a boat, I begin my sales pitch right away for a boat ride. "Don't worry, I can swim, row, and steer by the sun during the day and by the stars at night."

How could they refuse? I got my wish many times.

After such wonderful vacations, we return to Paris and to school.

THEN I READ bad news from Spain. Franco is winning. I must act.

Using small waxed coffee bags, I construct water bombs. These are destined for Franco's spies, who have infiltrated Paris and are walking under Tata's balcony. From my fourth-floor vantage point, the small bags of water are carefully dropped on any passerby who appears suspicious to my well-trained eye. It is quite a skill to hit a moving target. One must release the water bomb at the most precise moment. On impact, the muted noise, as well as the reaction, are impressive.

But then I am spotted. The concierge of Tata's building comes out to see what all the commotion is about.

"Little no good! You should be ashamed," she shouts up to me and menacingly points her finger. She's standing still. I can't miss, so I drop my bomb.

The last water bomb misses her by a fraction of an inch.

After that, things get completely out of hand. The concierge calls the police. When they arrive and take control of the situation, I am hauled off to the police station. Tata, who has been running some errands, eventually arrives and sorts out the misunderstanding so she can take me home.

After this unfortunate interlude, it is never quite the same with the concierge. She is out to get me, and I'm convinced she must be a Franco spy. One day when I come home from the park's little pond with my sailboat and clothing all soaked because I had fallen in the water, the concierge has her revenge.

She stops me at the door. "Little bum, I will not let you in the building with all that water dripping on my polished floor."

My response is less than polite.

When the concierge reports to Tata what I said, Tata slaps me on the face. The slap doesn't hurt me, but the very thought that I have offended Tata jabs my heart.

I try to explain. "Alberto and Marius say that all the time."

"You are my nephew. We are in Paris, and you are a gentleman. You can say that in a boat with them in Collioure but not here." The firm expression on her face presses the words into my mind.

"I understand. Like Papa always says: 'When in Rome do as the Romans do.'" Then I tell Tata that when I grow up, my wife, Aurora, and I will take care of her. We will have a home near a sandy beach with a boat, a dog, a car, and a plane, in that order of priorities.

IN 1937, Tata and I visit the Paris International Exposition many times during its run from May through November. This world's fair, the

Exposition Internationale des Arts et Techniques dans la Vie Moderne, stretches from the Seine across Champs de Mars and Trocadéro, with the Eiffel Tower center stage.

People come from all over Europe and the world to the grand event. Flags wave from every nation of the world, and countries exhibit their unique culture in art and technology. Monsieur Picasso's mural *Guernica*, a huge painting that depicts the atrocities of Franco that are still going on, is definitely the talk of the Spanish pavilion.

Rising prominently over the fairgrounds, on the east and west sides of the Eiffel Tower, two pavilions seem to face off—Germany and the USSR—with huge, striking statues atop them. On one side, a man and woman—Soviet Communist workers—are caught in motion, about to step off the building. On the opposite side, the German eagle sits even higher, perched on a swastika. The statues seem defiant and menacing, one threatening with a hammer and sickle, the other with a swastika.

Tata takes a long look at those statues.

"There is going to be a long, terrible war. You will have to be brave, Tatiou," she says sadly. Tata—the prominent figure in my life—is so tiny compared to the towering statues.

"France planted the seeds of this upcoming war in the last one," Tata explains. "The Versailles Treaty was only a twenty-year intermission to raise another generation of gun meat. And in reality . . ." she adds reflectively, "World War I never stopped. Now, it is just continuing."

Tata is one of the few people who can see the dark clouds of war rising slowly on the eastern horizon, long before the terrifying shadow is cast over the entire world. Too soon, her prediction will become a reality. At first, the Soviets will be allies with Germany and enemies of France, but soon these allies will turn on one another, facing off like those statues at the Paris International Exposition.

I understand some of what she is saying and know that war is a serious matter, but I'm not sure what I can do or how my own world might change. For now, I will enjoy every moment we have together.

MONTHS LATER, Tata has a great surprise for me. We meet Grandfather Henri and go to a jazz concert in Paris, featuring Django Reinhardt.

This live music is like nothing I have ever heard before. It seeps in, all the way down to my bones. I'm beside myself, jumping up, down, and sideways, shaking the whole row of chairs. Holy mackerel—do I love jazz!

Tata has a piano in her apartment that she plays wonderfully. I have only heard her play classical pieces so I am surprised that she loves jazz, too, which makes for a lively discussion about music between her and Grandfather Matisse throughout the evening. Grandfather plays the violin and the bass and seems to enjoy jazz as much as I do. I don't want this night to ever end.

But there is one more surprise for me after the concert when Grandfather Henri asks me if I would like to meet Django Reinhardt. With a twinkle in his eye, he ushers me backstage to one of the dressing rooms. Inside is the jazz star. I'm stunned to realize by the way they greet each other that he is a friend of my grandfather.

"And what music do you like, little fellow?" Django asks me.

"Yours, Monsieur!" That's the truth. *I can't go wrong with that answer,* I think.

"And what instrument do you play?"

"The bass that is in our attic. It is much bigger than me, Monsieur."

He smiles. I must have given the right answer. On that very special day, I realize for the first time that my grandfather must be famous. How else can he get invited to Django Reinhardt's dressing room? Grandfather Matisse has to be a big celebrity. As we leave the concert hall, I look at my grandfather, deeply impressed and with newfound appreciation for him.

FOR SOME TIME things seem to be going well, and then I take up roller-skating.

The four steel ball-bearing wheels on each skate are terribly noisy on the sidewalk. Noisy is normal for a boy my age so I do not realize how nerve-racking the sound is when I skate back and forth under the concierge's window. This doesn't endear me to the already cranky concierge and generates many complaints to Tata.

I really don't mean to upset the concierge, so I have a sudden inspiration. I will skate down the inside staircase from the fourth floor all the way to the first. My plan works well, and I make it from top to bottom without falling. But I don't consider the noise I'm making. The racket is many decibels above the concierge's tolerance. This time I've really blown it. She raises such a fuss that Tata has to send me to live with my parents, who have just moved from Collioure to Issy-les-Moulineaux, the same Paris suburb where Grandfather Henri has a large estate.

I stay in my parents' apartment for a few months until Tata's building management finds an anti-Franco concierge, one more in line with my political views, not to mention more tolerant of a difficult child.

During this time, I make an awful discovery. I overhear big people talking of Franco and the atrocities in Spain. How will I ever marry my Aurora?

In the winter of 1938, my parents receive word that Aurora has been beaten to death by Franco's men because she fought on the side of the Republicans. Her father and brothers were also killed in action, a few months into the Revolution. When I hear them talking about this disturbing news, I am devastated.

For years I've plotted how I can dethrone Generalissimo Franco and reunite with my sweet Aurora. I had to save her. And alas, now it can never be. Yet I vow I will find a way to avenge my lost love.

I BEGIN ORGANIZING the opposition against Franco. Gérard is too young for active duty, so I recruit him to film the whole operation for the benefit of the weekly newsreel at the local cinema. Move over, Cecil B. DeMille! However, my little brother is not as dedicated to the cause.

"Gérard, pay attention! You must set the camera over there."

I point to the best locations and give him a hand installing the movie camera that I have built myself, using items from around the house. My mother has been looking for her special wooden toolbox and her magnifying glass for a week. And my father doesn't know why his big alarm clock is missing—I needed some essential parts that were inside of it. The phonograph crank has mysteriously disappeared as well, but it is all for a noble cause. My magnificent movie camera is ready to film a hero for the glory of Spain and the honor of my beloved Aurora.

"The objective, Gérard, is this greenhouse where Franco and his ferocious soldiers are entrenched within."

My brother is momentarily impressed, but then he wants out.

"It's too dangerous," declares a prudent Gérard.

"No, it is not! You are only the reporter. The one who is doing the fighting and taking all the risks is me!"

"I need to go to the bathroom." Gérard tries every trick in the book to dodge his duties.

"Not now! I must take the greenhouse first. Look through the viewer and turn the crank slowly."

Then I announce with enthusiasm, "Ready to roll!"

To make it more realistic, I have requisitioned "hand grenades" from the elements of the family radio. The dry batteries are heavy lead cylinders, perfect for my purposes. Ammunition is such an important part of any battle. Franco will finally pay for separating me from my Aurora.

"Lights, camera, action!" I shout.

From the greenhouse, Franco and his men shoot at me. Bullets are flying everywhere, but I am invincible. I charge. I dodge the bullets. It's all very scary. They get a real surprise when I start throwing grenades at them. The glass panes of the greenhouse shatter with such realistic cracking sounds. Glass is flying all over, making quite a racket.

Papa hears the noise and comes to investigate.

"He made me do it" is my brother's defense.

Franco makes his getaway as Papa comes toward me to deliver prompt retribution. But then, a sudden change of fate. I am saved by Gérard's plaintive cry.

"I made caca in my pants."

The priorities change. What luck! My father curses as he places Gérard on the table to clean him up.

"You, Pierrot. Stay right there. I'm not through with you yet." At least this diversion is buying me some time.

Maman is out, as well as the maid, so Papa proceeds to undo the bottom of Gérard's knickers and immediately caca runs all over. Jean Matisse is not good at this sort of thing. The whole scene is hilarious. I go for my movie camera to get this on film.

But my father's aim is right on. His slap stings my cheek, and all I see in the viewfinder are stars. Even worse is that the film did not turn out good at all! Gérard messed up the film. I have let down the Spanish Republicans at the Battle of the Greenhouse.

The battle is over for now. But I am determined to fight on in the name of dear Aurora.

Monsieur Franco will rue the day.

Pierre H. Matisse

4

BLACK CLOUDS ON THE HORIZON

Some folk are wise, and some are otherwise.

TOBIAS GEORGE SMOLLETT

IN DECEMBER 1938, my life is about to take another U-turn. After being spoiled with Tata all to myself, she and Maman decide that I should attend the Lycée Michelet, a private school. This means it is time for me to return to live with my family full time. Gérard suffers from asthma, and his health is fragile. He spends most of his time inside the house reading. At Tata's, there was love, structure, and interesting studies with ample time for adventures, but now she is a forty-minute bus ride away. I miss her greatly.

I also miss Bouboule, who died shortly before I moved from Collioure. But I am happy to get acquainted with my new cocker spaniel, Mirasol de Glondes. When I come home, her tail wags frantically, and she quickly becomes my companion and confidant as well as a new partner in crime.

Our family's apartment is on the sixth floor of a new building atop a hill on l'avenue de Clamart. We have a long balcony from which we can see all of Paris. The panoramic view is spectacular.

Just a short walk up the avenue, Grandfather Matisse's estate is enclosed by a high masonry wall that has embedded shards of glass sticking out on top for security. There are two entrances made of majestic iron gates, one that leads to the mansion and the other to the studio. The three-level mansion, with its elegant stone staircase entrance, looks like a small-scale Château de Fontainebleau. There is a majestic green lawn surrounded by a circle driveway. Huge elms and plane trees grace the entire property.

I especially enjoy the two ponds on the grounds. The one I prefer contains water lilies and *poisson rouge*—twelve-inch goldfish—that I occasionally try to grab while standing in the water. There is a big garden with a greenhouse and a garage attached to the gardener's house. The estate is full of birds of all kinds. This is a paradise of nature, and when Maman and Papa are working there, Gérard and I are allowed to roam all over the grounds. None of the buildings are locked, which means there's much potential for adventures and many opportunities for trouble.

Along the crushed stone driveway leading to the studio are massive stone statues of nude ladies, many of them created by Papa, shaded by dense cypress trees. The studio is a large wooden structure with an office full of art books and artifacts such as African masks and all kinds of exotic costumes. Outside is a good-sized forge.

My parents construct another large building by the side of Grandfather Matisse's studio for their pottery business. The building contains deep cement containers for clay and three electric ceramic ovens. One of the ovens is so big that I can stand up straight inside of it.

Here, when I am not in school, I help my parents in their art studio. I think my parents keep me busy in an effort to limit my tendency toward mischief.

I become an apprentice sculptor, painter, and ceramist. We are always busy, and I learn a lot about art. I like to work, but because of my free spirit, I prefer my own projects. My personal plans rarely coincide with my parents' needs.

I spend a lot of time with two of my parents' employees. Brosse is a young Italian immigrant, a talented ceramist. After the war he will go on to work with Grandfather Matisse's old friend Pablo Picasso on his pottery projects at Vallauris in the south of France.

There is also a kind Belgian ceramist we call le Père Straten who makes all the plaster casts. He is an older man who has such wonderful stories about life, including women. This particular subject puzzles me completely. I do not understand the full meaning of his stories, but I understand that there is more about this subject than meets the eye.

Maman tells me not to listen to Père Straten because he could have a bad influence on my morality. Papa, on the other hand, says that I should listen. I agree with Papa. So on my two days a week off from school, I am covered in clay, with plaster of Paris sticking to my hair, and am gaining an informal education on art and women.

ONE DAY, GRANDFATHER HENRI arrives from Nice, where he lives most of the year. As he enjoys an aperitif with my parents and Brosse before dinner, they get into a deep discussion about art. I am fascinated, although most of what they debate is incomprehensible to me. What do they mean by *full form, controlled perspective, balancing masses, restraint?* Who wants to be restrained? *Lost contour?* If I lost it, I would just go find it. *Abstract definition?* I like this term so much that I decide to use it during my school art class.

"What are you talking about?" my art teacher says.

"You don't know what abstract definition is? Well, I guess my parents and grandfather are smarter than you are," I reply.

Strangely, my teacher does not care for my observation but then remarks that I am amusing on a dreary day. I am beginning to learn that I should be more diplomatic.

During one discussion with Grandfather, Maman, and Papa, Brosse says all art critics are jackasses. Grandfather Henri agrees wholeheartedly.

A month or two later, we all attend a *vernissage* (an opening reception for an art exhibition) for Grandfather Matisse's works. I dress like a Parisian gentleman. While standing among a group of art connoisseurs, I am introduced to a professional newspaper critic. I know exactly what to say.

"My grandfather Henri is a true artist, and he agrees with Brosse that all art critics are jackasses."

Maman's face turns red, and Papa slaps my face and throws me out of the room. I don't understand. My parents heard Grandfather Henri agree with Brosse. The art life is so complicated.

I AM CRAZY about aviation, and in the spring I decide to undertake my biggest and most interesting project yet. I will construct a glider—not a toy, a real one.

No one pays attention to me as I cut down bamboo on Grandfather's property and gather up my additional materials—string, rope, rags, a tarpaulin and sheet, an orange crate, and two umbrellas—which I store in the garage of the vacant gardener's house. This is where I do my calculations and most of my construction. When it is finished, I will launch myself into the sky from the second-story balcony of the gardener's house. I keep everything under wraps because I want this to be a big surprise for everybody. I imagine Pierre, the flying ace, showing off by gliding majestically over the Matisse estate.

I realize that my parents are somewhat suspicious when I overhear my mother say to my father, "I wonder what Pierre is up to?"

"He has been unusually quiet recently. No trouble at all," Papa muses.

"Which is scary," Maman replies.

Finally, the day arrives. I'm on the balcony, making last-minute adjustments to my invention. I glance down and see my parents walking by below me, unaware of what's about to happen. *How fitting*, I think, *that Maman and Papa shall witness this monumental event*. I straddle my orange crate seat and get comfortable for my first historic flight. My helmet, a copper mixing bowl borrowed from my parents' studio, is sitting on my head, just in case I have a rough landing. I am ready.

Certain of my success, I proudly announce, "Look! I am going to fly."

Suddenly I hear Maman shriek. "No, Pierre! Stop!" And I do. But it must be only a small delay. Once they understand what's at stake—my reputation and recognition as an inventor, aeronautical engineer, and aviator—I must resume my experiment.

Papa takes the stairs four steps at a time, while Maman frantically waves her arms and screams, "No, Pierre, no! You must not do that!"

"Don't worry, Maman," I tell her. *Women*, I think. Still, I haven't moved.

Papa has reached the balcony. *Perfect*. He can give me an added boost by pushing as I propel forward. Instead, he grabs me by my collar. My improvised helmet falls off my head, hitting the ground with an unsettling sound.

"What is that, Pierre?" my father asks, half-angry and half-smiling.

"A glider."

Doesn't he know a flying machine when he sees one?

"Are you crazy?" Papa's question is a little irritating.

It is well known that geniuses are never given the recognition they deserve. I try to explain. "Let me show you, Papa. It will fly."

"The one who is going to show you something is me, Monsieur Aviator. To begin with, this contraption can't fly."

He leans over the balcony's railing and calls down. "Louise, get out of the way."

Papa launches my glider over the side, and it falls straight down like a stone, smashing into pieces on the driveway below with a terrible noise.

I lean over the edge, and the sight of the dead bird is disturbing.

"Can you imagine what could have happened to you, Pierre?"

"Yes, Papa," I say, at a loss for words. *I could have been all broken to pieces inside the wreck.*

"From now on, you stick to balsa models. Understood?"

"Yes, but you see, Papa, there was no pilot at the controls." Eureka! I have found both the problem and the weak point in my father's demonstration. I *knew* my mathematical calculations couldn't have been that far off.

For quite a while, I am the joke of the family, and they call me Icarus after the Greek mythological character who escaped captivity by flying with wings made of feathers and wax. Icarus thought he knew better than his father and ignored the warnings of flying too close to the sun. When he flew too close to it, the heat melted the wax in his wings, and Icarus fell into the sea. Like him, I had to go back to the drawing board.

A week after my aborted flight, I find a book on my bed, *Aviation's Pioneers*. Inside is a note that reads:

To Icarus,
Please take note of how many pilots are dead.
We prefer you stay in one piece.

With love,
Papa and Maman

The book contains photos of crashed planes with each dead pilot's photo bordered in black. The images are a serious setback in my burgeoning aeronautical career. As I stare at the grisly images, it gives me pause and cools off my enthusiasm for inventive flying.

"I'll learn to fly when I am grown up," I declare, undaunted. For the time being, "later" sounds safer.

"YOU ARE UNDER ARREST! Hands up! Higher, please. Not a move or I shoot."

We are in Paris, but the orders are given in English. In the dark corridor, Mister William Sterny hides in the shadows. As soon as I open his door, he captures me.

From his wheelchair, Mister Sterny points a large-caliber pistol straight at my belly. He motions for me to walk into his office by waving the menacing barrel in the direction that I should follow.

"Careful. Don't be a hero, Mister Pierre. Sit here. Put your hands on the table, where I can see them."

I obey as I desperately try to understand every word of English he is saying. To give me a fair chance, Mister Sterny speaks slowly and pronounces his English perfectly.

"I have observed you for some time," he says. "I have deduced from your activities that you are a dangerous spy."

"*C'est pas vrai!*" I answer in French.

He aims the gun toward the ceiling and pops off a shot, making me jump.

"You are not fooling me. Now you pretend not to speak English. English, please, or the next shot is for you."

I correct myself fast in English, "I mean, it is not true."

He is interrupted by a noisy banging at the door.

"Monsieur Sterny, I've told you a thousand times, no shooting in the building. You're scaring the neighbors." It's his concierge, warning him in a friendly tone.

"Madame, I am dealing with a dangerous spy. I had to shoot," he calls out in French.

Thankfully, his revolver is filled with blanks. My private English teacher makes our lessons an adventure. Mister Sterny is an English World War I veteran.

He was seriously wounded during the Battle of Verdun, but when he tells me about the war, there are no hints of regret and anger. "Verdun had too many firecrackers; however, the wine had a definite bouquet while I was there. And then, there was this charming girl in the back country . . ." He married the girl, settled down in France, and received a comfortable wheelchair, which he says "was not a bad deal at all."

I am learning English by play-acting, and every lesson is a new scenario. Today is a spy mystery; at other times, there are pirates on the high seas, airplane pilots, cowboys, and adventurers. I love it.

Soon my uncle Pierre will be coming to visit us from New York. I am his namesake, and I must honor him by speaking English.

When Maman explains that Papa named me after his brother, I can't wait to meet him.

"He is Pierre Matisse, like me?"

"Yes, dear, next week there will be two Pierre Matisses in Paris," Maman says, shaking her head and adding, "I'm not sure any of us are ready for this."

I like the idea very much. When I meet the other Pierre Matisse, I find my father's younger brother to be kind and polite. He certainly speaks English a lot better than I do. I often ask him the same question: "How is America, Uncle Pierre?"

"Wide open for opportunity, my boy," he answers with a warm smile.

His answer has me thinking. Once I am sure he can understand my need for a newer, bigger country, I confide in him. "One day I will go to America."

"And what will you do there?" he asks.

"I'll become an American and get rich. Then I can buy Tata many beautiful gifts."

"That is a good-hearted plan. I'm sure you'll succeed," he replies, giving me a pat on the shoulder. He doesn't laugh, but instead takes me seriously. This Pierre understands and believes in me. We already have the same name, and someday I know we will share the same country.

IN THE SUMMER of 1939, we are on our last family vacation, visiting all of our relatives. I have had my color lesson in Nice with Grandfather Matisse, kept a low profile at Grandmother Amélie's, and now am at Grandfather Milhau's, where he breaks the news that France is now at war with Germany.

Immediately the walls of France are covered with official posters: *Ordre de Mobilisation Générale*, every fit man has to report immediately to the army, navy, or air force. The posters also include the requisition of horses and mules as well as cars or any other items the French government needs. Now everybody has war on their mind.

A few days later, I am sitting with my best and most admired war connoisseur, le Père Goudreaux, Grandfather's gardener and *l'homme à tout faire* (an all-around man). He was a fighter pilot in the last Great War, and I love hearing his war stories.

After finishing his first glass of white Bordeaux, he is doing a plane preflight checkup. At two glasses, he is taking off. The sky is black with the Red Baron and associates. Three glasses later, the Germans are plummeting in droves to the ground, their planes in flames.

"So as I said, Pierre, I am in the sun. The enemy can't see me. I dive. Then—*tac-tac-tac*—smoke is coming out of the fuselage."

This is my kind of man. I sit on the edge of my chair. "Tell me more, Monsieur Goudreaux."

"But the enemy is on my tail, bullets flying all around me."

"And what did you do?" By now I am sweating.

With consummate acting skill, Monsieur Goudreaux moves his hands in the position of the planes in the air. It is all so realistic that I have goose bumps down my back.

"I dive. So does he."

"And then?" I want all the details.

"I make a loop."

"Ho!" I shout, gripping the arms of my chair with both hands. Monsieur Goudreaux turns his empty glass, the fourth one, upside down. The sky is now the ground, and the ground is now the ceiling.

"Suspended by my safety belt at the top of the loop, I see a three-winged Fokker passing in my firing sight. I pull the trigger. Nothing happens!" He takes a deep breath to cope with a persistent hiccup.

Then . . . "My machine gun is jammed!"

I am beginning to worry about who is flying the plane during these few seconds of suspense.

"A fraction of a second left, I clear it. *Tac-tac*. Only two short bursts. He goes down in a flaming spiral."

My heart leaps. By now I have lost count of how many enemy planes the ace has shot down.

"Now I am on the next one's tail. It takes only a small pressure on the trigger. *Tac-tac-tac*. This one blows up in little pieces all over the sky. I must have hit his gas tank. My work is done for the day. I head home."

I am so relieved that he lands safely.

"Excellent, Monsieur Goudreaux. This is precisely what I'm going to do. One loop, *tac-tac-tac*, and Hitler's pilots will be kaput."

"Not so easy, Pierrot! The problem is that we don't have enough planes," he tells me in confidence.

"Why don't we make more planes, Monsieur Goudreaux?"

"Because then we won't have enough pilots to fly them," the expert replies.

What a dilemma! War is so complicated—a lot like art. I have, however, worked out a solution. That night I find Papa.

"Papa, Monsieur Goudreaux said . . ." I begin, but he interrupts before I finish my sentence.

"Pierrot! You have better things to do than listen to le Père Goudreaux. He was only a cook for a bombing squadron."

My World War I hero has just been shot down, flames and all. No loops? No *tac-tac-tac*? Monsieur Goudreaux is, for me, the first serious war casualty. Soon after, Papa is mobilized and on his way to join his regiment.

WHILE MAMAN GOES TO PARIS to take care of the art business, Gérard, Tata, and I stay with Grandfather Milhau from September to December of 1939. One day, out of the blue, I think of my beloved cocker spaniel, Bouboule, and something breaks open inside of me. I am beside myself with tears as if all the fears and sorrow and memories are unleashed within me—from Aurora's death to Papa leaving to losing my sweet dog and best friend. World War II is starting off on the wrong foot. Tata tries to comfort me, but for a time I cannot escape the grief that wraps itself around me.

When we return to Paris in December, all of France has turned crazy. Paris, the City of Light, is in total blackout at night. We tape or glue paper to the windows in a futile trick to give some protection against bomb explosions. There are many people living here who still have fresh and horrific memories of the previous war fought with the Germans on French soil.

But we have a wonderful surprise in early 1940 when Papa comes home on leave. My hero looks magnificent in his uniform. Papa is a sergeant in an engineering unit specializing in camouflage. Unfortunately, his leave is cut short when he gets word that his unit has been ordered to the front. All of us are devastated; Maman is in tears, and Gérard and I join in.

I think of the World War I veterans in Paris. We call them *les gueules cassées*, the broken faces. Is something terrible like this going to happen to Papa—or something worse?

Papa quickly puts things in order and boosts everybody's morale.

"France is going to win this war in a short time. I'll be back early in the spring," Papa declares with an air of confidence that clears the black clouds lingering in our minds.

Nevertheless, when Papa leaves, a nasty vise twists my heart. I have a hard time holding back my tears as he reminds me of the words he said to me on the beach, the day the war began. "Pierre, you are a man. As long as I am gone, you will have to take care of your mother and Gérard."

I give Papa my solemn word to do exactly that. I am eleven years old and will be the man he needs me to be.

What concerns me is the lack of French planes mentioned by le Père Goudreaux. I must solve this problem pronto. I have a brilliant solution. We will bluff the enemy.

"Why not paint hundreds of planes on carefully selected fields? When viewed from the air, this should scare even the most daring *Boches*," I tell Papa. I am certain that when Luftwaffe Marshal Hermann Goering evaluates the odds against such massive numbers of French airplanes, he will surely roll over and surrender. Et voilà! The war is over!

My father listens with a patient smile. "Excellent strategy, Pierre. I'll pass it on to the general."

When I discover that Adolf Hitler has been in cahoots with Franco, who took my Aurora, I am beside myself. Adolf Hitler had better watch out. My target list is growing.

5

A FUNNY WAR

In war as in love, everything goes.

OLD FRENCH PROVERB

EVERYONE IS AFRAID of aerial bombing raids on the big population centers. Some evacuation efforts have been implemented. However, the war takes an unexpected turn, and suddenly everything is quiet from September until April. There is no shooting, no bombing, no offensive in France. People call this *la drôle de guerre* or the Funny War.

We get used to this quiet war; Hitler is on the march elsewhere. Gérard stays with Maman at the apartment on l'avenue de Clamart, and I return to live with Tata, visiting Maman on weekends. *Maybe this war will not be so bad after all*, I think.

People begin to say things like "Hitler will calm down. It will be over soon, without damage."

Everybody except Tata, that is. She firmly states, "It's not over yet. Wait and see."

"They can't stop this war before I get to Franco and his accomplice, that infamous Adolf Hitler. These two monsters will pay dearly for Aurora. I will see to that," I reply.

From 1939 until the bombing begins, the war sirens are tested every Saturday at noon. The long and mournful whine is a sinister noise that immediately brings on fear. Occasionally, they even scream in the night. *Alert! The Germans are coming to bomb us*, the sirens say.

Whenever we are awakened by the sound, we grab our coats from the closet or a blanket and race to the underground shelters in the apartment building in our nightclothes. It is dark, cold, damp, dusty, and very scary down there. Piles of black coal are stacked in one corner. Tata tries to comfort me by holding my hand, and I pray for courage.

"I want to confront the Fritzes in the open air," I tell her. Defying them one by one is my style, but they never come.

After a few weeks, nobody bothers to race to the shelter when the siren goes off. Surely the Funny War will end by spring, people say, just in time for the lilies of the valley to bloom, *n'est-ce pas*?

I AM NOW ENROLLED in the rue d'Alésia School for boys. The windows are big so I can see the misty Paris sky through the branches of the large plane trees. Instead of studying, I daydream of my own future heroic war exploits once I join the French air force.

Our teacher, Monsieur Brouchard, is a skinny, tall, ascetic man with a yellow face and a nose so long I'm sure it can split a stone in two. His dead eyes never smile. He has no sense of humor whatsoever. Even his clothes are always gray. We have given him a nickname, Brouillard, meaning "fog." Monsieur Brouillard never raises his monotone voice one octave above dull. Even his speech sounds like a muted foghorn. He carries himself as if there's no hope and no excitement left in this world.

One day we hear the latest official gossip. The Germans are going to bomb Paris with mustard gas. The authorities decide to issue gas masks to every citizen. Monsieur Brouillard must take our whole class to the location where they will fit us with our gas masks.

"Everybody stand behind me, understand? I am taking care of this. That means *you*, Monsieur Pierre Matisse."

These are his last controlled words. Ahead of us, an official distributes gas masks to another class. Monsieur Brouillard raises his right arm and stands like a statue. He doesn't move. And neither do any of us.

His face turns from yellow to violet purple. Suddenly, Monsieur Brouillard shakes a menacing fist at the official and blasts him with his foghorn voice. He starts foaming at the mouth. His angry words come out, loud and clear.

"Pigs! You there! Yes, you! You are not going to do this to my children. I will not permit it! Do you hear me? Never! You idiots! Never! Never!"

He is right beside me, looking twenty feet tall. I realize that he is not talking to the official. He is spouting vulgarities at our enemy, yet there is something dignified about him. The other boys and I are stunned into silence.

Someone calls the school principal, who arrives promptly. He tries his best to calm down Monsieur Brouillard but without much success. Eventually, they call the ambulance.

"You will nev—my chil—" He is unable to finish a sentence as they guide him away.

I return home from school with my gas mask in its gray canister. When I open the canister, an offensive stench of mothballs mixed with decaying rubber stings my nostrils.

I tell Tata what happened with Monsieur Brouillard. She can't hold back her tears. He is a good man and a dear friend of hers, she says, and he was badly injured by mustard gas in 1916 near Verdun. The poor fellow had a massive nervous breakdown.

The next Sunday we go to the hospital to visit him. When Tata lets the attendant know whom we are coming to see, the lady tells Tata, "Madame, flowers are out of the question for your friend. He associates the perfumed fragrance with mustard gas and immediately goes into a rage."

Tata understands and hands the flowers we brought to the attendant. "Very well. Keep them for yourself and put them on your desk."

This is the saddest thing that I have ever heard. To deprive a man of the enjoyment of flowers is criminal. World War I has done this to Monsieur Brouillard!

When we come into his room, he greets me with a faint smile. "Ha! Pierre Matisse, the dreamer."

Seeing Tata, he begins to grow agitated again, ranting about wars involving children. "Ah! Henriette, if you only knew. They want to gas my children. Never! Never!"

Soon it is time for us to leave. I later learn that when the war begins in earnest, Monsieur Brouillard goes crazy and is placed in an insane asylum.

After this tragedy, none of us ever refer to him as Brouillard again. He becomes a true hero to us.

EVERY WEEK DURING SCHOOL, we rehearse the gas mask routine. In spite of my ongoing efforts to aerate the wretched gadget, it reeks of chemicals. With this abominable contraption on my face, I feel caught in an atrocious rattrap, which instantly triggers claustrophobia. During our school practice, one student or another either vomits into his gas mask or faints. A nurse is always at the ready for the casualties.

We do the routine in groups. When the doors open, one group marches out while the next marches in for the test. Once inside we are supposed to keep the masks on our faces for a few minutes. It's an eternity! I decide to volunteer to be the first in our group. I march in, put on my mask, then join the group exiting, skipping the test entirely. I'll take my chances if a real gas war situation arises.

Eventually, the officials discover that these masks are defective, perhaps sabotaged. They were manufactured in Austria under the Nazi regime. We go through the process of exchanging our masks for another brand that seems no better than the first.

Eventually the German planes show up in the night. We hear the engines roaring just over Paris. They don't drop a thing. Anti-aircraft guns fire some shots at them, but nothing much happens. There is no harm done to either side.

Later, they become more daring, coming in broad daylight. But nobody pays much attention to the enemy's air force anymore.

ONE SUNDAY AFTERNOON the German airplanes come in greater numbers than usual. This time, they do drop something—tracts. Tata and I are running errands when the little propaganda pamphlets flutter down from the sky. They are well printed and quite attractive with red covers. Written in French, they boast of the might of the German forces. The tracts do no physical harm, except for one unfortunate man who is hit by an unopened package of a hundred or so and is killed on the spot.

When Tata and I return from some errands, we see our concierge, Madame Bigot, standing in the front of the building, excitedly addressing a small crowd of passersby. We can't help but hear her anti-tract speech. She is standing there, all of four feet tall and skinny as a rake, shaking a fistful of the little red pamphlets above her head. She reads from the propaganda pamphlet in her high-pitched voice, adding her own colorful commentary.

"So you have thousands of tanks and planes, Adolf? Well, so do we! And come spring, we are going to kick your arse, regardless of your arsenal."

She throws her shoulders back and raises her head like a true French general.

She continues to rile up the crowd with her posturing and crude comments. She is a master of timing and suspense. Tata approves of the concierge's patriotism but not her vulgar language. With Tata standing beside me, I have to resist clapping and yelling bravo at the woman's antics.

"Pierrot, I think it's time to go up to the apartment," Tata says at last. As we climb the stairs to the fourth floor, Tata bursts out laughing. She looks at me, and I start laughing too.

When she finally can control herself, she says, "Pierrot, please do me a favor. Do not ever imitate her language."

"Tata, I am going to write French tracts to drop on the Germans, but mine are going to be better and illustrated with my own art."

"You do that, Pierrot," she says in a soft, tired voice.

SOMETHING HAS HAPPENED TO PARIS. There are no more visits to the museums now. They are all closed. All of the ponds and park fountains have been emptied of water because they shine at night and can be used to guide enemy aircraft. There is no more sailing my sailboat on the ponds. Tanks line up the whole length of Boulevard Brune.

"Those tanks are too small. They won't do," I overhear a World War I veteran say, a man with one leg who has four military decorations carefully pinned on his coat.

Piles of discarded scrap metal are left at some street corners to be collected. This is a war effort to melt down metal and make new armaments. In one of those scrap piles I find a discarded rusty revolver—a big one, probably a forty-five caliber. The mainspring is broken, but otherwise the menacing black barrel is quite intimidating. I bring it to class in my leather book pouch.

At school we have a new teacher to replace Monsieur Brouchard. I don't like him.

"Perhaps Monsieur Pierre Matisse would like to repeat, for the benefit of the class, what I just said?"

Did I hear my name? Distractedly, I turn my eyes from the cloud out the window where I am pursuing a Messerschmitt that has been evading me for the last few minutes.

"Would you please wake up, Monsieur Matisse, and be kind enough to share with us what is so interesting outside the window?"

I instinctively reach into my pouch and pull out the massive handgun, placing it firmly on my desk.

"Maybe *you* can tell us why *you* are not at the front fighting with my father?" I rudely demand of the teacher, thinking of Papa lost somewhere on the front line.

At that, he panics, running for the door as if his behind is on fire.

"I knew it! He's a coward! The gun isn't even loaded," I declare to the petrified class.

My classmates burst into laughter, releasing their fear. I quickly pack my books and gun, as the principal arrives to take me out of class.

I am expelled from the school, which ends up closing two months later. After giving me a stern lecture, Tata takes the education of her impossible nephew firmly in hand. From now on I attend Tata's private school at home from morning to evening. There is no more fooling around. I learn more in the next two months than in my two years of formal schooling. On Fridays I speak only English because on this day Tata understands only Shakespeare's native tongue.

My dear Tata gives me an invaluable gift—the desire to learn and the ability to teach myself anything I put my mind to. This priceless treasure will serve me well throughout my entire life.

ONCE A WEEK I visit Maman and Gérard in Issy-les-Moulineaux. Maman is alone now in the studio with only Père Straten to help her. Brosse is on the front lines with Papa. My mother struggles to keep the family business going. I notice how her wonderful smile is gone, and worse, she looks tired and worried all the time.

A few months into 1940 Papa comes home again for a week's leave. What a hero! Papa's leave appears to pass like a few hours. Before he returns to the front, we have a talk alone, man to man. Papa says, "War makes you old before your time. Come spring, this war is going to start in earnest. Pierre, you have no choice except to be a man. The games will no longer be games; they are going to be for real."

"Yes, Papa."

From this day on, Pierrot Tatiou is gone. I am Pierre Matisse, a man like my father with serious responsibilities. In war times children grow up fast. Papa leaves, and suddenly I feel like a very old man.

IN JUNE, WHEN I am staying with Maman and Gérard, Hitler's planes awaken us from our sleep. This time, they are not dropping tracts but bombs!

We feel the concussion of a bomb hitting a target. Our apartment rocks like we are in an earthquake. When the sirens finally fade, we go outside and see chaos everywhere. Only one block away, a six-story apartment building has just been hit. Half the structure has crumbled down into the street. The other half still stands precariously, looking like it will topple down at any moment.

I hear someone screaming and glance up. On the sixth floor of the building, I see a bedroom cut in half and a man, unharmed, is in his bed. "Please, get my pants. They are on the street!"

Down below, firemen and volunteers dig through massive blocks of stone and brick, risking their lives to save buried victims.

We cannot walk far. The entire street is blocked by the rubble. I keep a protective eye on Gérard and Maman, but there is so much smoke coming from all around Paris where bombs were dropped. I am praying to God that Tata is safe. On the sidewalk, blankets cover the dead. Some are much too small to be lying there dead. I immediately think of Monsieur Brouchard. He would not like this—his children have been bombed.

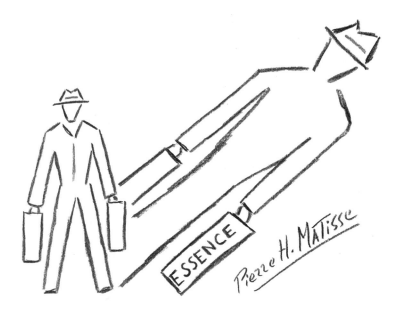

6

LES BOCHES ARE COMING

Necessity hath no law.

OLIVER CROMWELL

A PERFECTLY WAXED wood floor is to the French what a perfectly clipped lawn is to the English. The French wonder why the English are so obsessed with their green lawns. The English wonder why the French keep on polishing their *parquet ciré*.

"Be careful with my waxed floor. Take your shoes off, and put on your slippers," Tata's maid tells me. She comes once a week to take care of Tata's apartment and stay with her until I come home from school.

I don't like this maid and give her an insolent reply. "We should invite the Boches with their boots to walk on *your* floor. They will all slip and break their necks, and we will win the war."

"Little monster! I am going to report you to your aunt."

"Your floor is like a skating rink. Last week I almost broke my back on it."

She leaves, muttering angrily about me under her breath.

But then the inevitable happens. Somebody takes a bad fall, and it's Tata! She slips and breaks her hip. Tata is immobilized by a plaster cast, confined to her bed, which is moved to the living room. Every time she winces or grows pale from the pain, my stomach is torn apart. I want to save Tata from every kind of pain.

"If Aurora had been your maid, this wouldn't have happened," I confide to Tata at her bedside.

Soon after Tata's injury, the wail of the sirens echoes through the middle of the night. Now we take them seriously. Tata cannot move to go to the shelter.

"Pierre, you must go to the shelter," she orders me firmly.

"No. I am *not* going." This subject is not open for negotiation. I will not leave Tata behind.

"Pierre, you *are* going right now. I want you to go down right away!"

"No."

"Why not?" The tone of her voice softens.

"I'm staying with you," I answer more gently, yet still full of conviction.

She is no longer telling me anymore; now, she is pleading. "This is out of the question."

Tata picks up the phone by her night table and dials the concierge. "Madame Bigot, could you please be kind enough to come up to escort Pierre safely into the shelter?"

The sirens stop screaming. All is silent. The concierge arrives, a little short of breath from climbing the four flights of stairs much too fast.

"Pierre, down you go," the concierge states. "One, two, into the shelter, let's get cracking. Now!"

When I refuse to move, she slaps me. I turn my back to her and face Tata. Then the concierge lands a perfect shot in the middle of my behind with her foot.

"I am not going. I will not go! I am staying with Tata."

"Obstinate, eh?" she says. A second sharp slap from her burns my other cheek.

"I am not going, Madame Bigot," I mumble between my tears. "Tata needs me. My duty is here."

"Mademoiselle Escousse, we'd better face it. He will not go."

The concierge gives me a knowing smile as she turns to leave. She understands it's my duty.

It is dark and strangely silent for a while. Then we hear a faint annoying noise coming from somewhere in the night that grows steadily.

Soon noisy airplane engines are roaring in the sky—lots of them. Far away, heavy anti-aircraft guns start firing. On a roof close to us, an ack-ack gun begins shooting a barrage of tracer bullets, punctuating the sky with a deadly rhythm. Now the roar of the planes and the blast of the guns become louder, while at the same time we hear the unmistakable whistling sound of bombs falling, just above our heads, it seems.

"Pierre, my darling, get me a glass of water, please."

Tata's voice is firm, without a trace of fear, while I am hopelessly shaking from head to toe. I go to the kitchen and see that the glasses on the shelves are shaking too. I take one, fill it up, turn around, and spill its contents on the floor, so I go back and fill it again. This time I make it back to Tata without losing a drop. It's a small victory over my fear.

"Thank you, dear. Now, come sit here on the bed with me."

"No! I want to sit on the chair," I say in desperation, trying to control my panic and shaking. I know that the shelter would be the safest place to be, but I will not go down there without my beloved Tata.

"Not on the chair, Pierre. On the bed."

Slowly, I obey her. I know that I will shake the whole bed, which, to my shame, I do. Tata takes my quivering hand and proceeds to tell me a story.

"In 1643, at the Battle of Rocroi during the Thirty Years' War, General Condé is mounted on his horse, surrounded by his staff of officers. The enemy batteries—much too close for comfort—are firing. Shells are falling all around and coming closer."

She pauses, then raises her voice a decibel so that I can hear her over the noise that is getting louder outside. "General Condé's whole body shakes a *lot* worse than yours does now."

She stops. Something whistles high above our heads.

"It is a bomb, Pierre." Her voice is calm as she squeezes my hand more firmly. There is a bright flash, and the windows vibrate from an infernal noise. We hear plates in the kitchen fall from the cupboards, shattering on the floor. Above the *pom-pom* of the guns, Tata continues her history lesson.

"Every staff officer is looking at General Condé. He turns to them and firmly states, 'Body, shake as much as you want, because if you knew where I am going to take you, you certainly would shake even more.' Then he gives the orders to move even closer to danger."

We hear more whistling, followed by explosions and flashes of light. The walls shudder, and more glass shatters.

Finally, the dreaded engines' roar fades away. The silence of the night returns. After a few minutes, the siren announces that the danger has passed. We have survived another bombing raid.

IN THE STREETS OF PARIS, panic reigns supreme. *Rumeurs du jour* are served all day long.

"We have been betrayed," says the taxi driver.

"There are spies everywhere," a street merchant tells us.

"In Belgium, the Boches have bayoneted babies," the street sweeper states with conviction while leaning on his broom.

"Their tanks are huge. They run over everybody in the roads," the postman tells us.

I join the war effort by putting my artistic talent to something useful. I participate in a national contest to create a patriotic poster. Mine depicts a French couple (the man wears a traditional beret), both dressed in blue, white, and red, dancing on a broken black swastika. I am quite certain I will be the number one poster artist.

When the jury chooses a different design, I tell Tata, "The contest is rigged by undercover spies who are all over France."

We hear contrary news reports from the front lines, all of which are unsettling. Newspapers have big blank spaces in them, officially censored by the French government. Not only is there nothing to read, we can't believe anything there is to read anymore.

However, one thing is clear: The war situation is going from bad to worse. The roads all around Paris are jammed with refugees from

Belgium and the northern part of France. The refugees travel south in cars, horse carts, and on foot, carrying a few prized possessions. These poor people have the horrors of war etched on their faces.

Throughout France, an indescribable panic with a capital *P* rumbles through us all. The desperate hope is that *somewhere* along this retreat, the French army will stop the Nazis and push them back into their own country.

Grandfather Milhau sends an ambulance to Paris to transport Tata to his home. I will go to stay with my mother and Gérard. Leaving Tata in her terrible condition is very traumatic for me. I look back at her building and wonder when she and I will be reunited there again. It is truly a miracle that Tata makes the journey safely, and with the Germans coming closer to Paris, it is even a greater miracle we receive a letter to confirm that she does.

WE HEAR MORE bad news in July. "The French front lines have collapsed. The French government is moving from Paris to the town of Vichy." Then the radio stations and newspaper offices close down. Paris must fend for itself against the German invasion.

Air raids are constant now. Maman refuses to be chased into the shelter by the Germans. Every night there is no sleep for Paris. Maman, Gérard, and I ride out the raids in our sixth-floor apartment. I keep my promise to Papa, helping Maman and Gérard to be brave.

We have had no news from Papa for the last two months. No one knows where he is, and we are all worried sick about his well-being. The rumors are that the casualties on the front are heavy. The Germans are taking French soldiers prisoner by the thousands.

I console my mother by saying that Papa is very smart and very brave. With these qualities, he will survive anything. If he is taken prisoner, he will surely escape. I am confident nothing will happen to my father. Papa is a hero. Hitler's men are no match for his cunning strategy and unwavering bravery.

Finally, we must flee too. Maman and Papa have friends in Bordeaux, the Marrots, who have offered us asylum. It was arranged before Papa left so he would know where to find us if we were forced out of Paris.

I help my mother pack our big car. On the roof she securely ties the massive antique Spanish table that was her mother's, her cherished possession. The car is packed with suitcases inside and in the trunk. Our gardener/chauffeur, Monsieur Jacques, has agreed to drive us out of harm's way. The trip from Paris to Bordeaux is normally a three- or four-day drive. It will take us almost two weeks to get to our destination.

The roads are packed solid with the remnants of a defeated French army in retreat and a civilian population in the throes of an uncontrollable panic.

My mother wakes in the backseat. "Why are we stopping, Jacques?"

"Over this hill is a small village, and the road is narrowing." This seems an acceptable answer to Maman as she sinks back against the seat and closes her eyes.

We move at a crawl up a hill and stop again after a few yards on the top. Less than a mile down the hill is a small village with a main street and a half-dozen narrow side streets. From where we have stopped, we can see all the way to the center of town.

It is like being in a theater. I see miles of human ants crowding the roads, laboriously moving junk to apparently nowhere. The spectacle is incredible.

"What are they doing?" I ask Monsieur Jacques.

"Looting. The village has been abandoned."

Now I understand what I am seeing. People are running from one side of the main street to the other, entering stores and houses, coming out with all kinds of things. They dump items in the middle of the sidewalk, rummage through it, and pick out anything that appeals to them. I see people throw away belongings from their vehicles or carts and replace them with stolen goods.

"They are thieves," I say to Jacques, shaking my head in disbelief.

"No, Pierre. They are just patriot looters. If they don't take it, the German army will."

Suddenly, out of the sky, two planes come from nowhere.

"Look at that!" I say, watching the fighter planes with the black crosses on the bottom of the wings and a smaller swastika on the tail. They dive, following the slope of the hill close to the road. The planes, like everybody else, are heading downtown. *Tac-tac-tac* . . . We have the best balcony seats for this terrible show.

Now under fire, the people in the village abandon their goods and run for cover. Ahead of us, halfway down the hill, two soldiers jump out of a small French military truck covered with a green tarpaulin. One pulls out a big rifle with a small bipod attached to the front of the barrel. He rests it on the right shoulder of the other soldier. The planes circle for another strafing pass. They fly so close that I can clearly see the pilots' heads. The planes fire, and so does the soldier.

"He hit one! He got one!" yells Monsieur Jacques.

One of the planes disappears to the east. The other small monoplane rolls sideways, a stream of smoke coming from the fuselage. His motor has stopped. The plane seems to stand still as if suspended in midair, then he glides, finally belly landing in a garden on the outskirts of town.

For the first time, I wonder about our safety. We'd be easy targets at the top of the hill if other German fighter planes want to pluck off more civilians.

"He survived!" Jacques exclaims.

I lean out the window to see. The pilot, apparently unharmed, opens the sliding hatch of the cockpit. But from the little village, the crowd moves like a tidal wave toward the downed plane. In minutes, the small aircraft is surrounded.

From his cockpit, the pilot is trying to climb out of the airplane. We hear the roar of people shouting and cursing as they reach the pilot. They lift him over their heads, then the pilot disappears inside the circling mob.

I watch in dazed horror as he is torn apart limb by limb. A French officer shoots his pistol in the air to stop the madness, but it's too late. It happens so fast. The ants have killed the big insect. I feel sick inside.

"What is it, Jacques? What's happening?" Maman asks. I am thankful that she cannot see very well from the backseat. Gérard has slept through the whole thing.

"Nothing we could help, Madame Matisse. It is the war. An enemy pilot has just been killed." Jacques is keeping his vow to my father to protect my mother, not volunteering any unnecessary grisly details.

"How horrible!" she replies, leaning forward toward the window.

The line of cars in front of us creeps forward at last. I do not look at the downed plane.

"Clutch in, first gear in, up and to the right, hand brake out, slow on the gas pedal," instructs Monsieur Jacques. He gives me a wink, hoping to clear the horrific sight from my mind. I wink back. We are partners now.

"Are we stopping here, Jacques?" Maman asks.

"I would not advise stopping in this village, Madame."

"Only for food and drinks, Jacques," my mother says, trying to see the village ahead.

"No, Madame, not here. It is not safe. There is a small town about six miles away. We'll spend the night there."

"How long until we get to Bordeaux?"

"If we are lucky, one very long day more, perhaps two. At this pace, it's hard to say for sure, Madame."

The road clears somewhat, and we move slowly through the village. Here and there, on the pavement, I see large puddles of blood, a sinister testimony of the victims of the planes' strafing. Monsieur Jacques makes a wide circle around an old car on fire. The acrid smell of burning rubber, oil, and paint is thick, and we cover our noses.

On the sidewalk a little girl is crying as somebody cleans the blood off her mother's face.

At an intersection, an open truck turns in front of us. My eyes widen as I see two bodies lying inside. One corpse is missing a leg, with the remaining leg dangling pitifully over the back of the truck. As the vehicle lurches forward, a shoe falls off its bloody foot.

Monsieur Jacques curses between clenched teeth.

We are forced to follow the truck for some time. I cannot move or speak. Jacques grips the steering wheel even tighter, and I can see tears running down his cheeks.

This is not really happening, none of it. But it is.

I hear Maman sobbing softly in the backseat. She is finally aware of the tragedy around us. Fortunately, Gérard is still sleeping. *This is good,* I think. Perhaps he can remain a child for a while longer. But something has been taken from me in these moments. An innocent faith in people and my personal safety are stripped away. *Where is God?*

The question in my mind leaves quickly. I am not willing to relinquish all hope. God must be tending to more pressing needs elsewhere, I reason. Surely He will come soon. As I realize we may not survive this war, I say a silent prayer for Tata, Papa, and all of our family. And I ask God for courage to take care of Maman and Gérard, as I promised Papa I would do.

Monsieur Jacques slowly navigates the car around a number of wrecked vehicles obstructing the road as we finally put the village behind us. Fortunately, the truck is no longer in front of us.

"Pierre, tell me about your invention," Monsieur Jacques inquires.

"I am not inventing anything today." I cannot get the images of what I have seen out of my mind.

"So tell me about your aunt Tata." Jacques valiantly tries to divert my attention from unpleasant thoughts.

I think of Tata. I hope her hip is healing and that she and Grandfather Milhau are safe from the Boches in Saint-Georges-de-Didonne—that is, if anywhere is safe from them.

"In 1917, during World War I, she got la Légion d'honneur," I mutter. Dwelling on Tata gives me strength.

"Really! And what was that for?"

"She evacuated all the children in her school during a bombing raid in Paris, saving all of her students."

"Tata must be quite a woman!"

I cannot help but grin. Behind me, Maman has grown quiet. "She is the best, Monsieur Jacques, the best," I say. "And she doesn't even shake when the bombs fall."

"Ha! And what about you? Do you shake, Pierre?"

I glance at him. "What about you, Monsieur Jacques?"

"Just a little bit, Pierre," he says with a smile.

"Like you, Monsieur Jacques, I shake just a little. But Tata, she does not shake at all."

"An amazing woman she must be."

"Truly, Monsieur Jacques, she is *very* brave."

As we continue toward Bordeaux, haggard infantry soldiers are on foot, on horseback, or in trucks towing artillery guns. I see demolished or partially burned army and civilian vehicles of all kinds in roadside ditches.

Thousands of civilian refugees jam the roads in battered cars, horse carts, bicycles, or push handcarts, the poorest of them walking with nothing but a backpack. The overwhelming majority are old people and women with their babies and children. In one cart, I see a mattress, chairs, a table, and a framed picture of a bride and groom. The army has requisitioned almost every decent vehicle available.

Gasoline becomes scarce. Eventually, we run out. Not a drop is available in the villages or among the refugees crowding the roads. When we are forced to stop, Jacques tries to make sure there is an inn or bistro nearby where Maman and Gérard can stay, before he and I return to the car and sleep. Somehow the next day, we have gas again, and we slowly merge into the bumper-to-bumper traffic that never lets up. When one road becomes impassible, we find another road heading south to access. Sadly, every person is thinking of his or her own survival, so there is little camaraderie or communication with others on the road.

WHAT MAMAN DOESN'T KNOW is that our chauffeur is often risking his life to steal precious gas from French military trucks at night.

One night Monsieur Jacques explains to Maman, "Madame, I need to go look for some information on the best route for tomorrow. I would like to take Pierre along. It inspires more confidence if I have a kid with me."

"Wouldn't you rather wait until tomorrow morning in the daylight?" she asks.

"No, Madame. Believe me, it's safer at night."

My mother gives me a long look and then agrees reluctantly. Once we are alone, Monsieur Jacques explains and justifies the mission to me.

"The army doesn't need gas. They need to stop running and stay where they are to stop the Boches right now, here, in this very place."

Monsieur Jacques is talented. It doesn't take him very much time to find an army truck with the necessary jerry cans. Once his target has been selected, he sets me up as lookout. He hands me some money and gives me instructions. "Pierre, if a sentinel or a soldier comes, run toward him and keep him busy asking if he knows where your father is and where you can buy some food."

An hour later Monsieur Jacques is back with a can of gasoline that we carry to the car. The next morning, Jacques makes up a story for Maman of how he was able to get the needed gas for our continued journey. We do this a few times.

But then one night it seems to take him forever. I grow anxious sitting in the dark. Suddenly I hear shots being fired. I leap to my feet and look all around to be sure no one is coming. Monsieur Jacques still doesn't appear, and I am certain he has been killed.

Then I see him, emerging from the darkness. His hands are empty, but he is alive and uninjured.

"No wonder we are losing the war," he says, breathing hard. "Those guys are such poor shots."

We return to the car, which is hidden in a peach orchard. Maman is awake and has been worried sick. She sends me straight to my bed in the car.

IN THE MORNING, Monsieur Jacques approaches Maman to explain the situation. "Madame, there is no more gas available at this time from here to Bordeaux."

"So! What do you suggest, Jacques?" she asks.

"We wait, Madame. Have patience. When it is safe to move, we will go. Now we wait for the right conditions."

Late that evening, Monsieur Jacques wakes us up. "It is time to continue to Bordeaux."

He drives two kilometers on a small back road to the place where the shooting occurred the night before. The army trucks have gone, and the place is deserted.

Monsieur Jacques stops the car, and I follow him to an outcropping of bushes. Hidden under some hay are three cans full of gas that he had stashed earlier.

"Madame, we have to throw these suitcases away to make room for the gasoline."

"You must be crazy. No, I'll never do that!" Maman replies.

Monsieur Jacques has had enough. "In that case, you are on your own; I am walking away."

When Maman does not relent, Monsieur Jacques does just as he says.

Turning his back on us, he walks down the road. Finally, my mother runs after him.

"Please, come back," she says.

"The suitcases go?"

"Yes, but I'll tell my husband about this."

Monsieur Jacques nods his head. "Fine with me. Fair enough, Madame Matisse!"

We are crawling through stop-and-go traffic along jammed roads, only able to go about twelve miles per hour. In one place it takes an entire morning just to cross a bridge.

"What are the soldiers doing with those wires along the bridge?" my mother asks Monsieur Jacques.

"They are setting explosives to blow it up."

Maman looks surprised, watching the men roll out large spools of wire. "Why would they want to do that?"

"To slow down the German army that is not far behind us." He puts the car in gear, and we move a little faster.

As we continue, Jacques glances my way where I am sitting in the front passenger seat. "Pierre, pay close attention to how I drive. If something happens to me, you will have to drive."

Then he adds sadly. "This time we can't stop them. Les Boches are coming, Madame."

7
THE BIG BANG

The childhood shows the man, as morning shows the day.

JOHN MILTON

THE HEAT IN THE CAR is stifling, even with the windows down. We no longer try to clean ourselves because water is too precious. When we are fortunate, we can get water from streams or from fountains in the villages we pass through. Our stomachs are beyond the point of feeling hunger because our meager food supply is gone.

Mostly, I want to drink an ocean.

Gérard and Maman are dozing in the backseat of the car. In the front seat, I am numb, somewhere between a nightmare and a dream. There seems to be no reality.

"Pierre, tell me more about Aurora, Marius, and Alberto," Monsieur Jacques requests, as he navigates the car at its slow pace.

"I have already told you those stories a thousand times," I lament.

"Tell me again." He tries unsuccessfully to wipe the sweat running from his forehead into his eyes, dabbing at it with an already soaked handkerchief.

"No, I am too thirsty." An intolerable languor takes hold of me. With the roads jammed, the gas running out, the search for food and water, and trying to avoid the advancing Germans, we've been traveling for almost two weeks.

"There is nothing more to drink. But in an hour we should come to a small town. Shortly we will have plenty of food and water, maybe even a cold lemonade."

"You said the same thing at the last town, and there was nothing there."

"This one will be different, trust me. Talk to me, Pierre. So you want to be an inventor. What are you going to invent?" Suddenly he starts slapping his cheeks.

His actions get my attention. "Why are you slapping your cheeks, Monsieur Jacques?"

"These abominable flies are driving me nuts," he says.

"I don't see any flies." I open my eyes wider, looking around to confirm. There are none.

"Maybe you should open your eyes, my boy; you seem to be half-asleep," Jacques says.

"And so are you!" As soon as I let go with this smart reply, I regret it.

Monsieur Jacques straightens up and grips the steering wheel. "That was borderline insolence, little Monsieur Pierre Matisse. Do you know that?"

"Sorry, I didn't mean it to be," I reply sincerely. I look down at the floorboard. He is such a nice man, and we would be lost without him. I am ashamed to have treated him poorly.

"No harm done, Tatiou," he says softly. I am grateful that he understands my lack of control.

Ahead of us, the already slow traffic stops. On the right, I catch sight of a partially burned army truck.

"Property of the English Royal Air Force. They have burned it so that the Germans can't use it," comments Jacques.

THE NEXT DAY we finally arrive in Bordeaux, completely exhausted but without a scratch.

The Marrots live in a mini-castle, comparable in size to the one on Grandfather Matisse's property near Paris. I roll out of the car, thankful to be able to stretch my aching legs. Maman seeks out her friends immediately, but when we enter the big house, we are shocked to find that it is packed wall-to-wall with children, mothers, and grandparents. Every room is chaotic. There are makeshift beds all over the floors.

"This is where we are staying?" Gérard asks me.

"I believe it is," I reply.

Madame Marrot graciously welcomes us—three more weary Parisian refugees. Maman, Jacques, and I quickly unpack the car. Jacques is staying nearby with a friend of the Marrots and bids us good-bye. He takes the car with him and will hide it for safekeeping.

After having some food and drink, we almost feel human again. We are gathered in the living room when a door is slammed somewhere in the house. A little girl about four years old jumps and screams at the sound and starts shaking uncontrollably. Her mother hugs her and tries to soothe her.

"She has been shell-shocked on the trip from Paris," her grandfather explains from a chair nearby us. He puffs on an abominably smelly cigar, which makes my stomach roil with nausea.

"Your cigar stinks so bad it could stop the Boches," I tell him.

"Pierre, be polite, would you please?" Maman scolds me.

"The truth comes from the mouths of children," a woman sitting nearby declares. She disapproves of the offensive cigar too.

An older man comes into the room. His huge white beard makes him look like Santa Claus, and he gives the impression of someone in authority. "Good news. We are safe here," he announces. "With no troops to defend it, the mayor has declared Bordeaux an open city."

"What does that mean?" a young pretty woman asks.

"According to the Geneva Convention, the German army cannot bomb this city," Santa Claus answers.

"Are you sure the Boches know that?" another lady says with a skeptical look on her face.

"Of course. They can enter the city without fear of opposition, so why should they bomb us?" Santa Claus explains.

That night Bordeaux is bombed. Apparently, Hitler has written his own convention. We sit in the dark living room of the mansion, huddled together. Some people cry and others pray. Whenever a bomb hits the ground, the mansion shakes, and we hear glass shatter. The little girl cries louder and shakes even more and cannot be comforted until long after the planes have disappeared into the night.

The next morning, we inspect the damage. Fortunately, the bombs were small and dropped haphazardly, so the damage to the house is minimal. As ordered, not a single shot was fired against the enemy.

The psychological impact, though, is devastating to the citizens of Bordeaux. The famous wine city feels betrayed. Only the glaziers enjoy a few months of thriving business as they repair the windows of homes throughout the region.

AFTER A COUPLE OF DAYS, things settle down, and we join the household routine. Gérard and I are given chores to do. I am responsible to walk to the dairy early in the morning for fresh milk, then pick up baguettes at the bakery about four blocks away.

One morning, the streets are deserted as I set out for my daily routine. Strange. When I turn a street corner, I see a German armored scout car. At the same time, someone fires at me. Terrified, I drop the aluminum milk container I am carrying and run all the way back to the house. So much for the Geneva Convention.

"The Boches are here. There won't be any milk today," I shout as I burst into the mansion.

"What happened?" Maman asks, hurrying toward me to see if I have been hurt.

I tell everyone about the scout car and the shots being fired and end it by announcing proudly, "And I was not shaking!" It was true. There was no time to be afraid.

That day, the German army takes up quarters in the abandoned French army barracks in Bordeaux, located near the Marrots' house. The Nazi officers take over some of the best hotels and residences for their stay. France has been taken, but the war is not over yet.

IN BORDEAUX, the Boches keep every transaction very *korrect*, paying for everything they steal or confiscate with occupation marks. It is obvious they want to make a good impression. In reality, the marks have no current value in Germany, in France (at least in use between the French), or anywhere else.

The Germans buy everything in sight. Wehrmacht officers buy all the cars until none are left in the dealerships. Fortunately, there are not many for sale anyway. Jacques has hidden our car in a village nearby, under a pile of hay in a small barn to keep it safe.

The rumors circulate that the Nazi officers are purchasing fancy women's undergarments—French black lace corsets with red ribbons and black brassieres; silk stockings in any shade; dresses, the gaudier the better; perfume; and the best champagnes, liqueurs, fine candy, cigars, expensive canned foods, extravagant jewelry, and paintings. Once they are loaded up, the German officers mail the French goods back to their homes in Deutschland.

It becomes obvious that Adolf Hitler has traded butter for guns. Nazi Germany has very few luxuries until they requisition them from France.

After the officers take the lion's share, the high German command lets the low-ranking soldiers loose in Bordeaux's streets. Armed with their phony currency, these conquerors confiscate what is left in the shops. The selection is disappointing because the officers have been very thorough.

It's been a long haul from Deutschland to Bordeaux for these Germanic warriors. The campaign has made them thirsty. Naturally, they ask for beer in the cafés, restaurants, and bars.

But Bordeaux is famous for its wines, not beer. They drink wine until it is gone.

In the weeks to come, the nights are full of their guttural drunken voices, singing bawdy songs punctuated by pistol shots in the dark sky. The victors are having a good time. For now, France has lost the war.

The Germans cut France in two: an occupied zone and an unoccupied zone. We are stranded in the occupied zone. French bureaucracy remains and is nothing to laugh at, but the *Boche Bureaukrautsy* is a lot worse because the Germans are ultrabureaucratic.

We are all required to get new identification papers. Nobody can do anything without the indispensable German permit called *ausweis*, with its official stamped swastika and the certified signatures.

The trains and buses have stopped service. There are no newspapers, no telephones, and only erratic mail delivery. We have no news—only the Boches and the French bureaucrats know anything. It is questionable if what the French think they know has any credibility.

Maman, Gérard, and I are terribly worried about Papa. But everyone is looking for someone. Like thousands of other French women, our mother is looking for her husband. Has he been taken prisoner? Or worse?

Each day I accompany Maman to the official offices to find out what has happened to Papa's regiment. We read the names of those missing in action, the casualties, and prisoners. The lists are posted on the walls of these dreaded offices of despair. Father's name is nowhere to be seen.

Most times, Maman stands beside me, unable to look, so I run my finger down the list, searching for "Jean Matisse." Maman's face is pale all the time now, and I'm growing more worried about both her and Papa.

I also long to know the fate of dear Tata. I miss her desperately and don't know if Grandfather's city has been bombed or if the Germans have taken it over.

The world is falling apart around us, and an unsettling feeling grabs hold of me as I wait for the next bad news.

ONE DAY IN THE LATE AFTERNOON, after I have finished my chores, Maman calls me. "Pierre, come with me."

In the crowded Marrot house, there is only one place for privacy—the large main bathroom. When I realize Maman is heading to the bathroom, I fear this is about Papa.

We go into the bathroom and she closes the door, locking it behind us. Without preamble, she says very slowly, "Pierre, as of today your name is changed. You are no longer Pierre Matisse. Your legal name must be Pierre Leroy. Tomorrow I will enroll you in a boarding school. You will answer to your new name. Do you understand me?"

I do not understand. I hear her words, but they do not make sense. How can this be?

I am not Pierre Matisse? What is this name Leroy? Where did it come from? What have I done that is *so* bad that I have been kicked out of the family?

Yet these are Maman's absolute and precise words. They will be imprinted vividly in my mind for the rest of my life. I can still hear her nervous, quiet voice.

I am stunned and begin to cry. The sky has fallen on my head.

"I want to go and live with Tata at Grandfather's." The tears are pouring down my cheeks. "I want to go right now, today!" I scream.

"Tata is not well. She cannot take care of you," Maman says. Now she is crying too.

"I'll take care of her; she needs me," I plead. All the tears inside my body flow out, taking my very life with them.

"There is no transportation available, Pierre. You know that." She is giving me all this information in a monotone voice.

"I do not need transportation. I'm going to walk to Saint-Georges-de-Didonne. Now!" I shout loudly. I have made up my mind. I am leaving Bordeaux today. My mind is racing. I must find a good map.

"We are stranded here until we find out what has happened to your father." Maman continues to cry. "I want to keep the family as close as possible. Your school is in Bordeaux. We cannot all continue living with the Marrots."

Her voice fades away in my ears. I am twelve years old, and I don't know who I am.

Sensing that I will make her feel worse, I fall silent, and we leave the bathroom.

I am lost and completely devastated. *I no longer belong to Papa, Maman, and Gérard.* I am an outcast, a complete stranger, even to myself. I have lost my family without a single shot being fired. If I attempt to think anymore I will go insane.

8
NEVER GIVE IN!

Never—in nothing, great or small, large or petty—never give in, except
to convictions of honor and good sense. Never yield to force.

WINSTON S. CHURCHILL

I AM ENROLLED in the boarding school with this new name—Pierre
Leroy—that I blame on the war and the Boches. Whatever I have done
wrong, it is going to be that much harder to get my family name back.
I have one more reason to detest the Boches. Franco has taken Aurora
from me, and now, Adolf has taken my beloved Papa, and he's separated
me from my whole family as well. In my book, both of these dictators
have a lot to pay for.

I am leaving the crowded Marrot household the day after the devastating news, barely speaking to anyone. Maman and I travel by bus to the
school. I sit silently beside her, clutching a small suitcase and wearing
my best clothing.

When we arrive, I do not ask Maman how long I must remain here. I do not ask her anything.

In these days, children are extremely respectful of their elders. There are two well-defined worlds—children and adults. Parents call the shots. Children are not to be seen nor heard. We are taught to answer only when spoken to. Even a foolhardy daredevil like me rebels with great care—not too often, and only in desperation.

Maman leaves, and I am all alone.

I AM SHOWN AROUND, assigned a neat and tidy bed in the dormitory, and expected to be a proper gentleman. Meals are brought on silver platters by impeccably dressed servants, and we eat on fine china set on fine linen tablecloths.

To survive as whomever I am, I must pull myself together right now! *This Leroy label is absolutely and definitely unacceptable,* I tell myself.

Soon after arriving, I am walking down the hallway when a student stops me and introduces himself. "My name is Robert Mayer. My father is a doctor," he says with a certain air of superior arrogance I can't stand.

He is about my age, but any other similarity stops right there. He walks as if he has a broom handle stuck up his behind while some subservient valet is unrolling a red carpet out in front of him.

"I saw you talking to that fellow over there. If I were you, I would avoid him. He is dressed in common clothes." He stands posing, full of his importance, with the tone of one who knows about such things. "He probably comes from the proletarian class of the nouveaux riche."

In these few short seconds, I have taken a terrific dislike to this obnoxious snob.

Without losing his superb aplomb, he goes on, "What is your name? And what does your father do?"

That's it. He has touched a raw nerve.

"Listen, you stupid little clown's behind, I don't care about anybody's clothes. I'll talk to whom I please, and furthermore, this is what my father says to you." I let out my favorite expletive and watch his face turn the color of an overripe tomato.

"How dare you! How vulgar. I am reporting you to the principal right now."

"Please yourself, your excellency," I reply.

An hour later, I am in the library when they call for Pierre Leroy, but I continue reading. It isn't long before the principal comes into the library, calling once again for Pierre Leroy. I look around, curious to see who is in trouble.

"Aren't you Monsieur Pierre Leroy, little gentleman?" The man in charge is standing in front of me.

"No, I am Pierre Ma—" I stop as it dawns on me. "I beg your pardon, sir, yes, that is me."

The principal looks at me as if I have tried to escape prosecution.

"Will you please follow me to my office?" he says sternly.

I see heads turning in the room as the other boys silently watch us leave.

I settle uncomfortably into a seat in his luxurious office. The principal explains that this type of language will not be tolerated in this school, one of the finest French educational institutions.

"You are going to apologize to Robert Mayer."

I sit up suddenly. "No! Respectfully, sir, I will not apologize to that pompous, egotistical, cruel jerk."

"You what?"

"I will not apologize to him, sir."

He studies me a moment from behind his large desk.

"I see. You can't stand him, can you?" he says with a kinder tone.

"That is correct, sir."

"One more bad word from you, and you are out of this institution. Do you understand me?"

He has given me a break, but his tone is firm. He means it.

"Yes, sir," I reply as I am dismissed. I want to run from this building and go find Tata, but I can't let my mother down, no matter what has happened between us.

I FIND THAT MOST of the students at the boarding school have attitudes like Robert Mayer's. Somehow this crowd of elite upper-class, non-proletarian sons from old blue-blood money are somewhat ridiculous. There is something artificial about them; somehow they do not ring true to me. These snobbish buffoons are way too pretentious for my taste. I would rather rise early for my morning chores and eat whatever is available at the Marrot household.

Sadly, I realize I am alone in the world. I have no one, only the adventurous kindred spirits to be found within the pages of books.

When I am not in class, I spend time outside on the expansive grounds, which offer me both solitude and freedom. I take solace in my work, throwing myself into my studies and my art. Sometimes at night I lie awake wondering how Papa is doing. Is he alive? Will he return? What about Tata, Maman, Gérard, and my two grandfathers?

I start to pray, but my mind returns once more to the question: Will I ever get my name back? I have so many worries. I pray for everyone's safety, yet I dare not ask God for my deepest desire. I dare not even speak to God about it. I fall into a fitful sleep, thinking, *I am truly alone.*

"PIERRE LEROY, YOU HAVE A VISITOR IN THE PARLOR."

I have been keeping to myself for many weeks now, but I still am not used to this foreign name people call me. I hate being called by this last name. To me, I am still Pierre Matisse and do not want any part of this Leroy business.

After some confusion, I reluctantly go to the parlor.

When I see my visitor, I am overjoyed.

On this sunny day, Monsieur Jacques has come to visit me in my golden cage.

"On your mother's orders, I am taking you from this school today," he says with a smile. "Your mother has received word from your father. He was taken prisoner, but he has escaped."

This is wonderful news. I knew Papa would escape if he was taken prisoner.

"Your father can't come to the occupied zone," Jacques explains. "For the time being, he is keeping a low profile in the nonoccupied zone somewhere between Bordeaux and Toulouse." Papa is waiting for us to join him there.

I'm relieved that Papa is safe. He's alive, when so many others are not. Not only alive, but he has escaped from the Nazis like a true adventurer. The idea fills me with joy, but under the present circumstances, I am mixed up inside.

Will things ever be the same again between Papa and me? My thoughts are soaring as I thank God for saving Papa. Once he returns, we can sort out this name thing. God has answered the prayer that I could never ask for.

It doesn't take me long to pack up. As I walk out of the school with Monsieur Jacques, I glance back over my shoulder. I am freed from my prison.

FOR A MOMENT, everything is good again. We have a long walk ahead of us before we catch the bus. The trip to the Marrots' house takes the entire afternoon.

Along the way, Jacques explains what lies ahead. "Your mother has obtained the necessary travel permits. First, we get your mother and little brother and make some quick preparations, and then we are going to meet your father."

"He is not my father anymore," I mumble, knowing that Monsieur Jacques surely knows about my humiliation.

"Well . . ." He ponders this for a second or two. "Take my advice, Pierre. Perhaps not legally, on paper. But in reality, all this name business is strictly academic. One's father is one's father."

"I want my father like it was before the war."

Jacques is silent, closing his eyes as if to think.

Before he can answer me, my feelings burst out. "I don't know where I stand anymore!"

"You are too young to understand certain things," Jacques says, giving me his most serious look.

"But I want to know everything, Monsieur Jacques," I tell him earnestly.

"Impossible! Nobody knows everything. I do not know everything."

"Tata knows everything," I say. There is nothing in the entire world that Tata doesn't know.

"If anybody in the world knows everything, yes, it would be her.

You're right." Jacques smiles kindly. He trips on a small stone on the road, but his expression is blank. He isn't paying attention to where he is walking. Then he mumbles, "What rubbish! Jean Matisse was there to welcome you into this world with your maman, and a very proud papa he was, at that!"

I stop dead in my tracks and stare at him.

"What did you say, Monsieur Jacques?"

I want to hear these words again. I *need* to hear them. *Papa was proud of me.*

"Nothing, Pierre, nothing. It is none of my business and wrong of me to mention it."

I don't ask again, but I mull over what he said. It is a burning question in my mind.

"I have a plan, and I need your help, Monsieur Jacques," I say. "I have saved every bit of spending money that Maman has given me while I was at school. I need to stop someplace on our way to the Marrots to purchase two gifts—one for Maman and one for Papa."

Jacques understands the seriousness of my mission. We enter a little shop that still has a few wares left after the Germans' shopping spree. With Jacques's approval I buy a silver pendant for my mother and a *couteau a cran d'arrêt*, a high-quality locking knife for Papa.

I confide to Jacques that perhaps Papa will forgive me and want me for a son again. Jacques mutters something about adults that I don't understand before he turns away.

I hope that someday, once this war is over, I'll have done enough penance for whatever I did wrong to become a full-fledged family member, with the same name as Papa, Maman, and Gérard. As a guest, I think it is at least proper to bring a gift to my hosts. I'm too afraid to ask if I can call him Papa and ashamed of whatever I have done to be removed from the family. These two nicely wrapped gifts will be a token of my goodwill.

SOON JACQUES AND I arrive at the Marrots'. I am glad to be back with my mother. I give Gérard a pat on the back when I see him, and he seems happy to see me too.

Suddenly I am panic-stricken, and when I have a moment alone with

Maman, I ask her to send me to Tata. I feel uneasy about my future in the Matisse family. I'm not one of them anymore. I can sense this with certainty.

"You cannot go to Tata right now. Your job, Pierre, is to help Monsieur Jacques," Maman tells me.

Throughout Bordeaux, it is impossible for the French to find a drop of gasoline, even if one has the right authorization papers. Impossible, except for Monsieur Jacques. He does not tell me, but I suspect that he is siphoning gas from German trucks.

THE NEXT MORNING AFTER BREAKFAST, Jacques leads me outside the mansion to a bike that is leaning against the side of the building and hands me some French francs.

"Pierre, take this bicycle and go to several hardware stores. Buy five one-liter turpentine cans, one each at five different locations. It doesn't have to be done all today, but try to finish quickly."

The bike is a good one that I haven't seen before. "Where did you get this bicycle, Monsieur Jacques?"

"I borrowed it. Now ride only in the eastern part of town and only for the cans."

"Why?" A man has to know the details.

"This isn't a bicycle to play with," he says abruptly.

Over the next two days, I ride the bike to get the empty cans. Following Monsieur Jacques's instructions, I keep a low profile, looking out for Nazi soldiers and avoiding other shops and groups of people as much as possible. On the first day, I buy three cans, transporting them one at a time back to the Marrots' house. On the second day, I must ride a little farther to get the last two cans from different stores. As I am coming back with the final can, I hear a voice behind me, yelling in French. "Hey, that's my bicycle! You, with my bicycle. *Voleur!* Thief! Arrest him!"

I pedal so fast I almost lose one can as I make a quick turn to get away. I reach the mansion, out of breath and exhausted, after taking numerous detours and roads to be sure I am not being followed.

As soon as I see Jacques, I say, "You stole this bicycle! Why didn't you tell me?"

He gives me an indignant look. "Are you accusing me of being a thief?"

"Well, no. But this bicycle belongs to somebody else."

"Stolen? In a war nobody steals . . . we only requisition," he states, obviously offended.

"What is the difference between requisitioning and stealing?" I want to know.

He paces along the building, beside the bicycle. "We need it more than he does. So . . . we borrow it whether he likes it or not, so to speak." Monsieur Jacques makes his explanation sound quite logical.

"Ah, okay," I say, but my disapproval must show on my face.

"I will return his abominable bike this evening. Anyway, we don't need it anymore; we are leaving tomorrow afternoon." Although I completed my mission successfully, Monsieur Jacques's tone clearly says, *Whew! What a pain in the neck this kid is.*

I feel better. The bike will be returned.

I DON'T SEE MONSIEUR JACQUES again until the next evening. He motions me outside, where there are two bicycles waiting. These bicycles are different from the one I used the day before. We ride along the road silently, carrying the tin cans, which now are filled with gas sloshing inside them. Monsieur Jacques's nighttime mission has been successful. It reminds me of the nighttime adventure in Spain with my father when I was seven years old. As we ride, I cannot help but think of Papa out there somewhere . . . and of this Leroy business.

There is no doubt in my mind I have done something really bad. But what? Something sinister must be hiding somewhere in my past actions. I feel dirty, untouchable, like I have a contagious, shameful disease.

Obviously, only Tata will put up with me. For everyone else, I am an embarrassment and a burden.

Where did that Leroy name come from, anyway? I don't dare ask Maman for fear that the story might get worse.

"Pierre, will you pay attention! You are always on the moon." Monsieur Jacques sounds angry as he tears me away from my thoughts. He never speaks to me this way, so he must be tired. Then I hear him say, "This gas is serious business."

We have been carrying these tin gas cans on the bicycles half the night with only the moon and stars to light our way. The tires on the dirt and gravel road are the only sound I hear.

"Where did you find these bikes, Monsieur Jacques?"

"Holy mackerel, Pierre! You don't have to know everything, do you?" His impatience fades away immediately. Softly, he adds, "Borrowed, my boy. Honest. Not requisitioned, not stolen. Only borrowed." His weak voice sounds suspicious to me, and I am not convinced that he is telling the truth.

"Are you afraid the gendarmes will arrest us for stealing these bikes?" Jacques asks.

"These bikes are too good to be anyone's but a policeman's," I reply.

"Why mention stealing again? That's an obsession with you. I will personally return these bicycles tomorrow to their legitimate owners, for goodness' sake!"

We finally make it to the barn where Jacques has hidden the car. After uncovering it from piles of hay, Monsieur Jacques carries a tin to the gas tank. He pushes an old felt hat down inside the big gas funnel.

As he works in the darkness, I hear him muttering. "We've got to get out of Nazi France whatever way we can. I can't stand it here anymore. I don't even trust this Boche gas. Some of the French resistance fighters are putting sugar in it." Leaving nothing to chance, Monsieur Jacques pours the gas through the makeshift filter in the funnel.

"What does sugar do to gasoline?" I lean down beside him to watch him work.

"Fabulous things, my boy, fabulous. It wonderfully plugs the Boches' carburetors. Put the caps back on those empty cans tightly. We are taking them with us."

"Did you put sugar in their gas?" This idea is a juicy one. I have to know.

"I am *too* busy now, but maybe one day I'll win this sweet war with sugar."

We both burst out laughing at the thought.

"Sugar in their planes would be nice." I'm ready to volunteer for that assignment.

"Maybe, one day. Yes! One of these days." I know he is thinking out loud.

In no time, everything is shipshape, the door is open wide, and we're ready to drive out of the barn. The problem is, the car won't start. Jacques pulls out the hand crank.

"Pierre, sit behind the wheel. When I say go, turn on the car, and apply a touch of gas."

For a long time he turns the crank patiently without any result, not one word out of place. But through the dirty windshield, I can see his patience is being taxed to the limit.

Suddenly Monsieur Jacques tightens his fists, and he walks away from the car about three meters into the moonlight. Slowly, measuring his steps, he comes back, stopping just inches from the obstinate machine. He points a menacing finger toward the hood. Containing his rage as much as he can, he proceeds to talk to the reluctant car.

"Listen, you abominable piece of dung, I have had it with you! Now I will go directly to Number One. You'd better watch out. See!"

He raises both arms dramatically toward the spiderwebs hanging under the barn's roof.

"Now hear me! It's me, Jacques." It takes me a moment to realize he's not talking to someone in the rafters; he's talking to Number One—God. "I have been stealing gas and bicycles for a month. I have never asked You for anything for me. Right? Good! Now I have to get two kids and their mother out of the Boches' clutches. I gave my word, straight and true. Now today, this rotten motor will not start. Please, help me."

End of prayer.

Monsieur Jacques takes hold of the crank and gives the uncooperative car another dirty look for good measure.

"Car on . . . a touch of gas," he calls to me. His hair is so disheveled that he looks like a madman, although a very tired one.

After a few backfires and hesitations, the motor roars to life.

"Easy on the gas!" he commands, with a smile from ear to ear. I cheer from behind the wheel, careful to follow Monsieur Jacques's instruction.

As he comes to the driver's side door, Monsieur Jacques raises his head and arm upward, shaking his head from side to side in a combination of relief and disbelief as he says, *"Mon Dieu, mon Dieu, merci."*

He puts his hand on my shoulder. "A piece of advice, Pierre. When nothing works, you try God. Sometimes that is all it takes. But do not abuse it because He is always terribly busy, especially now."

I crawl out of the driver's seat, listening to the engine purr. Monsieur Jacques sits on a bale of hay trying to catch his breath. He looks straight up to the roof's spiderwebs, joins his hands together, and simply says, "Thank You."

He looks at me. "Whether you get your request or not, never forget to say thank you. Remember, it always could be a lot worse. You say thank you, too, right now."

I put my hands together and say, "Thank You." It is my first real prayer of thanks and a spiritual lesson I won't forget.

With the car full of gas and running well, Jacques turns the engine off, and we hide it once again, which is no small feat with Maman's table still strapped to the top. Then we ride the bikes back to the Marrots'.

My mother has a few more days of frustrating finagling with the French and German authorities for the necessary permits to travel more than a hundred and fifty miles. Then Maman, Gérard, and I say good-bye to our friends at the Marrot mansion. Monsieur Jacques is ready, stolen Boche gasoline and all, for the trip to the nonoccupied zone.

Thirty-one miles from Bordeaux, after passing many German military roadblocks and enduring numerous inspections of our papers, and six miles past the roadblock at the demarcation line, we stop at a little hamlet off the main road.

Papa is here!

9

A LULL IN THE STORM

A flower cannot blossom without sunshine,
and man cannot live without love.

MAX MULLER

HE IS SEATED on the terrace of a small bistro dressed in a wrinkled suit much too small for him, even though I can see that he has lost weight. His face is pale and weary. But in spite of his appearance, when Papa sees us, his face breaks into such a radiant smile full of joy that I cannot hold back my tears.

My war hero is waiting for us in this small village nestled in the French countryside.

Monsieur Jacques stops the car. We leap out and race toward Father. This reunion overwhelms us all. We are all smiling, laughing, and crying at the same time.

Monsieur Jacques greets Papa with tears in his eyes too as he hands him the car keys. He appears proud to turn over the car and its precious cargo intact to his boss. Papa's expression is full of enormous gratitude as he gives Monsieur Jacques a hard pat on the back.

"Thank you, Jacques," he says, swallowing hard.

Suddenly, it hits me. We have all made it safely into unoccupied France.

There is an awkward moment between Jean Matisse and this new Pierre Hateful-Name. *How do I address him now? Father? Monsieur? How do I solve this?*

We don't discuss it. It is not necessary, for he grabs me in his arms and kisses me. My heart takes over, and with eyes full of tears I say without hesitation, "Papa, I missed you so much!"

When the emotions and stories calm down, I pull out my small gifts. "To remember this day, I have a gift for you, Papa, and another for you, Maman," I declare solemnly.

As I give them their gifts, my mother's face glows, and I can see she is touched. Papa takes the little knife without saying a word. He opens it and touches a finger to the blade, then he ties it carefully to his key chain. A tear runs down his cheek, and he rubs it away with the back of his hand.

I don't know what to say. Neither does he.

Jean Matisse treats me the same as always, and seeing him, I know I'll always love him as my papa. But we both resent my last name; Papa's demeanor says it all. I can't shake this nagging ill feeling about it. From this day on, our relationship enters a new dimension—Papa is also my best friend.

Monsieur Jacques must be on his own way. The good-bye is quick between my parents and Jacques. It is a painful parting for all of us. I'm sorry to lose such a loyal friend. Together we have had many incognito adventures, and without him, we would not have made it from Paris to Bordeaux and eventually to Papa.

After a short break, we are all set. Papa takes the wheel, and I am beside him in the passenger seat.

"Where are we going?" I ask.

"Toulouse," Papa says, which means to Grandmother Amélie Matisse.

My excitement fades slightly at this news. We have all survived, we have Papa back, and we are safe in unoccupied France. But we are headed to the rule of Madame Matisse. Before the war, when Tata and I went to visit her and Grandfather Henri in Nice, she insisted I call her Madame Matisse instead of Grandmother.

Secretly, I have given her a nickname: The Great. In private, Papa calls her the Queen Mother.

The Great Queen Mother is a tall and massive woman, large-boned but not obese. Her face is strongly defined and harsh. I imagine she might have been beautiful in her younger years, but unfortunately she has lost her feminine magic. I can't help but compare her to the one I really wish to see. Tata. She is beautiful because she is beautiful on the inside. Tata is charitable, understanding, and kind to everybody. Tata understands everything. The Great chooses to understand nothing, except her power and prejudices.

We arrive at her estate two days later, using the last drop of the Boches' gas that Monsieur Jacques provided. The other members of Madame Amélie Matisse's clan are already there: her inseparable daughter, Marguerite, with her son, Claude. Madame Matisse greets my father and his acceptable son Gérard warmly but barely welcomes Maman and me.

We are now under her house rule. Grandfather Henri will not be joining us. Since early 1939, he and Madame Matisse have been legally separated, which doesn't surprise me. Who would want to live with Amélie? I'd overheard that Grandfather Henri grew tired of petty family problems generated by Amélie. So Grandfather Matisse is alone in Nice, far enough away from Amélie to find the peace he needs to concentrate on his art.

Madame Matisse is always accompanied by Marguerite and The Great's Pekingese dog. Whenever her son Pierre is mentioned, she calls him "l'Américain" in a cold and loveless voice, which obviously delights Marguerite, whose expression clearly reads, "He is out. I am in." As far as Papa goes, his mother's comment is "Give Jean a piece of wood, a hammer, and some nails, and he will leave you in peace the whole day."

The Great's trademark is a famous cane, always in her right hand. A symbol of her vested power, she handles it like a baton of command. In the style of all the great tyrants of Europe, Her Highness reigns supreme on the Toulouse estate. Her subjects, besides the family members, are a gardener, a loyal Yugoslavian couple, Albert the butler, Mary the cook, and an assorted variety of tradesmen—all of whom must toe the line.

WHILE WE ARE STAYING HERE, I spend as much time outside as possible, far from the house. I perch comfortably in a tree with a book, reading some Sir Arthur Conan Doyle mystery in English or pretending to be a solitary world explorer. Gérard and I never quarrel, but most of the time our interests send us in different directions. Claude and Gérard are closer in age and temperament so they spend time together. And for some reason, Claude and I can't stand each other. We often quarrel, and I'm tempted to fight him. It seems that ignoring one another is the best plan. However, my disdain for The Great's grandson only deepens her dislike of me.

One morning, Papa takes me aside with a gleam in his eye. "Pierre, today is the anniversary of my marriage to your mother. We have to make a big bouquet of flowers to give her."

"But there aren't any flower shops around to buy flowers," I say with disappointment, thinking of Maman.

"We do not need flower shops, my boy. We are going on an adventure in the countryside to look for wild ones."

Since I have already spent much time exploring the surrounding fields, I know the truth and must break it to him. "The past few weeks have been so dry, it is going to be impossible to find any wildflowers."

"You say *impossible*? What kind of negative attitude is that? For us, *impossible* isn't an option, Pierre. Love and honor are at stake. All we have to do is be a little bit creative."

I am inspired and energized by this pep talk. If Papa says we must find flowers for Maman, we will do so, no matter what.

"Let's go find some beautiful flowers," I say enthusiastically.

A difficult mission with my father is always exciting for me. I love to do challenging things with him to prove my manhood.

We decide to split up in our quest, but after walking for two hours and covering many miles, I haven't found one flower worth picking.

At that moment, I spot a lovely villa by the side of a dirt road with a few lovely flowers in the garden. I pull out the few francs in my pocket and go to ring the bell.

When the door opens, I begin. "I would like to buy some of your flowers," I say to the owner of the house, launching into a convincing speech about my parents' anniversary and the importance of these flowers.

The owner refuses to sell them at any price. What an ogre!

Papa said we have to be creative, and the most creative person I have ever known is Monsieur Jacques. What would he do in such a tricky circumstance? Requisition? Borrow perhaps? Hum!

I head down the road, looking back at the ogre's villa. I cannot take what he won't sell; it's too dangerous.

After a few more miles of walking, I see a fenced-in cottage, far from any neighboring properties. It is magnificent, with a garden full of wild and cultivated flowers. I hear Monsieur Jacques sitting on my shoulder, advising me on the best way to handle the situation. I know better than to ask to buy the flowers this time. Instead, I look around first. Nobody is in sight.

But then . . . I am startled by a man-eating dog in the garden that bares its teeth at me and growls as I advance a few steps closer. The menacing growls get louder. *Why isn't someone coming out to see what's going on?* I wonder. But no one appears. The dog growls at me again, and now I can see he's straining against a chain.

After a furtive look in every direction, I'm certain no one is home. I quickly jump over the fence to requisition the flowers. I pick a few here and a few there, so I'm not leaving too many obvious bald spots. And where there are some voids from my "borrowing," I fill them in with some tall grass. Thankfully, the mean dog stops his nasty growling.

When I meet up with Papa, he cannot believe his eyes. He has not been successful in his hunt. However, my bouquet is beautiful and outrageously huge.

"Where did you find those, Pierre?" Papa asks in astonishment.

"Far away," I say instinctively, while my face turns as red as some of the flowers I am holding.

"I hope so," Papa says, looking at me with a knowing smile. He takes a good whiff of the flowers. "Your mother is going to love these. However, get this straight—it is all right to be creative, especially when duty calls and, only once in a while, for real love." I smile with relief, knowing we were in this together.

I follow Papa inside to the kitchen, where a maid helps us find a vase, and then we arrange the bouquet artistically. He is thoughtful as he works.

"I do not approve of stealing, Pierre, so do not make a habit of it. We understand one another, don't we, Son?"

Son. I look him in the eyes and nod my head. "Yes, Papa, we do. I did try to pay for the first flowers I found, but the owner wouldn't sell them to me."

"But a thief is a thief. If we had been caught, those beautiful flowers would be quite expensive. Enough said. Let's go see what your mother thinks of her loving *banditos.*"

Maman is in the reading room, and when we enter, Papa presents the bouquet to her.

"How did you manage this, Jean?" Maman asks Papa, and he smiles and takes her in his arms.

As I exit, I'm happy that I am able to help Papa.

TO AVOID THE GREAT'S FAMILY POLITICS, I spend as much time as possible alone, hiking in the surrounding countryside. If I feel the need for company, I join the neighborhood shepherds. Sometimes I don't return to the estate for lunch. My friends generously share their raw onions, garlic sausage, or delicious cheese with me, which I wash down with a tin cup of red wine and some tasty walnuts for dessert.

But when my activities are brought to the attention of The Great, she issues an edict at the royal dinner table one night.

"Pierre!" she practically roars from her throne at the head of the long table. "This is a respectable family. You are not to associate with shepherds, nor are you to wander aimlessly like a bum in the woods and country fields."

I don't know how to address her. The Great is out, of course. This much I know. Grand-mère is only reserved for Claude and Gérard. That leaves only two alternatives: Madame Matisse or silence. I choose the latter.

"You say nothing, Pierre! Do you understand what I just told you?" She continues to bully me while I keep my mouth shut.

The whole tribe is present at dinner, including Madame Matisse's beloved Pekingese sitting on The Great's knees. Even the dog stares at me with disdain and an air of superiority, as if to say, *Well! What do you say to that? How about an answer, Monsieur what's-your-name?*

I answer with a blank look. A long and uneasy silence follows.

I look around the table, searching for an ally. Marguerite's face clearly reads: You see, I told you that he was no good. Like mother, like son. Claude has a curious smile on his face. It reminds me of his mother's smirks and the insults she wages against Papa and Uncle Pierre. I'd love to put my fist right through that smile, but right now I've got other fish to fry. Gérard seems to be enjoying the show, confident that I am going to be spectacular. Papa and Maman stay out of it, probably afraid of retribution from The Great, but I can see that they don't like what is happening.

When I still don't acknowledge her reproach, The Great fires hostilities at me full blast.

"Do you know that it is insolent not to answer when you are addressed?" she spits out. I still don't respond. Raising her voice a few decibels she shouts, "You little barefoot Spanish bastard refugee, I am talking to you!"

That does it. Something in her words unleashes my rage. I don't mind being called "bastard," because I'm not exactly certain what it means, although I know it is derogatory. "Barefoot" is accurate, because I love to walk barefoot in the countryside. However, "Spanish refugee" is outrageous! I immediately think of Aurora. So The Great is on Franco's side?

Livid, I stand up and flip my cream cake upside down on the impeccably set tablecloth. And then words spill out of my mouth.

"You think you are a queen? No! Not at all! I will tell you what you are." Every dirty word I know flies out of my mouth. My patriotic Paris concierge and my pirate friends would be proud.

Mary, the maid, drops her tray on the floor, making marvelous sound effects that add emphasis to my wild, furious tirade. Everyone is in a state of shock. I'm shaking from head to toe, but I continue to glare at The Great with hatred and contempt. Papa calmly stands up, grabs me firmly by my shoulders, and leads me out of the dining room.

I yell at The Great over my shoulder, "You think that you do this and that. Your servants do everything, not you. Phony! Fake!"

I end by swearing in Spanish, which I feel is appropriate after being labeled a Spanish refugee.

Papa leads me to my room. He doesn't slap me or reproach me for my insubordination. Instead, he calms me down—the kindness in his voice opening a floodgate of tears that course down my cheeks.

"I want to go live with Tata," I say. "I am leaving early tomorrow morning."

I'm still shaking and feel so cold and tired. Amid my sobs, I express my remorse to him. I am sorry because I have let down Papa, Maman, Tata, and Aurora by my behavior.

Papa is quiet. He stands beside my bed, looking out the window to the horizon for quite a while. Finally, I stop sobbing. Then, patting my shoulder lightly, he leaves to rejoin the family. I can only guess the reaction there, and I don't dare leave my room to find out.

Papa returns to my room much later. Again, he is silent as he sits at my bedside, lost in thought. Eventually he says, "You cannot go to Tata now. It is not possible, Pierre. But we will leave Toulouse soon, my son."

These are his last words before he tucks me into bed. I hold on to the last two words tightly until I fall soundly asleep.

Papa doesn't ask me to apologize to The Great Queen Mother for being so insolent. After the big showdown, she and I never speak to each other again, beyond one-word acknowledgments.

She does exact revenge by banning me from the royal table and ordering me to take all my meals with the servants. The Great has a lot to learn; I eat in peace with the servants, who are always kind to me.

OVER THE NEXT FEW WEEKS, my sleep is punctuated by a horrible recurring dream.

I'm in a bright red room without windows or doors. The floor is red with blood, but there is a pile of tangled white rope. The walls, the ceiling, and the floor are moving inward, reducing the size of the red room, closing in to crush me.

There is only one escape from this terrible room. The white rope leads to a tiny hidden manhole. The escape route can only be found by disentangling the white rope.

I realize the blood that covers every inch of the red room is from former victims. I frantically try to straighten the tangled rope. But the room continues to get smaller, faster than I can sort out the saving rope. I am going to be crushed to death. Panic sets in fast, followed by a claustrophobia that triggers an unbearable anxiety attack.

I wake up screaming, in a sweat, and terrified that I'm dying.

Maman or Papa rushes in to comfort me. I realize now that the last few months of adventures have finally taken their toll, with the main culprit being my incomprehensible name change. I have no identity. I feel alone, with no idea who I am. I'm an outsider, an impostor, an untouchable; one who doesn't belong here or anywhere else. One who should be dead.

The same red room traps me again and again. I fight for a way out. The way to a better life is courage. With unbending courage, I take this horror on the chin like a man and never mention the details of my nightmares to my parents, except that I'm afraid to die. I am certain my parents never realize how devastated I am by the loss of the Matisse name. If they do, they must not know how to handle it any better than I do.

Shortly after we leave Madame Amélie Matisse's household, the nasty nightmares fade away and never return. I beat the blood room alone.

10
FAREWELL TO THE SUITCASE

Everyone lives by selling something.
ROBERT LOUIS STEVENSON

THE NAZIS HAVE cut France into two parts—the occupied North and the unoccupied South. But not even the South is safe. There is still the Gestapo, the vile secret police of the Nazis. There are the informants, the shameful hunt for Jews, and the disappearances, sometimes of entire families.

Paris is no longer the capital of France. Instead, the city of Vichy in the unoccupied South is the new capital city. Vichy, apart from the vices the Nazis bring, tries operating like a normal, civilized city. The Germans hold two million French soldiers hostage, doing forced labor, which helps encourage the French to do the Germans' bidding. And with the Nazi emblem at every turn, no one can ignore the truth that France has lost the war—for now.

We certainly are not free. Among our restrictions, gas for private cars is out of the question. Resourceful Monsieur Jacques is not with us anymore to pinch fuel for the family gas-guzzler. The luxurious Delage that Papa got when we moved from Spain to France had been previously owned by the last French Republic's president. No wonder it drinks gas by the bucketful—when the president owned it, the taxpayers were forking over the fuel money!

Papa must leave the car in Toulouse, stored in The Great's garage. Maman, Gérard, Papa, and I head to the French Riviera via train.

At the end of 1940, the magnificent French Riviera scenery is still intact—as if we are in another world, where the word *war* is not even an entry in the dictionary. We settle in Mouans-Sartoux, a small village situated halfway between Cannes (where a film festival will begin six years later) and Grasse, the world's perfume capital.

Our home is a small two-story house with a spacious attic that I claim as my bedroom. The massive oak beam structure supporting the tile roof is reassuring to me and seems to protect me. Just above my bed is a big skylight. Every night I look at the stars until I drift to sleep. When it rains on the clay tiles, the sound is music to my ears.

Here, in this enchanted paradise, I rededicate myself to art. The Marrots have also moved here from Bordeaux. Their daughter, Odile, has artistic aspirations as well, and the two of us paint together. I create watercolor sketches of the spectacular ocean and mountain views. Through these paintings, something grows stronger within me, soothing the memories of the bombing raids in Paris and the traumatic exodus my family endured to get here.

When my paintings are done, I sign them *Tatiou*. I still refuse to have anything to do with that unwelcome Leroy name.

EVERY SCHOOL DAY from the winter of 1940 through the spring of 1941, I take public transportation to and from school in the city of Grasse about five and a half miles up a steep hill. Out the window, the landscape is breathtaking.

Grasse, like an eagle aerie, is nested on a slope of the lower Alps. From its high perch, Grasse overlooks hills covered with white jasmine fields as well as red and white carnations, stretching nearly all the way to the Mediterranean. It is here, in the perfume laboratories of Grasse, that the oil of the delicate jasmine flowers is extracted to produce the world's most luxurious perfumes. For miles around this charming city, the air is scented with the delicate fragrance.

Unfortunately, the bus service has been cut in half, with the remaining buses rarely on schedule, which makes it a challenge to get to school. The vehicles are *gazogène,* fueled by wood-burning stoves attached to the back of the bus. This marvelous gadget sort of works, but it is very slow going.

The buses are crowded beyond belief. If only one seat is available and ten people are waiting to be picked up, the driver won't even stop. However, we quickly learn to adapt.

One day, eight of us have been waiting an hour to be picked up, watching two fully loaded buses pass by. Finally, an old woman in our group, who has had enough, takes charge.

"Madame, give me your little baby. All of you hide behind that big bush over there. I will make the next driver stop."

The next bus, creaking under its load, comes puffing up the hill. Our commander is in place with the baby in her arms, standing in the middle of the road. The bus grinds to a halt, and the driver opens the door. Then the rest of us burst out of our hiding place and charge the door.

"I can't take any more passengers. We are full. It's the law!" the indignant driver shouts at us.

We push and shove until we're all inside, welcomed with colorful language.

Now, stinking of oil and fumes, the bus starts up the hill toward Grasse and its fresh, fragrant air.

Suddenly, smoke begins filling the bus. One of the gazogène stoves has burst into flames.

"Our tail is on fire! We are going to burn! Everyone out!" screams our driver as he pulls the bus to the side of the road. We jump out quickly and then watch helplessly as the bus burns to the ground.

We all must walk to our destinations. I do not go to school that day; it is closer for me to walk home. Since this is the only bus from

Mouans-Sartoux to Grasse, my formal academic education ends abruptly, just days before the school year does.

FOR ME, THAT SUMMER OF 1941 in Mouans-Sartoux is the eye of the storm. It's a reprieve from the war and danger. I spend the whole summer raising rabbits so our family will have some meat on the table. Ironically, when I go to the granaries to get food for the rabbits, the farmers send me home with bags of wheat germ. (Now that I think of it, those rabbits had to have been the healthiest animals ever! Even though we were starving and could have eaten the wheat germ ourselves, I guess we got it indirectly from the rabbits.)

I roam freely in the countryside picking grass for my rabbits and wild asparagus and mushrooms for the family table, stealing onions and ripe tomatoes from gardens—a risky but delicious business—and swimming in irrigation cisterns, which is dangerous when the gates are opened and water rushes in. I start a butterfly collection and enjoy pursuing them for hours, fascinated by the different shapes. I am impressed by God's creativity regarding their aerodynamic wings and the wind. On rainy days, I build model planes out of balsa wood to train for my career as a fighter pilot, which is going to make me a hero.

I don't often play with Gérard because of his poor health. After he suffers one particularly nasty asthma attack, Papa takes him to a clinic near the Swiss border. When they return, Gérard stays inside the house, per the doctor's instructions. It seems that the perfume country does not agree with his lungs.

It is a trouble-free summer except for one occasion when I tangle with some bees. While I'm gathering wild honey from a nest in a tree, my improvised gauze face netting rips.

When I return home, Papa is shocked. "What happened to your face, Pierre?" he asks. I don't realize that my head is the size of a pumpkin.

"Nothing. But look what I have. Two big bowls of honey," I proudly explain, holding them in my hands with fingers the size of delicatessen sausages.

Maman screams when she sees me. "What have you done?" She insists on taking me to the doctor, who identifies twenty-five stings on one hand

and thirty or more on the other, and gives up trying to count the number of stings on my face and head.

My face is so swollen I can barely see for a few days, and I run a high fever. But I never complain; besides, there is honey to enjoy. My pain is eased when Papa gives me a look that clearly says, "You are becoming a man, my son."

During this summer, Papa works on some sculpture projects. At times, I work as his apprentice and we get along well. Maman is painting and making ceramic figurines, and I help her, too, by taking them to Vallauris to be fired.

ONE NIGHT WHEN I CAN'T SLEEP, I overhear a conversation between my parents that gets my attention.

"Jean, this is insane. You shouldn't go. It's much too dangerous." These words make me listen more intensely.

"Nonsense, darling. There are no Germans or Gestapo in this area."

"On the contrary, I think it is crawling with spies and informants of all sorts." Maman's voice sounds close to tears.

"You are always afraid of everything. I gave my word."

"You are going to get all of us shot."

"I won't. But I have to do this, darling."

Silence. I can only hear my own heart beating in my ears.

Then I hear Maman again. "Promise me that it is the first and last time," she pleads.

"I can't promise that. Others are counting on me." My father's voice is firm.

I want to race down the stairs and go with Papa on whatever secret activity he's embarking on, but I know it will only aggravate an already tense situation between my parents.

"Can you promise me you will get out when it becomes too risky?"

"Of course! I'm not a fool, Louise. Come here, my darling." There is a long silence. I'm sure Papa is kissing Maman. Then I hear the back door closing carefully.

Through the skylight, the first quarter moon throws a pale light on my bed. Though Papa is off and away tonight, I feel comforted being wrapped in this light. I finally fall asleep, and when I wake again, the moon is gone, replaced by the Big Dipper, twinkling reassuringly. I whisper, thanking God for this beautiful display, that even through all the change here on earth, all is as it should be above.

As soon as I begin to drift back to sleep, that's when I hear it. A plane. At first, it is only a faint sound. *Maybe it's something else. Planes never fly around this area.* Then, no doubt! It is a plane.

I start shaking as fear grabs me. I'm frozen, listening for the whistle of bombs. But after a few long minutes, the engine's noise fades away. My knees stop dancing on their own. Then far away, from the southwest, the sounds of the flak guns bounce back and forth from hill to hill. A few dogs bark, and one howls long and mournfully. War has paid a visit to paradise.

The echoes of the guns fade away in the darkness. All turns quiet again and eventually, I fall back to sleep.

THE NEXT MORNING in our sunny kitchen, Maman serves large slices of bread covered with a war-thin layer of strawberry jam and coffee made of roasted black beans, made a little tastier with goat's milk. A tall, thin, good-looking man about Papa's age sits at the table talking softly with Papa.

Papa looks up at me and says, "Pierre, this is Monsieur Charles Dupont. He will be our guest for a few days."

"Bonjour, Monsieur Dupont," I say, extending my hand.

"My friends call me Charlot. You call me Charlot." His strong hand crunches mine.

"For a few days, you are going to share your quarters with Monsieur Charlot." Papa thinks for a moment and then looks me straight in the eye. "This is *very* important. Not a word about our guest to anybody." He pauses again and then makes things crystal clear. "Total silence. *Nobody* should know that Monsieur Dupont is here. Do you understand?"

"Why?" I am always questioning everything.

"The less you know, the better. Charlot is not here and never was. That is all. Do you have that straight, my son?"

"Yes, Papa, I do."

"Good." He turns to our guest and gives a quick wink to Charlot. "We can depend on him."

Papa knows I can be trusted. A sense of pride swells in my heart.

I spend the rest of the morning searching for food for my rabbits. It is the hot season, and we haven't had rain for weeks. I only manage to find a few tender dandelions. When I arrive home for lunch, Charlot is not there. He isn't at dinner either.

AFTER DINNER, I climb the stairs to the attic and discover Charlot busily hiding four medium-sized suitcases under the boards of the attic floor. He gives me a welcoming smile and greets me in superb Oxford English, "Hello, Mister Pierre! Good evening. Did you have a good day?"

I am startled. Charlot has the ability to go from impeccable French to proper English without the slightest trace of a foreign accent in either tongue! My surprise shows as I reply clumsily, "Good evening, sir." It takes me some time to get these three English words out.

"Could you be kind enough, old boy, to give me a hand to get this floor put back together?"

"Yes, sir."

Charlot completes the job by placing old broken pieces of furniture here and there over the loose floorboards.

"What do you think, Pierre?" Dust is sticking to the sweat that is running down his smiling face.

"Looks real good, Mister Charlot," I say in halting English.

"I think so too!"

He cleans his face with a towel and then, looking at me with a mischievous gleam in his eye, asks, "Have you seen any suitcases, Pierre?" Immediately, his expression turns as cold as ice, with no smile.

I shrug innocently. "Suitcases? What suitcases? No, sir, I have not seen any suitcases."

"Jolly good answer. A-plus."

His whole body seems to sag, and he looks very tired. "Today I rest. Tomorrow we start working together."

"Working at what, sir?"

"Your English is a bit rusty, my young fellow. You need practice, Pierre."

"Please sir, would you be kind enough to speak slowly? I only know a few words in English."

I had memorized this response before Uncle Pierre came to visit Paris, as a quick way to stay out of trouble with Tata and Monsieur Sterny for not learning my lessons well. Most of the rest of my English vocabulary has escaped me.

"No, little gentleman, I will not! You are going to have to get cracking and be serious about learning."

I only catch part of what he says but get the meaning anyway. Maman has asked him to give me some English lessons. While Charlot is with us, I will not have time to forage food for my rabbits. They will have to be content with table scraps seasoned with old hay.

Charlot makes himself comfortable on a pallet of straw, with a bedsheet that has been sewn on the sides, serving as a makeshift sleeping bag.

"It's not the Ritz, but it's remarkably comfortable, my boy," he declares with a broad smile.

DURING THE NEXT THREE WEEKS, with Charlot as my tutor, my English improves dramatically. He also has a miniature chess set, and he teaches me the fundamentals of this interesting game. The attic has become our clubhouse.

To thank him for his lessons, I offer to make a portrait of him in charcoal. He abruptly declines with a resounding authoritative tone that holds just a touch of panic. "No portraits! Absolutely none. Not even from memory. Do you hear me?"

But when he sees the disappointment in my face, he adds more kindly, "You can do my portrait, but only after the war is over, not before. You understand?"

It finally hits me. Charlot is an undercover agent, hiding from the Boches.

"Sorry, Mister Charlot, I understand. Only after the war."

These days, it seems everything good is being postponed until after this wretched war. I use my new skill in English to ask questions.

"What do you do, Mister Charlot?"

"I am a traveling salesman. I represent freedom. It's something like, let's see . . . I sell convincing peace arguments to the Nazis."

The grin on his face shows he is pleased with his statement.

"Are the peace arguments in your suitcase?" I glance at the floorboards where the suitcases are often hidden.

"Perhaps."

"May I see?"

"No, you may not! I demonstrate them only to potential customers."

"Isn't that dangerous?"

"Only for my customers when I close the deal."

I'm intrigued and want to know everything.

"Do you make a lot of sales?" I ask, studying his thin face.

He corrects my pronunciation on a few words, then adds, "Remember this, Pierre. Silence is golden. Do not ask questions; mind your own business. Just stick to your rabbits."

Then he elaborates, "If anybody asks you anything, take careful note of who he or she is in order to tell your father. Play dumb, ask them to repeat the question, tell them that you didn't understand. Finally, always say that you don't know."

"I understand." Truly I do not understand everything. However, one thing I do already know—one way or another in this war, if someone is not careful, he or she can get killed.

"In this kind of war, Pierre, it's better to appear—shall we say— slightly stupid."

SOME NIGHTS, Charlot disappears with Papa and returns just before daybreak. He then sleeps during part of the day. One day he falls soundly asleep on his bed during our English lesson. I want to surprise him, so I quietly keep busy, writing my homework exercise.

Suddenly, he becomes agitated in his sleep, sweating profusely.

His eyes are still closed as he begins in French, then switches to English, "*Jette les valises. Tout de suite.* Throw the suitcases. Now!"

He mumbles something unintelligible and then, "*Adieu la valise*"— farewell, suitcase.

Finally he screams, "No! No!"

Charlot jumps awake, soaked in sweat and visibly shaking. I can't disguise my shock.

"I'm sorry, Pierre. It's nothing. Just a little nightmare. Now let's see to this homework, then we'll play a game of chess."

One night when I return to the attic after finishing my chores, I find Charlot reclining on his bed fully dressed, with his back propped against a battered dark brown suitcase. The pieces of furniture that had been piled on top of the floorboards have been disturbed. He observes me looking at the suitcase and then glancing around.

"I didn't need the other ones—which were never there, Pierre."

"Are you leaving, Mister Charlot?"

"I'm not sure yet. I like the smell of jasmine. It reminds me of England, which is very beautiful in the spring with lots of flowers."

Rubbing his hands together, he says, "No time to fool around, little gentleman. Repeat after me, 'Silly Sally sold seashells down by the seashore.'"

"Silly Sally sold she-shells down the sheetshore.'" Somehow it doesn't sound quite right.

Charlot bursts out laughing. Slowly he repeats the tongue twister and says, "Again and again, until you get it right, young man!"

I fall asleep with my tongue in knots.

THE NEXT MORNING WHEN I WAKE UP, there is no suitcase and no straw bed. Not a trace of Mister Charlot remains. Underneath my pillow I find a miniature English-French dictionary with *Pierre* written on the first page. A note says: *In case of doubt, look it up in this book.*

When I reach for my sandals, I find Charlot's chess game in one of them, with another small note. "Checkmate, old boy! Yours."

Charlot came with five medium-sized worn-out suitcases. He left with only one. I recall three nights when he left the attic during the night. If that is one suitcase per outing, it leaves one suitcase for Papa. Curious, I discreetly look all around our house for the suitcase. I want to know what is inside. No luck. Papa must have hidden it very well.

A few years later, Maman tells me that Charles Dupont was his undercover name during the war. In peacetime, he was a French teacher at Oxford. Papa also told me after the war that Charlot had survived. He must have been a very good salesman!

AS WORLD WAR II tightens its grip on Europe, living conditions for its inhabitants become extremely difficult, even in our unoccupied zone. Transportation is slow, unreliable, and uncomfortably crowded. Food, soap, clothes, and other ordinary necessities formerly taken for granted become a rarity. Each winter is bad, and each spring is worse because last year's crops have been eaten. In the early spring of each year, we wait in line to buy seeds at the general store so we can plant them and grow food.

Like Charlot, the average person soon uses a suitcase as the main means of carrying goods. Paris is fed almost entirely out of suitcases in the last years of the war. On trains, buses, bicycle, or on foot, everybody has one—or better yet, two. The suitcase is king of Europe during wartime. Inside a bag, you might find a real supermarket: potatoes, melting butter, olive oil, and every kind of bean: black beans, white beans, brown beans. Beans are saving our lives. The phrase *C'est la fin des haricots! It's the end of the beans!* becomes the most feared doomsday expression.

The black market flourishes. Some are getting rich while others are thrown into abject poverty. The opportunists are black marketeers, who are open for business wherever they take their suitcases. The ultimate gold is cigarettes and tobacco.

Dry tobacco leaves become the currency of choice. With a few cigarettes, you can buy or bribe your way in or out of anything. Smokers will do anything for a cigarette, including trading their limited food ration for a puff of smoke. But everyone must be careful; thieves boldly steal suitcases left and right.

The French Vichy police chase the black market businessmen with their suitcases. Government agencies go after starving consumers to find and confiscate illegal suitcase goods, usually appropriating the goods for themselves.

The Gestapo is only interested in what is in Mister Charlot's type of suitcase—explosives, detonators, and grenades. Fortunately, there are so many suitcases circulating that adversaries can't possibly get their dirty hands on all of them.

Still, Charlot's suitcase nightmare becomes everyone's. We later hear that Paris is fed almost entirely out of suitcases in the last years of the war. If you lose your suitcase, you have lost everything. *Farewell to the suitcase!*

In these dark days, the loss of a suitcase is the end of the game. For some, it will be the end of their lives.

HENRI MATISSE BY Pierre H. Matisse

11

A PERFECT STUDENT

Do you believe in fairies? Say quick that you
believe. If you believe, clap your hands!

PETER PAN

THE SUMMER OF 1941 in Mouans-Sartoux comes to an end. We over-hear news about the war and the people we know who are missing or dead. Tata's prophecy of the coming war, made at the Paris Exposition, is now a reality.

For me, September means my return to a formal program of study. My parents enroll me in the Catholic Don Bosco Boarding College in Nice. The idle frolicking in the countryside has come to an end. It is time for formal education again.

From the first of September to July 14, 1942, I must remain locked in this institution. Freedom is what I miss most. *Give me liberty or give me death!* The American patriot Patrick Henry's words take on a new meaning for me.

Each day is regimented, and like clockwork I go from my dormitory to classes, to a short exercise period in the inner yard, to the study hall, and to the refectory for a meal—on and on, week after week, one month after another. The only relief is a movie every two weeks. After a month in this uncomfortable hole, I want out. But there is no easy way to escape, with the high walls all around the school and twenty-four-hour supervision.

Don Bosco is certainly not home to the fancy high-class society I encountered at the Bordeaux boarding school. In fact, Don Bosco soon reveals itself to be more like something out of Charles Dickens's *David Copperfield*.

ONE EVENING AT DINNER, I am sitting on the hard bench at my assigned table with eleven others. No one talks while a student reads a classical literature selection during mealtime. The reader's monotone voice is accompanied by the clinking of spoons and forks on plates.

At the head of my table is the school bully. For some time, he has been insulting me while stealing the best pieces of food right off my plate. He is taller, stronger, and older than me. Tonight, I have had it! Something has to be done. When he comes for my food, I stand up, take my steaming hot plate of spaghetti, and smash it into his face.

The priest supervising the meal jumps to his feet and shouts, "Shocking! How dare you! Both of you come here right now."

When the bully and I start arguing, the priest firmly grabs us both by our collars and drags us to the yard.

"Go ahead, sort this out between yourselves."

My behavior has been borderline insubordinate for some time. This priest thinks that finally I am about to get a licking to tame me.

My opponent, sure of his superiority, wipes the spaghetti sauce from his eyes. His moves are cocky; he's confident that he's easily going to mop up the yard with me.

I don't wait for him to get ready. From someplace deep within, I draw up all my strength, and every frustration I feel rises up. Realizing I will only get one chance, I hit my adversary in the upper stomach, right under the rib cage.

Without a sound, he bends over, folded in half. Now I must finish him off fast, or he will kill me. Using both hands, I grab the long scarf rolled around his neck and turn him round and round until he hits one of the marble columns decorating the yard.

Bang!

Again and again he hits his head. I am pleased. Things are looking pretty good. There is blood all over.

"Stop! Stop! Are you crazy, you little monster? You are going to kill him!" The priest on guard duty comes to rescue the bully, but I am in a fury. I kick the priest in the shins and when another priest comes to help, I kick him, too. Finally, a third priest arrives on the battlefield and slaps me on the face so hard that I land on the ground. I feel dizzy and rest my hands and head on my knees to stop the spinning stars from the blow and to catch my breath. I look up and get back to my feet.

The fight is over. Hands down, I am the champ. Apart from a burning red cheek, I don't have a scratch. I glance over at the bully. He is flat on his back, unconscious and bleeding from his head. This should officially remove my name from his victims list.

"You come with me!" I barely hear the order. The voice is muffled by the buzzing in my ear. The priest's slap was stronger than I first thought. Sometimes rage hides pain.

"You! To the director's office." Priest number three grabs my other ear and marches me to the office. Now both ears hurt.

"I HAVE HEARD only bad reports about you, Pierre Leroy. What do you have to say in your defense?"

I am a little dazed when I look at who is talking to me, seeing only an enormous red nose planted on a piglike face. It is the director, whom we students have nicknamed Piff, which in Parisian slang means "big nose." Seated at his huge mahogany desk with beady black eyes behind wire-rimmed glasses, he scrutinizes me.

"I do not like it here. I want to go back to my parents."

As soon as the words come out, it's difficult for me to hold back my tears. All this excitement is getting to be too much, and suddenly I feel dizzy again. I drop into an armchair across from the director, hoping to hide my weakness. I feel something crunch under my bottom.

"Stand up! You have ruined my biretta. And who gave you permission to sit down?" he says angrily.

Still wobbly, I stand up and look at the chair. Smashed against the seat is his ridiculous black hat lined with purple silk. The symbol of his authority is as flat as a pancake.

At this moment I don't give one whit about his crazy hat. I throw it on the floor and stomp on it.

Piff's eyes widen. He's completely flabbergasted. He has never seen a student quite like me. I pick up what's left of his biretta and throw it on his desk.

"I want out of this Devil's Island right now! You get that? And as for you and your silly hat, I say—" I let the insults fly uncontrollably out of my mouth in an array of languages.

I am feeling better. And I'm certain that this incident will get me thrown out of the school immediately.

"*Siéntese*," Piff orders calmly in Spanish. *Sit.*

"*¿Hablas español?*" I ask. I can't believe that this jail warden speaks a human language.

"I am Spanish. I can return the insults in eight languages." The director is almost smiling.

"Why are you in France, instead of Spain? Franco likes priests. And by the way, I hate Franco," I say. Tit for tat. I hope that a little political controversy will alienate him even more against me and expedite my expulsion.

He looks me straight in the eyes, hard, like a dark cloud passing over the sky, and then the sun comes as he smiles. "Tell me, Pierre, who won the fight today?"

"I did, sir."

"Ah! Good. By the way, I hate Franco too."

The director rings a bell, and a priest comes in.

"Take this gentleman to his quarters and keep an eye on him. At the first sign of rebellion or insolence, bring him back to me."

I never return to Piff's office. From that day on, the bullies leave me alone, and I extend them the same courtesy.

However, I make one last attempt to escape. I write Maman, telling her about the abuses to which I'm subjected in this awful institution. We have been corresponding regularly, and I know that she will not have Papa's attitude of "sink or swim." Our mail is censored both ways, so saying a prayer, I tie my letter to a stone and throw it over the high wall. Miraculously, she gets it, and her response comes back to me uncensored.

Dear Pierre,

I received your letter. Complaints read and noted. Never forget that I love you very much. However, at this time what you need to know is this: Nobody owes you a thing. Remember that. Sooner or later you are going to have to figure out life for yourself. Today is a good day to get started. Whether you like it or not, you are staying in Don Bosco until July.

Then, only if you have consistent good reports, you will spend the summer with us.

My advice to you is this: Make the best of it by studying seriously. Besides giving you a good education, it will make the time pass faster.

Your loving Mother

I read the letter again. The double-underlined *nobody owes you a thing* pierces me to the core. It sounds like total rejection.

I am on my own. Even though I am in Nice, it never crosses my mind to contact Grandfather Matisse. I know that he is too busy creating art.

With no alternatives left, I follow my mother's advice and bury my nose in my studies and library books.

Still, I am miserable. An unusually cold winter by French Riviera standards doesn't help. With no heat in the buildings, I'm cold to the bone day and night for several months. The fingers on both of my hands get chilblains, which are extremely painful. My fingers swell up like sausages and look frostbitten.

Our food supply is becoming meager. In the rice ration, there are rat droppings. It's the worst rice recipe I've ever eaten.

We all have lice in our hair. Even the weekly ice-cold showers can't chase them away. "The Boches brought the little critters from Germany," says Piff. We all scratch, scratch, and scratch some more.

ON ONE MOVIE NIGHT, the newsreel shown before the feature film is of the bombing raids on London, probably courtesy of the Germans as propaganda. The bombs fall and buildings explode beneath them. I watch with my hands clenched, vividly remembering the claustrophobic bomb shelter, the half-destroyed building with the man calling for his pants, the bodies covered by blankets and lined up on the street. I remember Tata telling me stories while I shook uncontrollably. I am not entertained or impressed by the movie and can't wait for it to end.

Piff always sits close to the projector during movie nights. If something is too risqué, such as a girl with a "big balcony," for instance, Piff blocks the lens with his new biretta. These priests love to censor to the point that even some of the library books have entire pages missing and certain classics are banned altogether.

Of course, the priests serve us a heavy dose of repetitious brainwashing. We must spend an awful lot of time at the church attached to the complex. I just can't get used to this church business. Instead of learning about God, I'm just bored to tears. The services are too long, and it is the same show every time. I don't feel God's presence in church at all. But then I find out that the choir boys are given red wine, so I quickly join the choir. Soon enough, someone notices that I'm a lip-syncher, not an actual singer, and I'm kicked out. Even though I adore music, I never could sing or play anything.

THIS EDUCATIONAL ROUTINE goes on like an annoying toothache. The only good moments are with my math teacher, Tosello, whom I nickname Hibou. *Hibou,* or "owl," is an appropriate nickname because he wears large-framed glasses over his unusually big, dark eyes.

Hibou reminds me of Tata. He has the same kind, intuitive eyes and seems to look straight inside your heart. This devoted gentleman is constantly worrying about the world in which *his children* will have to live, how they will survive and make a living after the war. "The world is mad.

What are my children going to do after the war?" he says to anyone who will listen.

One class period, instead of paying attention, I draw a caricature of Hibou. It's not a mocking drawing, but a serious character study.

Completely absorbed in my work, I don't hear him coming up behind me. As fast as lightning, Hibou whacks me on my back with his ruler while he snaps up my drawing with his other hand. Without a word to me or interrupting the class with my exposé, he walks straight to his desk and slides my drawing inside a folder.

When class is over, he asks me to remain. Alone in the empty classroom, he takes the drawing from his desk. Without a word, he studies it for a long time.

"How much?" he asks with a serious face.

"It's a gift to you, Monsieur," I hear myself say.

"Then you must sign it," he says with a satisfied smile.

So I write Tatiou.

"Tatiou. Who is that?" he asks, puzzled.

"It's my real name," I state with conviction.

"Ha!" He pauses, then adds, "I understand."

Just like Tata, Hibou understands everything.

But then he explains at great length that although he supports the visual arts, his class is strictly about math, not art. From then on, I must adhere to his curriculum.

"Besides," he informs me, "an artist has to know a lot about math."

In the next week, Hibou proudly shows my drawing to the entire Don Bosco personnel, from Piff all the way down to the janitors.

Years later, I will learn from a former Don Bosco student that Hibou went insane and was locked up in a mental institution like Brouchard, my teacher in Paris. Both men seemed to love their students deeply, and when the war came, the traumas became too much.

ONE AFTERNOON, I accidentally spill nearly a whole bottle of black ink on my trousers. I am sent to the dormitory to clean myself up, but I don't have many clothes because of the war and the fact that I am growing taller. Alone in the deserted dormitory bathroom, I'm mopping up the mess when "Cockroach," the priest in charge of discipline, enters the bathroom. He is tall and austere and reminds me of Goya's drawing of Don Quixote de la Mancha. "Pierre, what happened to you?" he asks, seeming genuinely concerned.

"I spilled some ink. It is almost cleaned up," I reply, as I squeeze into a smaller pair of trousers.

"Those do not fit you very well," Cockroach says. "Come with me. I think I have something your size."

"That is nice of you, but I am all set now." I detest charity. I would prefer to steal than beg.

He insists that I follow him to his quarters, and I go halfheartedly. His room is clean and Spartan, a monk's cell. Apart from a small wooden cross above the headboard of the bed, there is nothing on the walls. A small dormer lets in a weak ray of light. He closes the door behind us, and I immediately feel ill at ease.

As he forages in the closet, a strange premonition tells me that something is fishy. He turns back, empty-handed, and sits next to me on the bed.

I try to move away from him. He is breathing heavily, and his eyes have taken on a strange look. This is getting very scary. I jump up, run for the door, hit the lock, and shoot down the stairs like a jackrabbit, not stopping until I am back in the classroom.

"What's the matter with you, Pierre?" Hibou asks. "You seem very upset."

"Nothing, sir. Just short of breath. I was running back too fast."

For a while afterward, Cockroach would glance at me with a certain uneasy look. I did my best to avoid him altogether or, at the very least, not to look him straight in the eyes. A few weeks later, I noticed that he seemed overly friendly with another boy about my age. I firmly made up my mind that once I was out of this hated place, I would never return.

IN APRIL, Maman comes to the school and takes me out of my jail for an entire day.

We are going to see Grandfather Matisse.

Even in wartime, Grandfather is tremendously busy, consumed with his passion for art, and difficult to see. However, Maman never needs to worry about that. Grandfather Matisse always finds time for my mother.

In the rooms where Grandfather lives and works, there is a large aviary with lovely songbirds and doves, plants everywhere, tables loaded with sketches, and painting tools in curious ceramic pots. Shelves are tightly packed with books on every subject. The rooms are decorated with everything he needs to create art. I like this artistic environment, which projects a sense of organized comfort, both homey and secure.

"Welcome, welcome, Louise. Ha, Pierre, look how you have grown," Grandfather Matisse says warmly.

He ushers us into his studio, where he has just finished a morning drawing session. I look around at the studio with its walls painted white, fascinated by the paintings and drawings spread everywhere. It probably isn't very different from the day Grandfather Matisse gave me my color lesson nearly three years before, but at that time I was focused only on impressing him with my box of paints and not on my surroundings.

Grandfather Henri and Maman start to discuss art, which is much too advanced for me to understand. Then he takes a sheet of paper and a piece of charcoal to make a point to my mother. The silence in the room is broken only by the soft sound of the charcoal, moving firmly on a great piece of white paper. Before my eyes, his simple movements reveal a beautiful drawing.

"If one wants to be good at anything, Pierre, one has to go back to the subject again and again. Practice, practice, practice."

"How do you learn to draw and paint so well?" I ask in awe.

"Would you like to learn?"

"Yes, sir." Grandfather has my full attention now. I watch his face soften and his eyes light up. He seems pleased as he continues, "It's surprisingly simple, Pierre. To learn to draw, one takes a piece of charcoal or pencil and draws."

He pauses to reflect for a second or two. "That is all there is to it. Let your heart guide you. Your hand will do the rest."

He squints at his drawing, his eyes behind his thick glasses scrutinizing it intensely.

"There are no secrets, Pierre. Of course, one has to pay his dues with work and sweat."

Grandfather pauses again. I feel something is about to happen and almost forget to breathe.

"And still there is a great secret. You have to do it every day. Doing the same thing a million times until you understand what only you inside yourself have to understand."

Like a cat stalking his prey, he stands up and slowly walks around the drawing, a half step at a time, looking at it from all angles while talking to himself. "Boring? Never. The light. The light is everything," he finally says. "Get me my stool, Pierre. I think I've got it."

He has captured a picture. In his eyes, his brain, his soul—most importantly, in his heart.

I know something out of the ordinary is happening. Creation. I get the stool and then stand still, silent. Maman does not move either. Except for the birds in their cages and Grandfather's right hand, nothing moves in the studio.

Grandfather Matisse works fast. Then he says, "Hum! Maybe. Hum! Not bad. Hum! Something is missing, perhaps?"

Then he turns to me. "What do you think, Tatiou?"

I back away, taking on the guise of a connoisseur. Slowly, without a smile, I reply, pausing at every word. "Maybe . . . something . . . missing. But I like it. What do you think?" I say, with a grin. Grandfather chuckles and gives me a good tap on my back.

"You could very well be right, Pierrot. Nothing is ever certain in art. The possibilities are limitless."

The day passes much too fast. This world of color and art encompasses me, and it feels as if my feet weigh a thousand pounds as Maman walks with me back to Don Bosco.

The hand strokes and images created on that paper by my grandfather stay with me. Whenever I want to escape my prison walls, I think of the day with Grandfather Matisse and Maman. I envision his hand with a piece of charcoal gliding across the paper, creating beauty. The light in his eyes is what I saw during Django's concert and our time together at the Carnaval de Nice. No words are necessary for a sense of wonder to be shared.

AT LAST, JULY COMES.

I have buried myself in books and in learning to survive, and as a result, I receive a record of good conduct with A-pluses in every subject. I must admit that the Roman Catholic education is first class.

I don't even look behind me as I leave the gray walls of Don Bosco for my parents' home. They have moved to a charming villa in the Cap d'Antibes on Boulevard James Willy. Beside the house, I see the azure waves and a little beach. The surrounding shoreline is rocky with sand-colored stones and cliffs, with coves that have white sand beaches. I have a whole bedroom to myself, the only one in the house with a balcony facing the Mediterranean. After Don Bosco, this is sheer paradise.

From my bed I can view and smell the blue sea as far as my dreams will take me.

Adventure and freedom are on my doorstep once more.

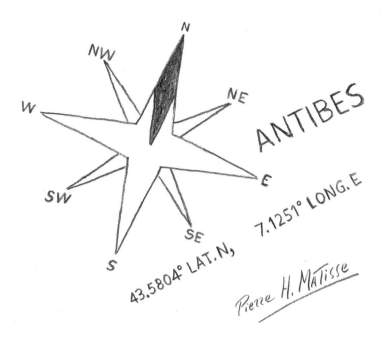

NW

N

W

NE

ANTIBES

E

SW

SE

7.1251° LONG. E

S

43.5804° LAT. N,

Pierre H. Matisse

12
DREAMS AND CREATIONS

Man cannot discover new oceans unless he has
the courage to lose sight of the shore.
ANDRÉ GIDE

I AM RESTING comfortably in bed, looking directly at the blue sea through the open French window leading to the balcony outside my room. The sounds and salty air of the Mediterranean flow over me. A southern wind blowing straight from North Africa is gently caressing my face. At night, the same window lets in the pale light from the majestic sky to guide my dreams and delight my senses.

For the first week or two in Cap d'Antibes, I spend most of the time in my room, quietly studying topographic maps of the surrounding area or reading. I am tired. Don Bosco's oppressive walls have drained my energy. By contrast, the blue line of the infinite horizon is too much for my eyes to take in.

After ten months of seclusion, one has to readapt to freedom. Tomorrow morning, before breakfast, I'll go for a swim in the Mediterranean to drown the last of Don Bosco's lice. Then I'll go swimming every day for pleasure.

My thoughts are interrupted by Papa, who has come into the room. "I have a gift for you, Pierre."

Papa hands me a box wrapped in blue paper decorated with boats, anchors, rope knots, and a compass rose.

"What is it, Papa?" I ask.

"Open it and see."

One look at the wrapping paper, and the effect is magical. Instantly, my blood begins racing. I have been brought back to life. Inside the wrapping is a book in English: *Moby-Dick*.

"Thank you so much, Papa."

I read it voraciously, finishing it in a few days. "It's a *whale* of a story!" I declare to Papa.

"That's what I thought too," he answers, with a smile. "Quite a story indeed!" he adds, laughing.

Now, I need a boat to live my own adventures, I say to myself.

THERE ARE ALWAYS interesting visitors at the Antibes home, artists from a variety of disciplines who live nearby. Sculptors, painters, cartoonists, musicians, composers, movie and theater stars—all of them colorful personalities. To them, everything is exciting; everything takes on extraordinary proportions. The conversations are always as fascinating as they are theatrically animated.

Picasso visits a time or two. He smokes like a chimney and is famous for having shot his pistol in the streets of Paris. I am impressed with him, but Maman is not sure he is the best influence on me. Picasso seems only to care about "la corrida" (bullfighting). He claims he does not care much for boats, which is inconceivable to me. But he adds that he did know of a painter who painted from a boat.

"Who?" I ask.

"Monet," he says, taking another puff on his cigar.

"I want to meet Monet!" I say excitedly.

"It's not possible," Picasso says sadly. "He swallowed the anchor before you were born."

"For once I want to meet somebody really interesting, but he died on me!" I reply, quite disappointed.

"That's life," Picasso says, adding a curt, "thank you."

Picasso and my father start laughing. The next day when Picasso shows Papa and me some of his newest works, I understand the humorous meaning of his "thank you." He is a great painter, and he's sitting right in front of me, very much alive!

Picasso likes to make fun of another occasional visitor's moustache—that of artist Salvador Dali. "Salvador is always trying to convince us that his crazy moustache is actually an antenna to contact the upper-up for inspiration."

After taking a sip of wine, he says loudly, "His moustache has nothing mystical about it. He waxes it way up so it doesn't get entangled with the sardines when he eats them!"

One painter whose stories I enjoy is Maurice de Vlaminck, a wild man among wild men. He raced motorcycles in his younger days, and I had even heard that one of them had an airplane engine for more power. I imagine him racing around a track and then suddenly flying into the sky with that extra boost. With his unruly red hair and big red beard, he reminds me of a large bear. His passion about anything and everything is outrageous, and he expresses his views just as fervently, whether he is discussing art methods, social edicts, or politics. When Maman tells me that de Vlaminck paints with knives, I immediately picture him slashing color onto a canvas with swords in both hands.

But my favorite family friend is Jean Effel, a renowned and successful artist. Before the war, his popular political cartoons depicting God appeared regularly in the magazine *Paris Match*. He owns a charming villa nested between some huge rocks on the extreme point of Cap d'Antibes.

ONE DAY EFFEL drops by our home for an *apéritif*. As usual, he is discussing politics, the war, art, and entertainment with my parents. When he sees me, he hands me a small leather pouch and says, "For you, Pierre."

Inside the pouch is a small brass compass. This is the real thing—a salty one, not a toy. I can't believe my luck. It's just what I need.

"It's too much. I can't accept it, Monsieur Effel."

But I sure would love to, I think.

"Yes! Yes! You can. It's for you because I hear that you are quite a sailor."

"Yes, Monsieur Effel. I can sail, steer, and row. Papa tells me that you have a boat."

"It's only a little dinghy, nothing fancy."

He knows what is coming.

"A dinghy? How wonderful!" I say excitedly. "Is it in need of paint? If it is, I'll clean it and paint it for you."

"Well, as a matter of fact, it is in bad shape and needs some attention. If your parents agree, you can come and work on it. The waters around the Cap are treacherous, so no boating without supervision."

I am thrilled with the offer. I can tell already that this is going to be an extremely good summer if I can get permission.

"May I go to Monsieur Effel's home, Papa?"

"Yes," he says. "But only after your chores are done each day. Tomorrow I will need your help the whole day."

I AM ASSISTING MY FATHER, a talented sculptor and true master at his art. Under his chisel, a massive stone takes the form of an exquisite nude. I never wonder how Papa can see something that beautiful in a block of wood or stone. That's what he does, and he does it extremely well.

Papa has his own style, characterized by a great purity of form. It is clear that he is searching for the very essence of real beauty without compromising for cheap effect. Whatever the medium—marble or wood—his eyes are sure, his hands firmly holding the chisel. With each hit of the small maul, a tiny chip of stone or wood falls away. On a piece of marble the sound is rhythmic and melodious—*tac . . . tic . . . tic . . . tac . . .* A masterpiece is coming into the world through the sound of music. It is the same method on wood with different notes and a different tune.

Papa is as gifted as his friend Aristide Maillol. Once the clay statue is finished, I help Papa make a plaster cast for a few reproductions. During these working sessions, we talk only about the work at hand. He has to have absolute mental concentration. I have understood this from the very first day I helped him. Mostly we communicate with hand signals and head nods, and Papa barks short and concise orders at me.

"Here! Hold this."

Papa is adjusting a measuring caliper and continues to give me orders.

"Yes! No! Not like that, Pierre. Like this."

It has to be done with the utmost precision.

"Sorry," I say.

"Get me more clay, and cover the rest with a damp rag," Papa instructs me.

I can see that he is thinking hard. The sculpture is not going his way.

"Your clay is there," I say, gesturing to a small mound, "and I have already covered the other batch."

"Good! Now you can start mixing some plaster." The tension is on. I have only a short amount of time before the plaster hardens.

"Right!"

"Clean those tools, will you?"

There is quite a mess to clean up because my parents are always working on something. In fact, I cannot remember a time when that wasn't the case.

Sometimes under the heat of creation, when working in marble, a chisel breaks and Papa's frustration is released. But there is too much to do, so the moment quickly passes.

"Oh well," Papa says, "I'm not making chisels—I'm making a statue. I could care less about a broken chisel here and there; it's part of the game! Pierre, pass me the big chisel!" His eyes have not left the marble. Like a surgeon, he holds out his hand, and I place the appropriate tool in it.

The matter of returning to Don Bosco has been dangling above my head like the sword of Damocles. I've been keeping a low profile and managing to keep out of serious trouble, anxiously waiting for the opportunity to bring up the subject.

Finally, one day in the studio with Papa, I speak my mind. "Papa, I don't want to go back to Don Bosco."

"We'll see to that with your mother," he answers distractedly.

"No, we won't!" I raise my voice. "We'll settle this right now between you and me."

"What!" I am startled as Papa drops his tool on the bench. "What did you say?" He looks outraged.

"I can't explain it to you. But on my honor, I have my reasons, Papa. I don't want to go back there ever again. Please trust me. I'm not going back to Don Bosco."

Papa stops working, sits down on a stool, and looks at me curiously.

"What happened there?" he asks quietly.

"I can't tell you the details."

"Are you okay?" He is looking me straight in the eye.

"I can't explain it, Papa. But it is okay as long as I don't have to go back."

He smiles, giving me a hug and a tap on the back.

"It's all right. You won't be going back to Don Bosco." He pauses, then says, "I understand that sometimes a man just has his own personal reasons."

That same evening I hear Papa quarreling with my mother. But by the end of the evening, they agree to send me to Antibes College, which is close enough for me to walk to. It is clean and has no walls enclosing it.

WHENEVER PAPA NEEDS ME, I help him, even though I am tired at the end of the day. Art is an intellectual pursuit, but the work is physically demanding because I am always picking up tools and moving things for him. Still, I know the contentment of contributing to something meaningful. Sometimes Papa says, with discouragement on his face, "I think that this statue is going badly. It's all screwed up."

"No! No! Not at all," I reassure him. "From that angle it's beautiful."

How can he doubt that this masterpiece is right? I am certain it is good.

Incredulous, he slowly turns around his creation, frowning, peering, critical to the extreme. When we are lucky, a faint smile lights up his face and he says, "Blast you! You could be right. I'll have to ask your mother's opinion."

Maman always agrees with me.

I help Maman, too—putting wood in the kilns, sometimes modeling, and, of course, cleaning up.

My mother, cloistered in her studio, is making a collection of small figurines, representing scenes from the turn of the century: elegant ladies in crinolines, carriages with drivers in top hats that are pulled by high-stepping horses.

I remember she also did a special edition of little statues inspired by Jean Effel's caricatures. Later, she creates a set of figurines depicting characters from Greek mythology. When these pieces are exhibited in an art gallery in Nice, Grandfather Matisse goes to the show. Right there on the spot, my grandfather makes ink sketches of Maman's figurines.

After a long day's work, Maman and Papa walk hand in hand to a small fisherman's bistro for an apéritif. It is not very far, just across the small harbor. One can see a mile away that they are very much in love.

While they are gone, I begin preparing dinner, according to my mother's instructions. I peel potatoes and carrots to boil them and make a salad, learning to put together a simple meal in no time at all. However, using an oven is beyond my abilities, and when it is needed, one of my parents takes over.

I begin raising rabbits again. It would have been nice to keep a few chickens, too, but there is no way to get grain to feed them. I also fish, and on lucky days I proudly return with a catch for the dinner table.

After all of my duties are done, I'm free to do my own things. I draw or paint landscapes or seascapes, while at the same time making innumerable plans to write the next what have you and earn the world's prestigious literary prize. Of course, after reading Ernest Hemingway, I realize that a writer has to have a lot of life experiences to have something interesting to write about. So I polish my English and make more plans to travel to America after the war.

When possible, I head straight to Monsieur Effel's villa and continue refurbishing his dinghy. As I work, I daydream about exploring the big oceans of the world after I install a set of sails on the small boat. Eventually, the dinghy is fixed enough to row it, and with Monsieur Effel's permission, I take Gérard for a little session on a calm sea. After a while this becomes too ordinary and I need more of a challenge.

ONE BLUSTERY DAY, Monsieur Effel finds me perched on the slippery cliff.

"What are you doing here, Pierre?" Monsieur Effel asks. "The weather is terrible."

"I am studying the waves, Monsieur Effel."

I am motionless, soaked to the bones by the spray of the waves crashing into the five-foot-high cliff, mentally calculating how I can handle the dinghy in such a turbulent sea.

I have it, I think confidently. *Put the bow at a ten-degree angle to the wind, taking the waves at quarter beam. Then turn only between two big waves, where the wind should be low. Nothing to it, that should work. I'll have to try this when nobody is watching me.*

"Pierre, come back. You are going to catch pneumonia." I can barely hear Monsieur Effel's voice—almost lost in the screaming wind.

"I'm coming!"

But Monsieur Effel sees a certain smile on my face and says more loudly, "You're not thinking about trying this small boat in this kind of sea, are you, Pierre?" He has read my mind. How does he do that?

"No, sir!"

He doesn't believe me. "The Med can be deadly, you know. It is absolutely forbidden to use the dinghy in any waves, however small. Strictly on a calm sea and only under adult supervision. Understood?"

"Yes, sir."

This time I try to be more convincing, while saying to myself, *We'll see about that.*

But I will need the right conditions. No Gérard, no adults, lots of wind, and the sea like a boiling pot. How exciting! I have to know if I am a real sailor, one who has courage and fortitude. I am growing up and getting stronger, but I need to measure up. Surely Papa and Monsieur Effel will understand.

Pierre H. Matisse

13
ADVENTURES ON THE HIGH SEAS

Sometimes it doesn't pay to be too smart.

PIERRE H. MATISSE

ONE STORMY SUMMER AFTERNOON, the right conditions come. The Med is cold, and a gale is blowing furiously from the southeast. No one is around to stop me. This day is all mine.

Sheltered between two short headlands of sharp rocks is a tiny cove, around twelve feet wide by twenty feet long. Full of confidence, I get in the dinghy and pull away. *Nothing to it*, I think, as I begin to row. *Now let's get to the real thing—the sea and me.*

In the open Med, holy mackerel! Up I go! Down I go! It's like riding a wild horse. I feel like a lion has me in its jaws and is shaking me savagely left and right. I realize that I am in serious trouble. The wind is pushing me out of control, the current is too strong. I can't possibly row against that.

The dinghy is taking on water by the bucketful. I have only a small tin can to bail it out. It takes all my limited skills to keep the boat from capsizing. My heart is in my throat, and panic sets in. It's all too clear— I am going to die.

I call for help. Only God can get me out of this situation, and now would be a good time.

"God, it's me, Pierre. I have disobeyed my parents, and I am a very bad boy. I have never asked You anything, but today I am stuck. Please help me."

A few moments alone with God can accomplish miracles. My panic is replaced by God-given courage. If I have to die, at least I'll die like a man. I don't have time to be afraid. The fight is on.

I pull on the oars as hard as I can. Deftly, I turn them parallel to the waves in an effort to keep the wind from tearing them out of my hands. A piece of jetsam a few yards away floats nearby. It's now drifting between land and the dinghy, heading back toward the Cap. *The current! It's following the current.* I have to follow the piece of debris.

I row with all my body and soul until my heart is pounding. The jetsam is going to shore, but for some reason I am not. I am caught in a trough between waves, and I can't see anything. The dinghy is like a spinning top, and I am disoriented. Abruptly, I am propelled on a wave's crest, and the wind hits me with such force that I can't breathe.

A big wave throws me sideways. Fortunately, I correct myself just in time to avoid capsizing.

"I lost the jetsam!" I cry out of frustration, not fear or despair—there is no time for them. My adrenaline is running full blast.

"Where is the stupid jetsam?" I scream loudly to no one but myself.

Then, I hear a banging on the hull of the dinghy. I can't believe it. The jetsam, remnants of a wooden crate with German lettering, is on the starboard side. I am getting closer to the shore, and I row like a madman. "Thank You, God," I say, "but don't leave me just yet, please? Maybe You can send a guardian angel to protect me."

Every time I am on a wave's crest, I can see Monsieur Effel's villa, so I aim for the cove. Am I making progress? Slowly, slowly, yes! The shore is coming closer.

Suddenly a big breaker takes me by the bottom of my pants and throws me brutally onto the rocks. The dinghy shatters into a thousand pieces, like an eggshell hitting a wall. I lie on the rocks half-drowned, covered in blood and chilled to the core.

I whisper a prayer through my chattering teeth. "Thank You, God! A million thanks. I'll never do that again."

I think that I hear a voice respond, "Really?" Is that heavenly ridicule, or is it the wind? It's only my imagination . . . right?

Somehow I manage to drag myself home. Fortunately, nobody is there. While I'm in the bathroom cleaning myself up, I hear Maman screaming. "No! It can't be him. He was told not to take the boat out in bad weather." She is getting hysterical. "No! No! He is not dead. Jean, tell me it's not true."

Some neighbors had spotted me in the cove. According to them, I had disappeared in the raging sea. They had run to the bistro for help to find my body. A half dozen people are running up to the Cap. This is not going well at all. Completely bewildered, I run out of the house to my mother.

"Maman, it's me. I'm here."

My mother almost faints, and everybody looks at me strangely. I quickly realize the problem—I am completely naked.

"What happened to your clothes?" Papa asks.

"They were wet!" I answer, shivering in the wind. "I took them off in the house." I turn and make a quick exit back inside. Once I am fully clothed again, it's back to work with Papa. Busyness keeps the lid on me.

I am grateful that I have survived, but how in the world am I going to explain to Monsieur Effel what happened to his dinghy?

"The good thing is, Pierre always inflicts his own punishment upon himself," Papa tells my mother.

"Until he kills himself!" is her curt reply.

"Don't worry. From now on, he's going to respect the sea."

LATER, MONSIEUR EFFEL ARRIVES at our house. When I apologize for the fate of the dinghy, he says, "I was going to give you the dinghy anyway, Pierre. So it's not a loss to me; you just lost *your* dinghy."

"Thank you. I think it is the nicest gift anyone has ever given me,"

I say, as the realization that I have destroyed my boat before I ever owned it sinks in. He laughs.

"What are you going to do now?" he asks, appearing quite interested in my next move.

I wait until Maman leaves the room.

"I am going to build a kayak," I tell him in confidence.

FOOD IS GETTING SCARCER BY THE DAY. The government has instituted ration coupons for everything: sugar, oil, butter, meat, bread, potatoes, rice. In fact, everything we need for living is rationed. If you need it, it is rationed. Sometimes, even with the coupons, you can't get goods. Even the black market operators are having difficulties. Papa has to be content with a small ration of cigarettes, which is the worst ordeal, reflected in his mood. I do my best to stay clear of him when I know he has no cigarettes.

We are all hungry. At night I can't fall asleep because my stomach hurts so much. The rationing system becomes more abominable: coupons are allocated by human classification. Babies receive little food. Children are allowed a little of that, so many grams of this, and not much more. Adults are on a slim diet, and seniors are receiving barely any food at all. But teenagers. Ha! Teenagers are classified J3 and are given the most, even more than adult workers doing physical labor. J3s are taken care of because when they come of age—about fifteen or sixteen—they will either be drafted into the army or be sent to Germany for forced labor. After all, Europe can't afford to run out of soldiers, or "gun meat" as Tata used to say. Even with the added ration coupons, I am always hungry, and the coupons aren't worth much when there is nothing to use them for.

The food coupons allocated every month don't cover much fresh fruit, which is nearly nonexistent. Who can remember what a banana or orange looks like? How do you describe the taste to a child who has never seen one? The unfortunates of war are sometimes fortunate. One day a British submarine torpedoes a German freighter close to Nice's harbor. *Boom!* The Boches' rusty bucket blows sky high. Among other things, the freighter is loaded with oranges on their way to Germany. Kindly, the current delivers the oranges, some still intact in crates, to their rightful owner—me—thirty miles away in Antibes.

I am constantly walking in the cove, looking for escargot and crabs, any fresh food from the sea. When I spot the oranges, I am enticed. But getting to them is tricky. The rocky shore is terribly slippery, and the weather has turned nasty. The sea can be mean—that much I have already learned. Yet I can practically taste the sweet, juicy fruit.

Apparently nobody else has noticed anything in the water, so I keep the secret to myself. I swim out to the crates and manage to salvage a few full crates, which I bring home in a wheelbarrow. I eat some at the beach and savor their taste, so refreshing compared to our usual diet of fish and beans. When I have retrieved them all, I will surprise my family with this treasure from the sea.

I go back the next day, and the next, snatching one floating orange at a time.

The weather remains foul, but I am obstinate. I have to get those last oranges. Who knows when another "orange boat" will be sunk? Between the swells is a nice batch, floating only a few yards away. I try to reach them for an hour or so with no luck. That's it! I'm going to swim for them. Tomorrow will be too late; they'll be gone. I can already envision Papa, Maman, and Gérard enjoying my spoils and sharing them with our friends and neighbors.

There is a lot of oily wreckage drifting all around me. I have a little net bag for my catch attached to my belt. The current is strong, but I get to the prized fruit and fill the bag almost full.

As I turn to swim back, something is in my way. It's like a big bag of rags. The material is a pale blue gray color. I see something red—a cross, then an arm and beautiful long hair. *A dead nurse!* I am horrified and swim as fast as I can back to shore.

When Papa asks me where the oranges came from, I explain how I got them. Some of the oranges last only a few days because they are waterlogged, while some last up to a week. Everyone enjoys the bounty, but I politely refuse the oranges when they are offered to me.

When Maman asks me why, I simply say, "I prefer bananas."

"I told you," a neighbor says. "It's the same story all the time. They are spoiling those J3s. He has oranges but he wants bananas. Typical!"

"If only they could sink a boat full of cigarettes," Papa adds wistfully.

I never tell anyone what else I saw in the water.

However, I accept my lone responsibility for having found this dead nurse, and I ask God to accept this angel of mercy into heaven with open arms.

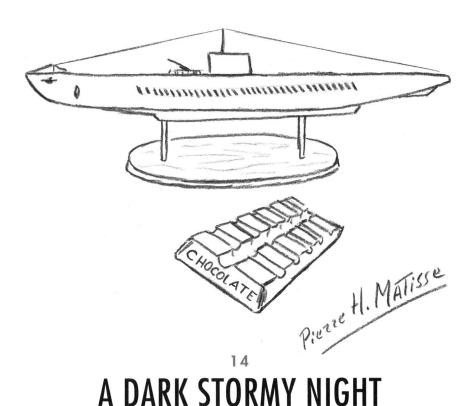

14

A DARK STORMY NIGHT

Everything is permitted, but don't get caught.

FRENCH FOREIGN LEGION SAYING, SIDI-BEL-ABBÈS

PAPA HAS NEVER really been a keen fisherman, but in the late summer he suddenly takes an interest in fishing. Not from the shore, but from a boat. He has made some friends among the fishermen in the community, and they often lend him a solid heavy rowboat with oars. It is large enough for us to attach a temporary short mast with a small lateen sail.

On one fishing trip, Papa, Gérard, and I row to a certain spot before Papa says to stop. Since I have been fishing these waters for a while now, I offer my opinion. "Papa, we are not going to catch any fish here. It's no good."

"We are fishing here anyway," he replies.

"But I like to actually *catch* fish," I say impatiently. "Look! There is not even a crab to eat the bait."

"Be patient!" Papa drops a sounding lead into the water to measure the depth.

What's wrong with him? I can't contain myself. "Papa, the east side of the Cap is the deepest point of the entire French Mediterranean, close to the coast."

"Pierre, you are getting on my nerves. Shut up and take a few bearings on the white house with the red roof over there and another one from the tip of the Cap."

I do as I am told. When he checks my nautical calculation, he smiles. "Right on the money. Our numbers match. Perfect!" When he nods in approval, my momentary irritation with him disappears, and I feel proud.

"I have a surprise for you, Papa." I pull out a sealed brown envelope from my pocket and pass it to him.

He opens it carefully. "Tobacco!" he says happily. "Where did you get it?"

"I requisitioned it from that farmer who charges exorbitant prices for his vegetables. He grows it secretly between the rows of tomato plants."

Papa's expression darkens immediately as the boat rocks on the waves. Gérard, sitting in the middle of the boat, glances at Papa, then me, then back and forth.

"So," Papa says to me, "it is not enough to steal dinghies from Jean Effel. Now you have graduated to grand larceny, eh?"

I begin my defense. "Monsieur Effel was going to give me the dinghy. And Monsieur Jacques said that *requisitioning* is the term for gaining necessities during wartime. Besides, that farmer will not notice a few missing plants." My eyes are riveted on the floorboards of the boat. I've been anticipating this lecture.

"It's not a legitimate excuse. You are strictly forbidden to steal or requisition anything. Do you hear me? You'd better shape up, Pierre. We went over this with the flowers in Beauzelle. I will not tolerate a thief under my roof."

His look burns into me as he waits to see if I have gotten the message. Once he's satisfied, he seems pleased with himself and, as the expression on his face indicates, perhaps even with me. I am certain that, deep down, he's very glad I helped myself to the tobacco leaves.

"By the way, where exactly are these tobacco plants located?" he asks with a grin, rolling a cigarette with my contraband.

Two hours pass without a single bite. I am bored to tears, and so is Gérard. Papa is spending most of the time smoking. No one says anything because sound carries too well across the water. We have packed water and a little bread, cheese, and onions, but this is emergency food only.

I have to do something. "Can I go for a swim, Papa?" I finally ask.

"Yes."

This is strange. Papa never lets me swim around the boat when we are fishing. But then again, we usually are catching fish.

"Can you swim under the boat?" Gérard asks me, looking over the edge of the boat. Although I have been swimming since I was a small boy, my brother has never wanted to learn. I love showing off for him.

"Sure!" I dive, splashing water on him and Papa. Gérard laughs, enjoying watching me disappear on one side of the boat and pop up on the other.

Papa bursts into thunderous laughter. What is the matter with him? He's not fishing seriously. Something is definitely *fishy* here.

As I climb back into the boat, he says, "Let's move out of here, Pierre. Go straight, one hundred and forty degrees."

"There are no more fish in that direction than here, Papa."

"As I said, one hundred and forty, my boy," Papa insists.

This doesn't make any sense to me at all. Gérard gives me a shrug and trails his hand in the water.

"This course leads directly to Corsica, Papa." I want Papa to realize that I know what I'm talking about.

"I know, Mister Pirate, but keep on going anyway." My father is going batty, no doubt about it. The lateen sail goes up and catches a light breeze that pushes us steadily along. The sky is cloudy, but here and there the sun's rays break through openings in the white cotton above us.

"Now put the bow toward the Cap, Pierre."

"That is even worse for fishing," I grumble. With this strategy the fish are safe. What a waste of time.

"I know," Papa says.

"When we get back, those fishermen will laugh at us, Papa."

"Let them laugh. Now, Pierre, do you know exactly where we are?"

"Yes, Papa."

"Could you get us back to the first place where the fishing wasn't good? I mean exactly."

I study his face. "Yes, Papa."

"Go!"

When we arrive at the initial fishless spot, I finally ask Papa, "Is this a game?"

"Yes, it's a game," he says, "but a very serious one."

Now I am extremely curious. "Tell me about it."

"Not now."

THE THREE OF US play this game a few times over the next week. We pack water and a lunch, and we "fish" in places where there is no chance of catching a thing. I have a good time swimming, and the navigation drill with my compass is fun. I wish Papa would try some other spots, but he seems obsessed with these two positions.

Finally, one day Papa and I go out alone. Gérard doesn't mind being left behind. Although he liked the first excursions, the truth is that he hasn't been too enthusiastic about water or boats since he saw me battered and bloody after the wreck of the dinghy.

When Papa and I get to the usual spot, he says, "Do you think you can get to these exact spots at night, Pierre? Right on the nose?"

He is calmly packing his pipe with some tobacco leaves that look very much like the greedy farmer's. I'm wondering if we have two thieves in the family instead of one. Papa notices the questioning look on my face.

"After further consideration of your actions, I asked the farmer for forgiveness and offered to pay for the tobacco. You were right; his prices are exorbitant. So I convinced the farmer that if he shares the tobacco with me, he has my friendship and silence on the secret crop." I should have known Papa would find an honest way to keep his supply chain going.

I grin and then answer his question. "With a little bit of moon, we can see the Cap. Then if the white house has a light in a window . . ."

"Correct; that's what I thought. We're going to try, but not a word to anyone. This is just between you and me."

"But Papa, the fishing is not better at night, you know."

"I know," he says. "We are not after fish, my son. We are after Adolf Hitler."

A shiver runs through me; I have goose bumps from head to toe. From the way he looks at me, I understand. Together, we are going to fight these rotten Boches.

Over the next week, strangers come to our home late at night. They stay a few moments, discuss something with Papa behind closed doors, then disappear into the night.

A FEW NIGHTS LATER, Papa asks me to give him a hand with a project in the cellar, so I follow him down the stairs. He walks over to a wall and says, "We're going to make a hole in this wall." The wall is dirt covered with brick and stone. Working together with a hand drill, sledgehammer, pick, and shovel, it doesn't take long to break through and create a three-foot-by-three-foot hole.

"Take that basket, shovel the dirt into it, and bury it in the garden."

I carry out Papa's instructions quickly and return to the cellar. There is something beside him on the floor.

"That's Charlot's suitcase!" I exclaim.

"Who is Charlot, Pierre?" Papa snaps at me.

"I don't know," I reply, realizing my mistake and looking at the floor.

"That's better," Papa says more kindly. "One slip like that and we are dead. From this moment, put this firmly in your head: You see nothing, you hear nothing, you know nothing, you say nothing. Clear?"

My eyes tell him yes before the words come out. "I understand, Papa."

By now, I know better than to ask questions. A doctor who is a friend of my parents has been arrested by the Gestapo. There has been no news from him since, and it is rumored that he has been executed. Other people have disappeared mysteriously, including an architect friend of the family.

In Nice, the Boches have rounded up a lot of Jews for deportation, but to where? Again, nobody knows, or if some do, they are not talking.

Papa opens the black suitcase, which contains a few pieces of underwear. Then he lifts the false bottom inside, revealing a shortwave radio. A side compartment inside the suitcase holds a small automatic pistol with a couple of clips. Papa puts the pistol and clips in his pocket, then we hide the suitcase in the opening in the wall. I spend the rest of the day piling up firewood in front of it.

SHORTLY LATER, I start school but look forward to the evenings at home when we gather around our regular radio to listen to the forbidden BBC broadcast messages, an ingenious cloak-and-dagger operation. The radios themselves are not illegal, but the program certainly is. During the broadcasts, coded messages are being sent, embedded in sentences, and Papa is concentrating, listening for certain things. I don't know what the messages are, so I interpret them in my own imagination.

"Uncle Arthur has the smallpox." *Somebody must be sick.*

"The strawberry jam was too sweet." *Gourmet food, my mouth is watering.*

"Grandmama gave birth to a baby girl." *Family problems coming on the horizon.*

"My sister is going swimming." *I'd like to go for a swim with her.*

"We are running without rest or dreams." *That's the war for you.*

"Toward the paradise of my dreams!" *That's a line from* Les Fleurs du mal *by Charles Baudelaire.*

Zeee! . . . *Brromm* . . . *Crac* . . . *Cheee!* . . . The Boches don't seem to appreciate Baudelaire's poetry. They are jamming the transmission with static.

Papa swears as he turns the knob to another frequency. "They haven't blocked this one yet, but it is coming in very weak." Papa puts his ear to the speaker. The sound comes, then fades.

"The day will come." *Enigmatic and full of promises.*

"Death to the cows." *Definitely threatening.*

"The sound of the guns will roar at dawn." *Musical harmony.*

"The beautiful girl is still waiting." *Maybe she is waiting for me,* I think with a silly grin.

Then the sound is drowned out by static at full blast.

Day after day and night after night, we listen to the same sentences, which seem meaningless to me.

THEN ONE DAY after we have listened to the broadcast, Papa tells me, "Tomorrow you are not going to school. You are going to be sick and stay in bed all day. Try to sleep. We are going fishing tomorrow night."

I can't fall asleep, but I do stay in bed, only getting up to eat and make short trips to the bathroom. By a preplanned arrangement between Maman and Papa, she and Gérard are spending the night with some friends.

Papa comes to the attic and says, "It's time." We both dress in dark clothes, with black knit watch caps pulled down over our foreheads.

"We look good," Papa comments dryly.

We slip silently out the back door and through the garden. We head for a small promontory by the seaside and follow the edge of the rocky beach to the small fishing harbor. Once in the harbor, we walk straight to the jetty, wait for a few minutes, and move until we are hidden in the shadow of a big crate.

There is no one around. A passing cloud obstructs the quarter moon, and I become uneasy. Am I scared? No way! I am a pirate. However, I whisper to my father, "What if we are caught?"

"The gendarmes know, so we won't be caught. We just don't want anyone else to know, especially the neighbors."

The moon is emerging from the clouds, and my courage grows stronger when I see it.

I feel a light tap on my shoulder. "Let's go. Stay in the shadows." Papa walks toward the end of the pier, where an old, half-rotted dark blue boat is tied ashore with equally rotten ropes.

"Bad choice. This one is pretty rotten," I dare to point out.

"That's the one we are taking. Jump in and get the oars in the gunwale. We are taking her out," Papa commands.

Once aboard I feel safe.

Papa unties her, and we quietly row out to sea, headed for the no-good fishing spot. It seems like we row forever, much longer than in the daytime. My arms are aching. The rocking of the boat makes me slightly seasick. Finally, from the dark shore, we see a faint light that appears on starboard, coming from a house on shore.

"We're close. Take a bearing on that window, Pierre."

Again, clouds shroud the moon. The Cap's outline disappears on the horizon.

Papa is not pleased that we have to wait.

From time to time, the clouds part and enough moonlight hits the Cap for us to check our position. We are at the right place. Slowly, the hours pass by.

"They are not coming tonight," Papa laments. We row back just before sunrise and moor the boat.

A WEEK LATER, it's the same story with the same boat. We spend a night on the sea with no results. Ten days later, we try again, to no avail. A month later, we are in the same position at the appointed time. The blue boat with its peeling paint is gently rocking in the swell, under the quarter moon.

This time something happens. A strange, gurgling noise approaches out of the darkness. Low on the water, a submarine suddenly appears!

There is hardly a sound, as she is running on battery power. My heart races. Whoa! This is exciting. We row toward the drifting sub.

A hatch opens, and I see men coming out. A line is cast, I grab it, and they pull us in close. No one says a word. Three men in civilian dress, each carrying a suitcase, board our small vessel.

"Cast off!" someone says.

Once we are a safer distance away, the sub disappears into the night.

"Straight on, for our house," Papa orders the crew.

Papa and the three men handle the oars, and I'm at the tiller. When the wind picks up and the sea starts getting choppy, we take on water.

"Gentlemen, please move toward the center and bail. The Mediterranean is quite unpredictable," Papa says. Morning is coming too fast for our liking, and the men row like mad.

"We have to get there before sunrise. Row harder," Papa commands.

The waves are higher, and we are taking on more water than we can bail.

"Everybody out!" Papa says. "We will have to swim. The house is just across from our landing spot. There." Papa points it out for the three men. I keep the boat steady with the oars while Papa removes the rudder and helps the men quickly plunge into the water with their suitcases.

When I start to get up and follow them, Papa says, "Pierre, stay with me. There is no time to moor the boat. We have to scuttle her."

We are far enough from shore for the current to take it away, so Papa rams an oar through the boat's rotten hull and sinks her before we swim back to the beach.

By the time we reach the beach, where the men have been waiting, I feel as if I am dragging chains with every step, and I'm shivering in my wet clothes.

"We're lucky it's still dark," Papa whispers.

Finally, we are home, soaked to our bones, but safe. One of the gentlemen opens his suitcase and says, "Cigarettes, Jean?"

Papa's eyes grow large as he looks inside—it's as if he is seeing a pirate's treasure. "Gauloises? Where did you get Gauloises?"

"We have everything, Jean." From now on, this man will be Monsieur Gauloises to me.

"Yes, we live like kings!" the tallest of the three men jokes.

"Travel first class, too," the blond one says with a grin.

Monsieur Gauloises offers me a bar of Spanish chocolate from the suitcase. I haven't experienced this luxury for years.

"Thank you. I'll keep half for my brother."

"Here is one for your brother, my friend," he says with a smile.

Before I can open my mouth to thank him, the blond man grabs the chocolate bars out of my hands.

"It's always the same thing with you, taking stupid risks," he says angrily to Monsieur Gauloises. "You were told not to have anything on you at all. That is a strict regulation." The blond one is mad as a hornet. He unwraps the chocolate and hands the treat back to me without the paper wrapper.

"Eat it. It's all right, but not a word about this to anybody." He wads the wrapper up into a small ball and throws it at Monsieur Gauloises.

"Burn it right away, idiot."

"The kid is safe," my father reassures the blond one.

I stuff both bars in my mouth like a ravenous wolf while they all watch me. The tension is broken when Papa bursts out laughing and the others join in.

I go into the kitchen to make coffee with the roasted black beans. We light the furnace and strip down. I string clotheslines in every room. The insides of some of the suitcases have gotten wet, so we also hang French and German banknotes on the line to dry.

"What is that?" I ask one of our guests, who is separating items from a pile of metal parts.

"A car jack," someone answers.

"It's actually a Sten submachine gun," explains the tall one, drying the components with a rag.

"We have something else for you, Jean."

Monsieur Gauloises hands a package wrapped up in a green, greasy, heavy paper to my father. Inside is a Thompson submachine gun. Things are taking an interesting turn. After Papa examines it, he hands it to me. I had only seen this kind of weapon in the movies, and after our long night at sea, eventually I fall asleep on the sofa with the Thompson lying in my lap.

I DON'T WAKE UP until late the next afternoon. Papa is sitting in the living room, enjoying a Gauloises. The Thompson is on the table, loaded.

"Eat something, Pierre. Those gentlemen have left some hot chocolate for you."

Hot chocolate. How wonderful.

"Where are our guests, Papa?"

"Still sleeping upstairs."

"When are they leaving?"

"As soon as the weather permits. This time, we need a dark and stormy night."

Papa gets his wish a couple of days later. Two of our guests leave late during the night in a torrential storm that not even a dog would be caught in. A day later, I guide the blond one in broad daylight to the railway station. Who would have guessed that they were British spies? They are all different nationalities—possibly Czech, Hungarian, and Turkish.

A week later they are nothing but a memory, with no evidence of their visit apart from the Thompson and the Gauloises cigarettes. They leave no traces, no names, nothing.

THERE IS NO MORE FISHING for quite a while. Life returns to normal—that is, war normal. Papa has smoked all of the cigarettes, but he now sleeps with the Thompson under his bed, and a coil of heavy rope is permanently on the floor beneath the half-open window for a quick escape.

One afternoon while Papa and I are in the studio, I take a piece of paper and draw a rowboat in a rough sea with five men aboard. I hold it up and am pleased with how it looks, realistically capturing our last expedition. Papa glances over to see what I am doing and rips it out of my hands, shouting, "Are you crazy? There must be no evidence of what has taken place here. Do you have that straight, little fool?"

"Yes," I say quietly.

"You write and illustrate your world-famous novel when the war is finished," Papa says, giving me a kind smile. "Okay?"

I nod, understanding completely.

The war is distorting everything. It's like life is on hold until the war is finished or until we are all gone because we have starved to death—whichever comes first.

But it doesn't seem like the war will end any time soon. Benito Mussolini (Il Duce), the Fascist prime minister of Italy, has been Hitler's buddy since the summer of 1940 and decides that he wants to expand his holdings in France. He sends the Italian army to occupy the French Riviera. These days we have the Gestapo undercover, a few of our own foreign guests running around, and now, the *Macaronis* (Italians), who think they run the place.

We hear from our secret BBC programs that the Boches are getting a licking in Russia. One evening we catch a Russian shortwave broadcast that mentions the French underground doing anti-German activities in our immediate area.

"We're getting famous," I proudly declare to Papa.

"Or infamous," he says with a frown.

15

HUNGER AT THE DINING TABLE

An empty stomach is not a good political adviser.

ALBERT EINSTEIN

THE FOOD SITUATION is getting worse. Even the black market's supplies are dwindling. Ever since we moved to the Cap, Papa and I have been able to put some fish on the table, but now there are no fish to be found.

"*Merde!* There are no fish in this cesspool. I told your mother that we should have gone to the Atlantic coast. She never listens." Papa, who rarely swore before, is using bad language regularly.

With very few cigarettes available anymore, Papa's mood, like everything else, is worsening. Something else is happening that disturbs me. Maman and Papa, who have always been so loving toward each other, are quarreling quite often. My mother is doing her best to accommodate everyone's needs, which is not an easy task.

Gérard doesn't complain too much, and neither do I. Come to think of it, nobody does, at least not away from the dining table. Unfortunately, at the table, everybody's nerves are on edge and dangerously close to exploding.

Every meal is a volatile ordeal that begins with an empty plate in front of each one of us. Maman silently serves whatever meager food she has been able to gather. She fills our plates according to the government allocations, slightly modified to her interpretation.

"Why does Pierre always have a full plate?" Gérard asks.

"Because he is a J3," Maman answers.

"I am hungry too," Gérard says. I am quiet, but I understand where he is coming from.

"This is ridiculous. I don't believe that Pierre should have so much to eat," Papa says bitterly.

Maman ignores his comment and calmly continues to serve us. She puts a hard-boiled egg on my plate, the only one on the entire table.

"Where did you get that egg?" Papa asks.

"I got it with Pierre's coupon."

"What about Gérard's coupon? And what about yours?"

"They have already been spent."

The tension is mounting, and I am getting uncomfortable.

"What about you, Louise? There isn't anything on your plate!" Papa points with an accusing finger.

"I gave my portion to Pierre and Gérard, Jean. Besides, I'm not hungry."

"This is intolerable! From now on, I'm distributing the food here. You get that?"

"No, you are not!" Maman screams.

The fight is on. My stomach is turning into a vinegar container, and I can't swallow a bite.

"What do you mean I'm not? I'll show you who the boss is around here!" he shouts.

"Jean, that's enough!" Maman screams five octaves higher.

I stare in disbelief. Papa is raising his hand to slap Maman.

"I dare you . . . just once! Do you understand?" Maman isn't backing down an inch. She stands there, defying him with a menacing finger.

Papa has met his match. His hand falls limp on the table. "Mon Dieu," he says sadly.

"Eat, Pierre!" Maman commands me, with tears in her eyes.

That evening I go to bed realizing that war can even come between a man and a woman who love each other very deeply.

I HAVE BEEN HELPING Papa with his underground activities, but I also assist Maman on some shopping expeditions.

"Pierre, listen to me, we are going to fool the butcher. Then we are going to do the same thing to the grocer and finally in the *boulangerie* (bakery). You remember our chauffeur, Jacques?"

"Yes, Maman, I loved him very much. Are we going to steal food?"

"Never in our life. Where did you get the idea that we are thieves?" she says, upset at my insolence.

"But Monsieur Jacques . . ." I say, before she cuts me off.

"We are only going to chisel the system, Pierre; just a little bit. Almost like Monsieur Jacques, but not quite so outrageously. We are going to call this strategy 'Monsieur Jacques goes shopping.'"

Before we leave the house, Maman paints my face with makeup. I look pale, like a corpse; the only color on my face is smudges of dark gray blue under my eyes. In my too-small clothes, my slimness is exaggerated. The plan is for Maman and her dying child to bring tears to the most hard-hearted shop owner's eyes.

"Monsieur Butcher, look at him; he is dying before his own mother's eyes. Do you have children, Monsieur?"

The butcher looks at me, then Maman, before wrapping up a bigger, better cut of meat in the paper. The same scenario is repeated at all of the other food shops. We cannot hit the same shops too often. We have to walk long distances to play a variation on the same theme to other food merchants.

"Monsieur Grocer, I am alone. The war took my husband. Now look at this poor child. Starvation is going to take my sons away from me." Maman is on the edge of tears.

Without this trick, the tears would be running for real. Once we are far enough from our mark, her face breaks into a radiant smile. Our shopping bags are getting fatter.

Maman decides to expand our repertoire, using her lovely figure as a lure. My mother is a beautiful, well-endowed woman.

"Pierre, you know that it's a crime to shoplift. Keep your hands off things," she tells me while she is bending forward to point out an item to Monsieur Grocer. Monsieur Grocer's eyes are riveted on my mother's d-e-e-p neckline.

"I understand, Madame, that these J3s are constantly hungry," he says, never letting his eyes leave Maman's balcony, but dropping a bundle of sardine cans on the floor. Could it be that his mind is not on his work?

"And who is not hungry for one thing or another these days?" she adds sweetly.

"Madame, this is a little extra for your son, but let's keep it strictly among ourselves."

Four of the precious sardine cans land in my mother's shopping bag. The grocer is quite a kind fellow. A few more items find their way into our basket, without a single coupon being handed over: a bottle of olive oil, a bag of beans, a few cans of condensed milk, a big wedge of cheese, and two eggs.

As soon as we are outside, Maman takes a moment to arrange her dress more modestly.

"Never let a woman play that number on you, Pierre," she instructs me seriously.

"I don't understand, Maman."

How dumb can you be at fourteen? Well, my only defense is that I know nothing about girls at that age. Anyway, my main interest is food.

"Later on in your life you will, Pierre. Just remember what I told you."

"Papa is going to find this funny," I add innocently.

"Don't ever mention this to your father, Pierre, or I'll kill you!"

When she sees my shocked look, she bursts out laughing.

"Monsieur Jacques would have liked your plan," I say.

"Monsieur Jacques, yes. But your father wouldn't appreciate this kind of humor."

EVENTUALLY even these pathetic tricks don't work. Copycats have ruined our business. Now every mother has a dying son, or sometimes three or four of them, with deep blue under their eyes.

At night I lie in bed and contemplate the sky full of stars. It is very late when Orion appears. Every time I see the sparkling outline of the hunter, I remember when Papa first pointed it out to me, which seems incredibly long ago. It is so extraordinarily beautiful, but I am restless because my stomach is keeping me awake. This heavenly dessert, however, helps me to fall asleep.

In the morning I have leftover soup for breakfast before I leave for school. But it only takes the edge off my hunger for a few minutes. I walk to school hungry. I study hungry. I walk back home in the afternoon hungry.

The disputes continue at the dinner table.

"Some starve while others stuff themselves silly," Papa says in disgust.

"If you hadn't exchanged your meat ration for cigarettes, you wouldn't be so hungry today, Jean," Maman replies.

"Well, I don't have a big balcony to drive the grocer crazy."

How did he find out?

"That's unfair, Jean!"

One could cut the air with a knife. Every day it's the same. I don't know what to say, what to do, or where to keep my eyes: On the other empty plates while mine is full? Or perhaps on the ceiling?

In spite of the embarrassing scenes, my mother insists on giving me more food than anyone else.

I feel that my father hates me. I call him Papa, and *still* my name is Leroy. I hate this ugly name, which keeps me separated from my family, but I can't muster the courage to ask my mother or father any questions about it. I sense a dirty mystery surrounding the detested name. Every time I have to answer to it, I feel uncomfortable. And now I have this J3 business added on, which is separating me even more from my father and brother.

Still, Papa and I have a bond, especially when we work together on an art project or are involved in some mysterious mission. I admire his courage and his honesty. Deep down, I love him . . . and I know that he loves me, too. But this war is getting to us—will it ever end? Will my family name ever be restored to me?

I write to Tata regularly and share all the news about the family and my studies, telling her about my recent art projects and that I am making progress with Italian and English. From time to time, we receive a parcel containing food that she has lovingly prepared. Eventually she has to stop because most of the time her packages are stolen in transit. It breaks my heart to think of the sacrifices she is making to save a few precious tidbits out of her meager ration to feed us.

Fortunately, she is with Grandfather Milhau, who loves her and will protect her. Nevertheless, I worry about Tata and miss her terribly.

Pierre H. Matisse

16

CURFEW À L'ITALIENNE

If a man hasn't discovered something that he will die for, he isn't fit to live.

MARTIN LUTHER KING JR.

THESE DAYS IT seems I am suddenly running a lot of errands for my father. The only family vehicle is a tired bicycle, so I either take buses, which are erratic, or more often resort to old-fashioned walking. We are all doing more than our share of walking. But whenever I can find a faster way, I take it.

"No! Don't take the bus, Pierre," Papa says. "The buses are searched too often by the police. For this errand, use my bicycle."

"The bike has a flat tire, Papa."

Laziness is taking hold of me. I think of any excuse to dodge the long ride up into the hills of the back country.

"I fixed it. Go to this address on the road to Vallauris . . ." Papa begins to explain the mission.

"Let me write it down," I reply, reaching for a pencil.

"No! You have to memorize everything. When you ring the bell, a man will come to the door. He looks Corsican and will be wearing a blue shirt with a button missing, the second white button from the top. Ask him for directions to the pottery."

"I know where the pottery is," I cut in.

"No, you don't know anymore, so you ask for directions. He will tell you that their work is lousy. Repeat the instructions back to me."

No problem, I think. "Small red brick house with a rusted gate, located after the railroad tracks. I ring the bell and ask for directions to the pottery. Work is lousy. Corsican; blue shirt; a button is missing. I got it, no problem."

"Pierre, pay attention! The second white button from the top is missing. Got that?"

"The second white button from the top is missing. I got it," I repeat patiently.

"Much better. Now, whether the Corsican is there or not, or if he doesn't have the right shirt, you still go to the pottery to get some modeling clay for your mother."

He looks me straight in the eyes and says, "If everything is right, the Corsican will give you a verbal message. Memorize his message, get the clay, and come straight back home. Pierre, you must be very careful. Be alert at all times to everything around you. Life is dangerous in these times." I can see the concern on Papa's face.

"When do I leave?"

"Right now. And keep an eye that nobody follows you either way."

Everything goes smoothly on my first mission. I find the house, the Corsican in the blue shirt with the correct missing button answers the bell, I ask for directions to the pottery, and he says they are lousy. But his "message" to Papa is very anticlimactic: "I couldn't get any cigarettes."

I expected something more exciting. I visit the Corsican several times, always returning with various messages about cigarettes. One time it's about the wrong brand, another time there is a big chunk of wood in the tobacco, then the quality is bad, the pack only has three cigarettes in it, and so on. I repeated his boring messages verbatim to Papa. *At least the BBC messages are more original,* I think.

AFTER CARRYING A LOT of verbal messages successfully, I graduate to small package deliveries. This is more to my taste: I can almost smell the adventure and maybe the possibility of becoming a hero like Papa. Why not?

"Create detours, Pierre. Don't use the same road too often. If you see any butterflies, stop for a while to chase them."

"I will, Papa."

"Good! And watch your back for anything suspicious. If you are followed, make your way back here very slowly, taking a few scenic detours."

I use the broken-down bicycle to deliver Papa's packages. I always manage to make it to my destination and back, but the bicycle always needs some kind of repair when I return. Papa doesn't complain; he just patches it back together so I can make the next run.

On Christmas Eve 1942, I am heading home after spending the day delivering "gifts" when I lose control riding downhill. I try to stay on the road, but I hit a bump, and the frame breaks completely apart. Thankfully, I have only a scratch or two, but the bicycle is in pieces. I pick everything up and carry it home.

When I arrive, Papa looks at Maman and announces, "What perfect timing. No risk at all." Obviously, Maman has been discussing my partnership with Papa, probably wishing I wasn't involved. She shakes her head, not the least convinced by his words.

MYSTERIOUS VISITORS CONTINUE to come and go furtively late at night. Sometimes Papa does his own errands, but he always picks a stormy night. Everything seems to be going very well, like there is no danger. Nevertheless, we can feel an uneasy tension creeping in all around us.

Maman has joined the underground games ever since we began hearing rumors about Jews being arrested and transported in train cattle cars to places unknown.

We all must keep our mouths shut at all times. The French police have tipped Papa off that the Gestapo is probably in the area looking for informants. Nothing is certain, but the rumors mean it's best to be careful.

One evening at ten o'clock, I get ready to take my post as a lookout while Papa is busy in the house.

"Pierre," Papa says, "go up on the hill and keep an eye out for the Italian patrols. If you hear or see a patrol, run and tell me. Otherwise, stay there until I come to get you. Don't fall asleep; keep a sharp lookout."

"Yes, Papa!" I sense the urgency in his voice and head out the door in a flash.

It is pitch dark. The sky is totally overcast; not even the moon is able to keep me company. From my vantage point, I can only guess where our house is. Standing there, I can easily hear anything coming from either Antibes or Cannes, and toward the eastern Cap's side where our house is located. Sitting on the grass, the time passes very slowly; it feels like this cold, gloomy night will never end.

My stomach starts aching, a little bit at first, but soon it hurts like crazy. Now what do I do? Despite the pain, I stay put. *Maybe the sickness will go away*, I think. It doesn't. Now I feel nauseated. Nevertheless, I keep my eyes wide open.

That's when everything happens all at once! I am sick from both ends! I glance in the direction of our house. It looks like Bastille Day. A kaleidoscope of colors is lighting up the sky. Blue, red, orange, and yellow flames are shooting out of the chimney like a gigantic blowtorch. *What is Papa burning?*

I am still sick with diarrhea. Then I hear something—running footsteps. An Italian patrol is coming.

Holding up my pants with both hands, I run toward our house to sound the alarm.

Another patrol comes from a different direction, and I am running directly in front of them. Scrambling up the pathway, I trip on a stone but get up quickly, making it to the front door. "Our chimney is on fire! Papa, come quick, the Italians are coming!" I scream as I bang on the door with my feet and fists.

Thankfully, the chimney has stopped spitting fire.

The door opens just a crack. "What is it, Pierre?" Papa whispers.

"The Italian soldiers are following me. I'm sorry, Papa."

The two patrols are closing in fast.

"You speak Italian, Pierre. You handle them," Papa says calmly as he closes the door.

My Italian vocabulary is limited, but when I am surrounded, I grab at words. "The furnace hasn't been cleaned for years," I try explaining.

"What were you doing on the hill?" The one who seems to be in charge questions me.

I think fast. "I had to go to the bathroom and . . . our toilet is plugged."

"Chimney on fire and jammed john—that's the French for you," a high-pitched voice responds.

"Boy, you tell Mama no lighting a fire in the house at night. Planes coming. *Boom . . . Boom . . .* Bombs! Fire *forbidden*. Lights bad! You hear? Planes bad. Bombs bad. Blackout good." The man in charge is taking a crack at speaking French to impress his troops. They all leave, still laughing, and I go in the house where Papa is waiting.

"So . . . you left them laughing. I knew you could handle it," Papa says with a twinkle in his eye and a broad smile on his face. Then he gets a whiff of me.

"Pierre, you stink!"

Papa is going to think this happened because I was scared. I have to explain.

"Papa, I was sick. I had diarrhea, the chimney burst into flames, and the Italians came—all at the same time."

"I understand, Pierre," Papa says. "I was in the toilet when you knocked at the door. I have a bout of colic, too. Your mother is sick and so is Gérard. The crab soup we ate this evening must have been bad."

There are no more patrols that night. Under darkness, Papa and I bury packages in the backyard of an unoccupied villa not far from our home.

"It is too dangerous to burn this stuff anymore," Papa says while we are digging.

"Yes! I noticed that right away from the top of the hill," I reply.

"So now we are getting smart, Pierre, eh?"

"Right, Papa," I tell him as he gives me a loving tap on the back.

"Well done, soldier," Papa says. A sense of pride runs through me. I am contributing to the war effort. Now that I am in the fight, Adolf Hitler's days are numbered.

Overall, the Italian soldiers are easygoing and nice people. It is evident that their hearts are not in this war. Their equipment seems as worn out as their threadbare uniforms. Like us, they are severely short of food. Mostly they fraternize with the French population, play music, and sing love songs. It doesn't take long before the troops blend in with the locals. Eventually, we don't even notice them. They have never arrested anybody that we know of.

In the south of France we like the Italians. However, they are hated in the northern part because they have allied themselves to the Nazis. Bless the Italians who occupied the French Riviera. If it had been a German patrol the night of the chimney fire, it would have been all over for us.

AFTER THE FIRE INCIDENT, I don't run any more special errands, but there is now something more interesting going on in Papa's studio. Very discreetly, he is building a mock-up of a railroad track made out of leftover wood. I help him cut, nail, and put this strange thing together. When we finish, Papa names the ten-foot track the "Hitler Express."

Late at night, we install the Hitler Express in the back of the garden, hiding it under a pile of compost made of vegetable peelings mixed up with well-aged, discarded rabbit litter. Papa says that the aroma should keep away any unwelcome visitors.

Sometimes, in the middle of the night, Papa asks me to shovel the compost off the track.

On one particular evening, it is pouring rain when Papa enlists my help.

"Perfect weather," Papa says. While I keep watch at a safe distance, I watch Papa and two mysterious men all dressed in black set up charges of plastic explosives and detonators on the track.

In my imagination I hear a big, black steam locomotive puffing and smoking—then *boom!* There is a violent explosion, followed by a huge fireball and SS soldiers running and screaming. "Kaput, you rotten Boches," I mutter quietly. Papa's firm tap brings me back to reality. "Pay attention," he whispers in a conspiratorial tone. Shivering from the rain, I return to my watch. It is a onetime demonstration, but what a show! From constructing the model, the men learn what they need to know for positioning explosives on a real track. These interesting interludes make me forget my growling, hungry, empty stomach for a while.

Not long after the track is blown up, I am coming home from school and see a surprise visitor leaving our house—The Great! We nod silently at each other, trading icy glares.

The Great is still very tall, powerful, and overbearing, but I think I detect a trace of concern on her face. She is in a hurry, stressed and tense.

It is clear to me that she is involved up to her ears in the French underground.

The dirty look she gives me in passing shows her disapproval of my own involvement in this dirty business. I'm sure she is thinking I am untrustworthy, a little Spanish refugee and rotten bastard who is not worthy of belonging to the honorable cause.

It will be the last time we ever see each other.

In 1944, more than a year later, The Great and her daughter, Marguerite, will be arrested separately by the Gestapo. All this time, I thought that The Great had been living in Toulouse, but it seems she has been traveling all over the country. This lady is definitely full of surprises.

The Boches have no idea who they are up against. It would be bad publicity if the Nazis shot the wife of a world-famous artist. Besides, the Nazis don't want to tarnish their image as art lovers. They are stealing art all over Europe, anywhere they can put their greedy hands on it. *Good for her*, I think. *She finally has an enemy worthy of her status.* There is no doubt in my mind that just by her open contempt, she will give the Nazis hell on a daily basis.

17

DETOUR TO PARIS

War is not a true adventure. It is a mere ersatz . . . War is
not an adventure. It is a disease. It is like typhus.

ANTOINE DE SAINT-EXUPÉRY

THE MEDITERRANEAN'S BLUE WATERS have never been so enchanting.
The fresh, salty wind smells so good and continues to bring the promise of faraway adventures. What a shame that all this beauty should be
spoiled by a senseless war.

Personally, I have made up my mind. As soon as the war ends, I am
leaving Europe for America. I want out of France, despite its beauty. This
continual bickering about ideological, social, and racial theories does not
interest me. I do not want any part of the persecution of the Jews, the
tyranny of the Roman Catholic Church, the Communist Party, or the
colonization of less powerful countries.

I don't hate anyone. I only want freedom and, like Uncle Pierre, I'm
certain I'll find it in America. I continue to prepare, brushing up on my

English like mad. One day while I am reading *The Adventures of Tom Sawyer*, I overhear a conversation between my father and a local detective in my father's studio.

"The Gestapo is everywhere, Jean. We can't cover you anymore."

"There is nothing to worry about. It's only gossip," my father says.

"Two days ago, I found the Corsican full of Parabellum bullets from a German automatic pistol. Gossip, you say?"

"We haven't dealt with the Corsican for quite a while because he was reckless."

"Another thing that disturbs me is your kid going in and out of every Maquisard resistance hideout in the area. Do you think that we are idiots?" the detective asks.

Papa throws the question back. "Whose side are you on, the collaborators' or ours?"

"We have to be cautious; our necks are on the line. A month ago they arrested one of our best police officers for terrorist activities."

"Are you trying to scare me?" Papa asks.

"You'd better be scared, Jean. You have to keep a low profile, or you're on your own. This war is going to last another two or three years."

"One more reason to push the Boches around," Papa says enthusiastically.

"At the rate you're going, you won't be around on victory day, my friend."

"All right. We'll keep a low profile for a little while," Papa promises.

"You'd better. And keep that kid of yours out of the way. I don't want to see him wandering in the wrong places."

A SHORT TIME LATER, my parents move me to a small boardinghouse close by, located in the upper part of the Cap d'Antibes. Papa explains it's necessary because I am being noticed and talked about, which is dangerous for all of us. I am still going to the same school, but I share a bedroom on the upper floor with another boy.

"Be good to Simon," the woman who owns the boardinghouse says to me. "It's very important not to mention to anybody that he even exists. He's a Jew. We are hiding him from the Germans." No problem here—I have had plenty of practice keeping secrets.

We eat in a huge dining room with the other pensioners, mostly war-stranded wives whose husbands have disappeared. The missing soldiers are not only from France, but Czechoslovakia, Poland, Italy, Belgium, and Spain and could be prisoners in Germany, deserters, or on some secret mission.

My roommate, Simon, does not go to school and never leaves the premises. He spends his days reading or playing chess against himself. He is pale and skinny as a rail and doesn't say much.

Still, I try my best to be friendly and get to know him.

Soon after moving in, I greet him and tell him my name, holding out my hand.

"My name is Simon," he answers without emotion or elaboration.

"Where did you live before?"

"Paris."

"Me, too." I can't get anything but a few words out of him.

"Why do you have a rope attached to your bedpost?" I ask curiously.

"If the Boches come, I will escape out the window."

"There are only Italians here. They don't bother anybody. Believe me, I know."

"No, you don't know," Simon answers, sounding depressed.

End of conversation.

ONE NIGHT I AM AWAKENED by a strange muffled noise. When I realize Simon is sobbing, I go to his bedside.

"What's the matter? Are you sick?"

"No!" he says pitifully, pulling the blanket around him.

"If you're not sick, what's troubling you?"

Now tears are pouring out. He is not saying a thing, just crying his whole soul out. I gently pat him on the back, and he calms down somewhat.

"My mother and father," he finally gets out between sobs and hiccups, "were arrested in Nice by the Germans a few months ago while they were attending an evening social event."

"If they didn't do anything against the Boches, they are in a work camp somewhere in Germany. They will come back after the war," I say, trying to reassure him.

"No! It's the train." Simon's eyes fill with fear.

"What about the train?" I say impatiently.

"My uncle was arrested with them. The Nazis put them in cattle cars on the train, packing them in like sardines." Simon's sobbing is getting worse. "The night they were arrested they were wearing evening clothes."

"I am certain that the Boches gave them blankets." I don't really believe that, but I am trying to comfort Simon. Even though I am not exactly sure what has been going on with the Jews, I am aware that bad things are happening.

"No. The train went slowly up north. It was very cold, and the people inside the cars didn't have any heat or food. My parents, along with many others, died of exposure."

"Who told you such a tale? It's only propaganda to antagonize the French against the Boches."

"No, it's true. My uncle escaped when the train was bombed in an air raid. His train car broke open, and he escaped. I saw him two days ago. He was hoping to hide here, but it's becoming too dangerous for the owner."

Simon's eyes flash with anger. "You Gentiles hate us!" he said, practically spitting the words at me.

"Hate? Where did you get that stupid idea? And what do you mean by *Gentile*? Are you insulting me?"

"If you aren't a Jew, then you are a Gentile."

"I see. So you Jews are racial theorists like Adolf Hitler, eh? You label yourselves Jews, me Gentile, the Boches call themselves Aryan, and we French call the Arabs Bougnoule. Then we start a war and kill one another because our tribes' names are different. This is insane. Have you seen anyone killed by bombs and machine guns?"

"No!"

"Well, I have and you should. Then maybe you'd stop calling me a Gentile. Did I ever call you a Jew?"

Simon looks at me, confused.

"By the way, what are you going to do about the Boches who killed your parents?"

"Nothing. What can I do against an army?" he asks with conviction.

"That's the problem. You have to fight and kill as many of them as you can . . . before they kill you."

"I am just a child."

"I have seen children our age dead. Today a J3 is a man. You fight to survive, or you die like your parents did."

"Are you fighting?" he asks shrewdly.

"What I do is none of your business. Do I look like a victim? Draw your own conclusions." I have learned to keep my mouth shut.

I go back to bed feeling very sorry for Simon. I have heard many rumors concerning the Germans mistreating the Jews—how they must wear a yellow Star of David on their clothes to identify themselves and follow a long list of restrictions and regulations. I have never seen anyone with a yellow star while I've been in the Riviera, and until my stay at the boardinghouse, I have never known a Jew personally. Simon is the first one I've met, and I see no difference between him and me.

I find this treatment of the Jews totally disgusting. One more mark against Adolf in my book. Ostracism is a terrible thing, and I know the pain, having endured a mild form with The Great's disdain for me.

One day I come home from school and Simon is gone. When I ask about him, the owner of the boardinghouse explains, "We couldn't keep him here any longer. It's too risky. But I found him a safer place in the Alps, close to Switzerland. From there, he might be able to cross the border to safety."

Pierre H. Matisse

18

MOUNTAINS AND MAQUISARDS

The world is a dangerous place to live; not because of the people who are evil, but because of the people who don't do anything about it.

ALBERT EINSTEIN

WITH THINGS HEATING UP with the Boches, my family arrives at the boardinghouse about a month later. I am being moved again, accompanied by Maman, to an undisclosed destination. She has packed two small suitcases, and after I say good-bye to Papa and Gérard, we start the journey by taking the bus to Nice. In Nice, we board an old train that has been barely maintained and is packed with people, thankfully finding seats further down in one of the cars. The steam locomotive chugs at a turtle's pace up into the mountains, and while Maman rests, I admire the incredible view out the window. When we finally get off at our stop, we walk for half a day to a small inn, where we spend the night.

"My poor Bunny Rabbit," Maman says as she tucks me in, before going to bed in the cold bedroom. She seems to have forgotten that

I am a man now and can't hide the terrible worry on her face. I lie there silently; I won't ask Maman where we are going or what will happen when we get there.

The next day we walk quite a distance before getting on a run-down gazogène bus. This time there are plenty of seats available. All day, the rusted wreck puffs up the mountain on twisting dirt roads between deep ravines. Finally, late in the evening, the bus pulls over near a small brook and stops. We get off and wait for about an hour, when just before dark, a stocky fellow with a mule appears.

"Madame Matisse?" he inquires politely.

"Yes, and this is my son, Pierre," she says, shaking his hand.

"So you are the little devil I've heard so much about, eh?" he says with a broad smile, sticking out a strong, calloused hand in greeting.

How would they know me in this remote place?

"Let's put those suitcases on the mule. We have about an hour's walk to our farm. My mother has prepared hot soup, cheese, milk, and her specialty—a beet leaf pie."

What did he say?

I am dead tired, but the air is crisp and fresh. I walk as fast as I can up the narrow trail, spurred on by the promise of food at the end.

Monsieur Mountaineer is a small man, probably in his midthirties, built like a black bear—as wide as he is high. His whole personality radiates strength, confidence, and courage. His face could have been sculpted with an ax—there are no weak lines to it—set off with piercing, inquisitive eyes and a nose that an eagle would envy.

He runs a small dilapidated farm with his widowed mother. Their home is nestled on the side of the mountain, right at the tree line, perched high like an aerie.

"I like it here," he explains to Maman as we hike. "There is nobody to boss me around and to tell me what to do."

"I was led to believe that the Maquis is very active in this area," Maman says.

"You believe right, Madame," Monsieur Mountaineer says proudly. "The Maquisards are giving the Boches a very hard time in these mountains. They can't get their tanks or trucks up here. Lately, a small Boche plane has been spying on us. We hide the more obvious things, and a few old women give them friendly salutes with their scarves."

"How long do you think it's going to remain safe?" Maman asks with concern.

"Oh, they'll never come here, Madame. Not to worry—we have the high ground. We know the mountain and can pick them off one at a time, like in a shooting gallery. Besides, the Boches are taking a beating in Russia, and they are short of men. And now Italy is giving them plenty of troubles. Hitler has better things to do than bother with us."

Finally, we arrive at the farm, where we are welcomed warmly by our hostess. She leads us directly to the table, laden with a feast. The meal fills my belly to twice its size, and I go to bed completely stuffed for the first time in as long as I can remember. Before I fall asleep, a little white mouse skitters across the floor, probably searching for leftover bits of cheese, hoping to fill his belly too.

THE NEXT MORNING I am awakened by the sound of rushing water— there is a stream close to the house. In the distance, I can hear a melody played by cows' bells echoing in the mountains.

Monsieur Mountaineer's mother is preparing breakfast while talking to Maman. "Madame, if he continues to eat like this, he is going to burst," she exclaims, with a twinkle in her eye.

As I take my seat at the table, Maman says, "Pierre, don't eat so much. You are going to get sick."

"But Maman, she says that I can eat as much as I like, and I am always hungry." I begin eating my breakfast like a pig, and plan to devour every morsel of food I can while I am here.

Monsieur Mountaineer gives me a kind look and says, "Let him eat as much as he wants. If he gets overfull, he'll throw up. It's as simple as that!"

I gorge myself silly and don't throw up at all, but an hour later, I am hungry again.

The first floor of the house is one large room that serves as the kitchen, living room, and dining room, and one wall is actually the rock face of the mountain. Above the massive sink is a clay spigot from which glacier-fed spring water flows continuously. The bedrooms are on the second floor.

The whole house smells of wood-smoked ham, which makes my mouth water, and the remaining walls are discolored by the brown smoke that escapes from the cast-iron stove connected to a chimney. The fireplace is large enough to easily roast a whole lamb.

Later in the day, Maman finds me and says, "Pierre, you have to stay here for a while. It's safer than anywhere else for the time being, and you'll definitely eat better." Maman seems satisfied.

The next morning before she leaves, I thank her. "I love you, Maman. Good-bye, and safe travels." The "safe travels" is my prayer for her, given with a long hug. Then she is gone.

I SOON REALIZE that Madame Mountaineer is definitely a character in her own right who never fails to surprise me. For one thing, she doesn't believe that bathroom facilities are necessary.

"If the cows can do it when and where they want, so can I," she states with conviction. "I don't much like city folks. They have no manners, passing you by without so much as a good morning." I quickly adjust to the no-bathroom approach, since there isn't one available anywhere!

To me, she is The Duchess. She definitely reigns in the kitchen, performing miracles of gastronomical delight on the cast-iron stove—beet leaf pies, lentils, marmot stew, crow soup, bean cakes, and huge loaves of bread. I have no idea how the three of us can possibly eat all the food she is making.

"The children are going to like this," she says one day while packing all her carefully prepared meals into woven baskets.

"What children?" I ask.

"The Maquisards."

"I've never seen any Maquisards here."

"In these mountains, we are all Maquisards. With your past, you fit in quite well, no?" *She knows?* She looks at me intensely, then adds with a laugh, "Now you are a Maquisard too."

In no time at all, I am fully integrated into the farm as the official cow herder. Going from bees to rabbits is an easy step, but graduating from soft, small rabbits to large cows with long, sharp horns is another matter.

Every morning I herd a dozen of them from the farm up to even higher ground to graze. The cows walk single file on a narrow trail, and I march behind them, wondering what I am going to do if one decides to make a run for freedom. On the left is a sharp decline two miles straight into the ravine, and on the right is a rock wall two miles high. But the cows know the way, so up we go. Once we are on the grassy slope, I constantly turn the herd, keeping them relatively close to each other. If a cow wanders away, I tap her gently on the back with my walking cane.

The first time I try to do this, the cow pays no attention. So I resort to stronger tactics and try to push her from behind as if she is on wheels. Suddenly, she kicks viciously and runs like a demon.

Swearing and screaming, I go after her. She eventually stops, and I stand at a cane's length away and tap her firmly. This time she responds and walks back to the herd. But now the rest of the cows are meandering in different directions. *How am I going to get them rounded up and back to the farm this evening?* I wonder.

But I don't need to worry. When it starts to get dark, the cows all head back to the farm on their own. After I get them safely into the barn for the night, I find The Duchess in her element—working in the kitchen.

"How did it go?" she asks me.

"Great!" I answer, tired but happy.

"We have cheese soup and beet leaf pie for dinner."

"Good! I've worked up an appetite from all this activity and fresh air."

After a few more excursions to the green slopes, the cows and I get to know each other well. It becomes so easy that I am able to take my small sketch pad to draw my models chewing their cuds against the scenic backdrop of the mountains. Unfortunately, one day when I am trying to round up a cow, one of her friends finds my sketch pad very tasty.

There is nowhere to buy another sketch pad, so my artistic endeavors come to an end. I'm not too disappointed; after all, I prefer to draw boats and the sea. Besides, The Duchess prefers that I concentrate on caring for her cows. When I tell her what the cow has done, she laughs heartily.

"Good!" she says, still laughing. "We'll frame the cow."

EACH DAY MY ROUTINE IS THE SAME. Then one evening Monsieur Mountaineer takes me aside. "How would you like to come with us into the mountains, Pierre?" he asks.

"I would love to!" I answer eagerly.

"I thought so! Try on these heavy shoes," he says, handing me a pair of French army walking shoes.

I smile as I pull them on. "They fit perfectly."

"Good. Tomorrow we head into the mountains."

It's still dark when Monsieur Mountaineer wakes me up. After a hearty breakfast and well wishes for the journey from The Duchess, Monsieur Mountaineer and I start up a trail with four heavily loaded mules, a different path from the one I usually take with the cows. It's dark and cold, and we travel silently, hearing only the sound of the mules' hooves on the rocky trail. When daylight finally comes, my feet are hurting. I have no idea how far we have walked, but the rough terrain and the borrowed shoes have taken their toll.

But then I look around. The view is absolutely breathtaking with mountains and valleys as far as one can see—some peaks are capped with snow. The natural beauty is so stimulating that I actually forget the pain in my feet. We stop for a snack of smoked sausage, The Duchess's delicious bread, onions, and garlic. It's a fabulous feast washed down with a poor-quality red wine.

"What do you think of it?" he asks, waiting for my opinion.

I don't want to seem ungrateful so I smell what's in my tin cup and pronounce my findings like a true connoisseur. "A little dry perhaps. Maybe a little too much tannin in it, but overall, it's good. I like it."

"That's what I told my mother," Monsieur Mountaineer agrees.

We continue walking, and my feet begin to hurt again. The adventure is becoming less fun with each step I take. Soon I start to hear men calling back and forth. Their voices are bouncing off the mountains.

"Eh! Oh!"

"Eh! Oh!"

"Eh! Oh!"

Before long, we come upon a small stone shelter located between a cold spring and a little ravine.

"I could have walked by and not even noticed it!" I say to Monsieur Mountaineer.

"It's a refuge for mountain climbers," my companion explains.

"Eh! Oh!" A man with a long rifle steps out from behind a big boulder and walks toward us.

"What have you brought us, Gaston?"

"Food, ammunition, and a big surprise."

Surprise? I wonder what the surprise is. Monsieur Mountaineer looks excited about it.

"What is it?" Long Rifle asks.

My guide pulls something out of one of the packs. "*A fusil-mitrailleur.*" It's a French-made machine gun/rifle hybrid, which I admire too. *The Boches are not going to like this.*

"Fabulous. Wait till the others see this."

When all of the supplies have been unpacked and taken into the shelter, I collapse on a bed of hay, fighting off sleep to observe this band of men. I am very cold, but curiously there is no fire to welcome us, so I ask Long Rifle, "Why can't we light a fire in the fireplace?"

"Because the Boches' planes will spot us, my friend," answers another Maquis, with two ammo belts full of bullets double-strapped across his chest. More men come in, all armed to the teeth. They joke, laugh, eat, and drink. Before long, they begin assembling the fusil-mitrailleur. It has a folding bipod attached to the front of the barrel so it can be anchored to the ground, and a large detachable magazine is inserted on the top.

"Take the clip out, you fool. Do you want to shoot the window out?" one man says to the other.

"I was just trying to see if it fits."

"It'll fit the Boches. Don't worry."

I fall asleep to hearty laughter.

THE NEXT THING I KNOW, Gaston is shaking me.

"Wake up, Pierre. We have to head back to the farm."

"It's still night. Why don't we go down later?" I say, still exhausted.

"We have to travel in darkness part of the way down because of the Boches' planes."

I dread the march down, but I am not about to complain, even if my feet still haven't come to terms with the land and these boots. The adventure is well worth all the suffering.

Gaston seems to read my mind. "Don't worry. No more walking. The mules are unloaded, so we can ride them down the trail."

After a breakfast of cheese and bread washed down with wine, we mount the mules and start out with our bellies full and our spirits high. The sky is clear, and I quickly find the constellation Gemini. As the sky gradually lightens, the stars disappear one by one. Now I can almost see where the valley is, and soon the snowcaps show up in the distance.

A few minutes later, it is light, although the sun isn't visible. *How strange.* At sea the sun comes early in the morning, but here in the Alps the sky king hides behind some big mountain in the east. The sun in these mountains is lazy like me; I would have enjoyed staying in my comfortable hay bed for a few more hours.

The air is so pure, one can see for miles. I spot a small hamlet nestled on the other side of the valley. Sprinkled here and there are isolated farms that look like miniature toys. With so much beauty surrounding me, it's hard to remember that there is a war going on.

Suddenly a marmot runs across the trail. My mule shies sideways, and I almost fall off.

"Stop dreaming, Pierre! Pay attention to where the mule is going!" Gaston says.

"Sorry!" I say, shaking my head to keep from falling asleep.

"We are going to take a shortcut down the mountain. Stay alert!"

We dismount and guide the mules, one by one, down a steep rocky slope onto a trail again.

"That saves us an hour," Gaston says with a smile.

We are riding again, but the trail is so narrow, it's scary. With a deadly precipice on the right, there is no room for a mistake.

"Faster!" Gaston orders.

"What's the hurry?" I ask, trying not to look over the edge.

"The Boches' planes. If they catch us here, we are in trouble, Pierre."

"In the month that I have been here, I've never even seen one."

"One more reason to get out of here fast."

I can see the pines that mark the tree line. *We're safe.*

"Run! Run, Pierre! Make her run faster to the woods," Gaston screams in a panic.

I don't hear any planes. What's the problem? But I make my two mules run as fast as they will go, which is not an easy task riding one and pulling the other. Gaston gets to the trees before me. Then he runs toward me, pulls me off my mule, grabs the two animals, and quickly hides them under a huge pine.

"Flat! Lie flat! Quick, get over here behind this tree trunk." He is shaking.

I can hear Papa's words in my mind. "Obey, don't question." I crawl over, turning my head slightly to glimpse a small plane through the branches, circling above us. It's an observation aircraft with a black swastika painted on the rudder that has cut its engine. That's why I didn't hear anything.

"He is gliding in order to surprise us," Gaston gasps.

"Do you think he saw us?" I ask apprehensively.

"I don't know, Pierre. But if he did, we're going to find out soon."

"How?" I ask, afraid to hear the answer.

"The Boches have a regiment of alpine troops about five hours from here."

After one more pass, the plane's engine restarts, and it flies west.

"We'll have to stay here until dark. It's too risky to move now," Gaston decides. "Go ahead and get some sleep." I don't have trouble at all.

When it is dark, Gaston wakes me up, and we get back on the trail. A few miles from the farm, The Duchess is waiting for us. She is wearing an ammunition belt full of red shotgun shell, and a double-barrel shotgun is slung over her shoulder.

"It is safe, Gaston," she says. "I noticed the plane too. It must not have spotted you."

I'm surprised at the shotgun. "I thought that the Boches ordered us to turn over all our guns," I say.

"The only thing I'm interested in turning over to them is the buckshot inside these shells," she replies, patting the ammunition. "Of course, they are welcome to try and take it anytime they want to," she adds with a defiant toss of her head.

LATER THAT DAY we are visited by some French gendarmes, the feared Vichy government police. I am in the cowshed brushing the mules when they arrive, and I can hear animated conversation coming from the kitchen. The Duchess is not afraid of the gendarmes, but things don't seem to be going well. I slip out of the shed and get closer to the house so I can hear.

"You are hiding two cows from the government requisition program," says a gendarme to The Duchess. "We could throw you in jail for that."

"I am a French lady! I will give the cows to the French but not to the Boches. What are you? Collaborators, perhaps?"

"Gaston, please explain to your mother that if you go overboard, we can't protect you and the Maquis."

"They are right, Mother."

"Let's make a deal, then. One cow." The Duchess makes her offer.

"No! The requisition rules say two," the sergeant insists.

"I am wondering whose side you are on," The Duchess replies bitterly.

"It's the war, Madame. We are trying to slow them down as much as we can."

"I don't want you to slow them down. I want you to kick their behinds back to Germany, killing as many as you can in the process. Who cares what they did to my husband, eh?"

"We know, Madame. We sympathize."

"The Boches killed him, and I want them dead, all dead. *Dead*, do you hear me?" The Duchess says, raising her voice.

I hold my breath, but everything calms down when the gendarmes accept a glass of wine.

The next day Gaston sets out to deliver two cows to the requisition services, where they will be slaughtered and used to make sausages for the German army.

As The Duchess and I watch Gaston leave with the cows, she says, "I never thought that I would see the day when I had to feed the Boches.

I hope they choke on it! One day they'll pay dearly!" she adds, filled with hate.

I suddenly miss Papa. I wish he could have been there with me, The Duchess, Gaston, and the Maquisards. He would have loved them and the adventure.

I LIVE ON THE MOUNTAIN for only two months; no place is safe for long. When my mother comes to get me, we take a different route this time—first a long walk to Grenoble, where we catch a rusty gazogène bus before another stop and a train to Paris.

This time we need the help of a *passeur* to cross in between the occupied lines since our papers are not up to bureaucratic standards. This gentleman, a professional smuggler by trade, makes a living by guiding people during the night to and from northern and southern France. His clients need to cross the demarcation line discreetly, to conduct their private affairs without any involvement with the authorities, whether German or Vichy.

Now we are back in occupied France with the Boches, heading for Paris where Tata awaits me. She has moved back from Saint-Georges-de-Didonne. The trip is long and uncomfortable, but otherwise uneventful. I am going to visit Tata, and I am very happy about that.

Maman, Louise, working at the kiln of the Matisse estate in Clamart, a Paris suburb

My beloved *Tata*

My dear friend Bouboule and me (age three) outside Maman's studio. We stayed out of trouble when I was busy as her assistant.

At age nine, I dressed up for this photo-booth portrait taken by Tata at the 1937 World's Fair.

Grandfather Henri Matisse in his home/
studio in Nice, where Maman and I would
visit and I went for a color lesson.

In January 1948, I sailed from
Marseille to Algeria to join my
commando paratrooper unit to
fulfill my military duty. The first
test was getting 800 men and a
herd of seasick cows there safely,
through a terrible storm.

Many of my days in the military were spent learning how and preparing to jump out of airplanes during commando operations. The parachutes we used were very dangerous. Today, they are referred to as "suicide parachutes" because you cannot control them.

A practice jump from a reclaimed German Junker (above). Thankfully, I landed in one piece (below).

Jeanne and me
on our wedding day,
September 23, 1995

Swingin' in the Rain is a part of the collection We'll Always Have Paris, inspired by Jeanne's and my favorite movie, *Casablanca*. I began this series with a painting, which I gave her on our first anniversary. To this day, I continue to create many images in many mediums, courting Jeanne artistically through my pre–World War II Paris—all part of our ongoing love story.

I channeled my inner Matisse in *Making Your Mark*, the first abstract cutout I ever created. It's signed in all four corners, allowing the collector to participate in the art by deciding which way to display it.

Wanting to paint wherever inspiration struck, I designed my own traveling easel. Photo taken in our backyard, 1996.

In 1998, I was fortunate to meet Prince and Princess Takamado of the Japanese Imperial Family (on the far left) and present them with this cutout, *O Japan, Land of Beauty*, which they accepted on behalf of UNICEF.

I designed this poster for Make Music America, raising money to purchase instruments for children across the nation who couldn't afford them. Jeanne and I are passionate about contributing art to charities and organizations that are making a difference in the world.

In 2000, Jeanne and I were in Las Vegas for a millennium art show. As part of our outreach to children, I conducted a hands-on workshop with the Clark County Schools gifted students' program. I designed a cutout, which the children helped me create and assemble. Then we each signed the finished work. I wanted them to understand and experience the joy they can generate by using their art to give to others. The finished artwork (below) was donated to the Sunrise Children's Hospital.

I was honored to be the painting instructor for my Duck Commander friends in Season 8 of *Duck Dynasty*. We all agreed Si was the perfect model.

Me and Si, wearing two of my favorite hats

After confirming my faith in Jesus Christ, I was baptized by Willie Robertson. Assisted by his wife, Korie, I emerged a "new Matisse."

Me in my studio, where visions become reality

I created this cutout, *Living Waters*, with the idea of using the image to raise funds for children's health organizations, before I even knew the true living water of my Savior, Jesus Christ. He said, "Those who drink the water I give will never be thirsty again. It becomes a fresh, bubbling spring within them, giving them eternal life" (John 4:14).

LIVING WATERS

THE ART OF LIVING WELL

The radishes of love

19

NIGHTMARE BY DAYLIGHT

If you have tears, prepare to shed them now.

WILLIAM SHAKESPEARE

MAMAN AND I arrive in the early morning, tired, dirty, and hungry. It is a dark, drizzling day in 1943, and Paris is depressing and drab, but not because of the weather. Boches are everywhere, and there are only German military vehicles and civilian bicycles on the streets.

There are no taxis running anymore, so Maman and I walk to the closest subway station. Along the way, we pass some buildings flying swastika flags. The subway is cold, and so are the people. The passengers either look up or down or have blank stares—it seems everyone is furtively trying to avoid eye contact. Soon we exit the subway and walk to rue Morère.

I stare at the door of the apartment building for a moment, catching my breath, then I rush inside.

Full of joy, I run up four stories, two steps at a time. My heart is beating hard, but not from climbing the stairs. I knock at the familiar heavy oak door, and when it opens I say, "Tata, it's me, Pierre!"

A very small, frail old lady is standing on the threshold. *Tata?*

My heart sinks from the shock of what I see. When I left Tata in 1940, I was twelve years old. She was so tall and I was so small. Today at fifteen years old, I am a giant, and she is so tiny. She is standing there looking up at me with her tender eyes, tears running down her face.

Maman stays with us for a few hours, reminiscing about our last great vacation together before the conversation turns to the war, collaborators, traitors, the Jewish persecution, and the food shortage. She will return in three days, and I must be ready to accompany her to my new boarding college.

After Maman leaves, I can't speak, and neither can Tata. I take her in my arms to hug her, and I can feel how thin she is, nothing but bones. I think about the food parcels that she sent us in Antibes and am so ashamed. She deprived herself to send food to Gérard and me. Today, I still think about all the women of Europe who sacrificed during the war so their children could eat.

I am delighted to find my old roller skates in the apartment. I put them on and go outside, skating on the sidewalk for about twenty minutes. I am exhausted! What has happened to me? Where did my energy go? I used to be able to jump up and down and run all day long. Now I am an old man who can't do either.

MAMAN DOES RETURN three days later, and after a tear-filled goodbye to Tata, we make our way to the agricultural boarding college near Fontainebleau where I am enrolled. It is a long walk from Tata's apartment to the train and then a half-day train ride to the college.

The school is called the Chateau, and it is housed in a magnificent castle situated on the bank of the Loing River. When Maman and I arrive, we are given the grand tour. There are luxurious gardens growing enormous vegetables and fabulous orchards containing an incredible variety of fruit trees. Grapes from one vineyard are used to produce fine wines, while another one grows the finest table grapes. The livestock is only purebred cows, a few champion bulls, blue-blood pigs, Aryan rabbits, angora rabbits, racehorses, racing donkeys, and chickens with a lineage dating back to Louis the XIV.

The agricultural engineering education is first class here, with the *crème de la crème* of France's agricultural engineers coming out of this institution. I hear that it was started by the rich family who owns the cognac champagne industry of France.

A person has to be connected in order to be accepted to this mecca of gardening knowledge. The Matisse family has pulled some strings to get me here. I am privileged and so are my peers. If an upper-class boy does not do well in academia, his family sends him here to become a fancy farmer. I am being sent here to maintain a low profile.

From the moment we arrive, Maman senses that I don't like the place. When we have a moment alone, she brings it up.

"Pierre, my darling, you might not like to be here, but you should be safe until the end of the war and you will eat decently," she explains.

"I prefer being in the Alps with The Duchess and Gaston," I declare flatly.

"It was becoming too dangerous," Maman says quietly. "Besides, I don't want you to become a barbarian."

"These people are so pretentious, Maman," I reply. "It reminds me of the college in Bordeaux."

"Please, Pierre, conduct yourself like a gentleman and promise me you will not get into trouble."

"I promise . . . but why can't I stay in Paris and live with Tata?"

"Tata is too old to take care of you, and you would starve there. Paris is unsafe, and your presence would place Tata in great danger." I know Maman is right, and her last point convinces me to end the discussion.

When we visit the refectory, I can't believe my eyes. There is food spread across tables as far as the eye can see, and you can feast on as much as you want—potatoes, roast beef, vegetables, fruit, and desserts. I can't believe that there is roast beef. Nobody eats roast beef in Europe these days, but they do here. Incredible! Of course, this changes my mind about the place immediately.

Finally, it's time for Maman to leave. She has a long journey back to Cap d'Antibes. As she kisses me good-bye, she says, "Every month you will have a weekend pass to visit Tata, Pierre. So that's not too bad." And then she is gone.

AS MUCH AS I TRY, I can't get adjusted to the school, especially the people. I keep to myself as much as possible. When I have permission, I go for long walks in a forest on the property, but it's rare. A retired French colonel, whose discipline is strict, runs the Chateau like a Swiss clock.

When I am not in class, my job is to care for the chickens and the rabbits, which is arduous work. I start at six every morning, and I have two hours to feed about fifty chickens and fifty rabbits, clean up their manure, and finish any other tasks related to their care. At eight o'clock, breakfast is served, followed by study time and garden work. Most of the gardening is done with hand tools, not machinery. Lunch is at noon, followed by a half-hour siesta. Then it's off to botany classes and to the fields for the afternoon, finishing up with evening animal care. By dinnertime, I am extremely hungry and exhausted, but I must study after dinner until I collapse in bed around nine. For six days in a row, everything is repeated. On Sunday, I only have to see to the animals' needs, so there is a little more time to rest. Still, I don't like the regimen.

Despite the abundance of food, I am always hungry. Actually, we all are hungry. We work so hard outdoors that it builds a monstrous appetite in our young developing bodies. So the temptation is there. Once in a while, I suck an egg on the sly. Once I even stole food from one of the dogs' plates in the rear of the kitchen, which was quite tasty. Even the dogs are eating like kings. Here and there, I chisel the system for food—a cup of milk snuck directly from a cow, or if the occasion presents itself, a cup of gourmet goat's milk.

I can't wait for my first leave to go to Paris. The time passes so slowly here, and with Tata, so fast.

FINALLY, A MONTH GOES BY, and I have my first weekend pass. This time when I see Tata, I feel awkward and I don't know what to say. Mostly, I feel guilty for not having written more often during the three years we were separated. When she and I had last parted, I was a child. Now she is getting back a teenager who is somewhere between a boy and a man.

But slowly we reconnect. I rediscover how extraordinary Tata really is. Her loving-kindness and wisdom are a wonder to me. Every move she makes and every word she says, however ordinary they are, take on extraordinary dimensions. She is pure love. Each moment I am with her is magical and gives me a peace of mind that I haven't had in years, not since I was a little boy on the train with her traveling from Collioure to Paris for the very first time.

And yet, in the back of my mind, there is the burning question I have about the awful Leroy name. I am still deeply wounded by this name change, but when I am close to her, it doesn't hurt as much. I am tempted to ask Tata what she knows, but I am so thrilled to be with her that I don't want anything to come between us. Here with her, I feel that I am in the eye of the hurricane—it's quiet, peaceful, and tranquil, and there is an overall aura of serenity that I don't want to disturb. I sense that she, too, doesn't want to waste these precious moments we have together with anything disagreeable.

One thing that Tata has never forgotten is my love of books. "Before I forget, I have a book for you to take back with you, Pierre. It's called *Maroussia*."

"What is it about, Tata?"

"It's the story of a young Russian girl about your age. She belonged to the Russian partisans' resistance during the Napoleonic invasion of Russia in 1810."

"What happened to her?"

"She was caught by Napoleon's soldiers, interrogated, and tortured, but she refused to talk. Convicted of underground activities against the French occupation forces, she was shot by a firing squad."

"I'd like to read that book, Tata."

As she hands me the book, she says, "Remember this. There is nothing new under the sun. History repeats itself again and again. Men don't learn, Pierre. They just don't learn."

She pauses, shaking her head. "I want you to survive the war, Pierre. Be careful. It's not over yet, and it's going to be a very long one."

"I understand, Tata."

THIS WEEKEND IS almost like the old days. Tata prepares delicacies from the little that she has, even finding flowers for the table. When she puts a plate of radishes in front of me, tears well up in my eyes. This is what she served me when I came home for lunch that first day of school years ago. The presentation is just as it had been then: The radishes are like little red jewels with artistic white cuts on the sides, garnished with a few green leaves for a sweet, loving touch. Small slices of bread covered with a thin coat of butter are also arranged on the plate. Where did she find butter? No one has butter in Paris.

I am touched by everything on the table. Tata has gone to so much trouble to show her love. The cloth napkins are smartly rolled in their brass rings, sitting on the flowery tablecloth. Every radish says "I love you" a million times over to me. I will never forget those radishes. It was a feast that didn't just feed me physically, but also fed my heart.

When we finish, Tata says with a smile, "Another meal that the Boches won't have."

We talk of one thing, then another, mostly small, unimportant things. Every gesture, every pause conveys so much. The time passes quickly like a strange dream in slow motion. There is music in the air, yet everything is silent. Graciously, Tata moves around tending to little details here and there.

On Sunday evening, out of the blue, she says to me, "Pierre, I can see that when you marry, you'll be good to your wife."

Yes, I think. *And my wife and I will take care of you, just as I vowed when I was a small boy.*

THE WEEKEND IS OVER, and I have to catch my train. It's too much to ask Tata to go to the station with me, but she walks down the stairs, and we say good-bye in the entryway of her building.

"I will see you in a month," I say, giving her a kiss. She slips a small parcel into my hand.

"Take this with you, Pierre."

I give her one more hug before the door closes behind me. I hate leaving, but she assures me my family will be moving back to Paris in a few weeks, and soon we can all see one another.

When I open the small parcel on the train, I gasp. There is chocolate, cookies, a few cans of sardines, condensed milk, a pot of strawberry jam, and roasted bread. Tears begin to stream down my cheeks. Where did she find these treasures? How much did she have to pay or give up from her own rations to put together this incredible treat?

I read *Maroussia* on the train back to the Chateau, learning that French soldiers can be as cruel as the hated Boches. As Tata has told me many times, "Perspective is relative to where one stands." How true that is.

Back at the Chateau, the farming routine rolls by day after day. I am only living for my next visit to Tata. Unfortunately, the next month's pass is canceled because the train to Paris has been bombed. Impatiently, I wait for another month to pass.

I have something extremely important to tell Tata, something that I've never told her to my satisfaction. How do you say "I love you" to a saint? Yes, I know that saying the words "I love you" is simple enough. But how can I begin to match her giving love with my taking love?

She is so small, so frail. I am so tall, so strong. I have promised her that I will take care of her. Promises, promises. The small house for Tata, the car, the dog, the sandy beach, the boat to take her sailing, all pie-in-the-sky promises. All lies, and I am guilty of them.

IT'S A BEAUTIFUL early morning in the late spring, and I am working in the fields when the supervisor comes over to me.

"Pierre, you have a visitor at the Chateau."

"A visitor? I'm not expecting anybody." Could it be Tata? It's only a few weeks before I can visit her again. Maybe she couldn't wait that long either.

"Is it a nice old lady?"

"No. It's a man."

I enter the majestic castle's hall and Papa is standing there. What a surprise. I haven't seen him for a year. When we last saw each other, our relationship was rocky. I had begun to rebel against a few things, affirming myself, I suppose. I don't remember exactly which trivial issue triggered the dispute, but things went from bad to worse.

A painful memory comes flooding back.

OUR HEATED DISCUSSION has escalated quickly, and Papa is about to slap my face.

"Nobody slaps my face anymore!" I tell him firmly.

"That's what you think!" he answers.

I grab a bottle off the table and tell him menacingly, "You touch me, and I'll defend myself with this." He is standing three heads above me, strong and powerful, but I am not backing down.

"You do that and I'll lay you out like a carpet," he retorts.

"Try it," I reply calmly. I know Papa is not himself today. He has had a little too much wine at the bistro. However, I've promised myself that this is it; I am holding my ground. Honestly, I couldn't tell you what my reasons really were for this behavior—youthful rebellion, the stress generated by famine and war, or the loss of my father and my identity. Most likely, we are both feeling many of the same stresses.

Finally, Papa's head seems to clear and he comes to his senses. "Let's settle this like gentlemen. Put down that bottle and go to your room now."

"If you give me your gentleman's word not to touch me, it's yes. Otherwise, respectfully, it's no!"

"You have my word, Pierre. Now go to your room."

I put the bottle on the table and go to my room. This regrettable incident has stood between us all this time.

PAPA HOLDS OUT his strong arms to me, and we silently embrace. Just as with Tata, I don't want to let go. Then he says in my ear, "Your aunt is gravely ill, Pierre. She wants to see you."

"When do we go?"

"Get changed. We are leaving for Paris right now."

It is a long walk to the railroad station. We follow the Loing riverbank to a bridge, which is a long detour.

"I thought that you would like to walk through the forest on our way to the station, Pierre."

"Yes, Papa, I love the forest. It's so peaceful," I say. "And we have plenty of time. The train doesn't leave until seven thirty."

The weather is superb—not too hot, not too cold, just perfect. Flowers are in bloom everywhere. The birds are singing, and the light breeze from the south is invigorating. Papa and I stop at a little inn by the riverside for lunch. There isn't much on the menu, so we order a salad that comes with an atrocious dressing, and we wash it down with a homemade beer.

"We call it *frenette*," the owner says. "It's made of ash leaves."

"It's pretty good, but it's not quite up to a Cabernet Sauvignon," Papa says with a smile.

"It's the war, Monsieur," she replies sadly.

I am surprised that Papa seems so relaxed even though he doesn't have any cigarettes or a glass of decent wine with his meal. Ordinarily, he would be venting his frustration.

We chat about unimportant things, such as my life at the Chateau. It's merely small talk. *What's the matter with him?* We used to talk about serious things like boats or art, past adventures full of danger and funny moments. *Maybe we should quarrel,* I think. *At least that would be lively.* However, I am not going to start anything. Once again I have Papa back in my life, if only for a few days.

BY MIDAFTERNOON we are walking in the beautiful Fontainebleau forest all by ourselves. The sun rays are filtering through the centenarian oak trees, where birds are flitting from branch to branch. Our footsteps scare a rabbit that vanishes into the underbrush.

"Remember, Papa, when Tata rented a country cottage in Moret-sur-Loing and we used to go hunting for rabbits at the edge of the forest? It's not very far from here."

"I remember when you took a shot at a rabbit with my sixteen-gauge, Tatiou, and fell on your behind," he replies.

"Yes, I did." Neither of us is laughing or smiling. We should have been. Something is drastically wrong.

The road weaves between some birch trees as we walk in silence. My father begins to slow down. Then he puts his right arm around my shoulder and holds me tight.

"Pierre, you have to be brave."

For what? I feel something very bad is coming my way.

"Tata died in her sleep two days ago. She didn't suffer," he offers simply.

I go numb and cannot speak.

He tightens his grip. "I had an aunt too, Pierre. I loved her very much. She died when I was about your age. I understand completely."

Words are not coming easily, and Papa has to clear his throat a couple of times. We are there, the two of us, in the big forest. I can see birds moving through the air, but they are blurry and I can barely hear their songs.

The silence is sliced by a blue jay's shrill scream as it crosses our path. I walk straight ahead. I look straight ahead. I can see the sun playing hide-and-seek through the canopy of the forest, but its warm rays are not touching my cold heart. Suddenly, everything becomes blurry. It's still beautiful, but I can't see it anymore. My eyes are full of tears. I don't stop walking—I can't. I walk and walk and walk. I want to kill my pain by walking until I drop.

ADOLF HITLER, DICTATOR

BENITO MUSSOLINI, DICTATOR

JOSEPH STALIN, DICTATOR

FRANCISCO FRANCO, DICTATOR

PIERRE H. MATISSE, AMERICAN

Artistic rendering of signatures by Pierre H. Matisse

20
IS HE OR ISN'T HE?

To be, or not to be: that is the question.

WILLIAM SHAKESPEARE

"HOW DID HE TAKE IT?" I overhear Maman ask Papa as soon as we arrive home.

"Like a man, Louise. As I expected."

When she sees me, Maman takes me in her arms. "Poor Bunny Rabbit," she whispers tenderly.

I cannot cry because I am still completely numb. When I talk, I cannot hear myself saying anything. When I walk, I cannot feel the ground under my feet. There is no reality, only an immense void.

I have to go to Tata's apartment to see for myself that she is gone. When I arrive, I slowly climb the stairs and open the door with my key. Her things are there, in their proper places. A book of poems is open on her bedside table. But Tata is not here. That is when it hits me brutally, with full force. *I will never see Tata again.* I am traumatized and I want to die too. How can I enjoy the beauty of life if there is no Tata to share it with?

The sky is gray and overcast for Tata's funeral. While we stand at the gravesite, a German Dornier bomber roars low above the cemetery. I don't even raise my head. No one can hurt me more than I am hurting now. The flowers that I throw on Tata's coffin are discarded hope to me. Tata was so good. Silently I pray, asking God to receive her in His warm embrace.

A few days later, it's time for me to return to the Chateau. Maman has gotten my suitcase ready. "You'll find a lunch inside, Pierre," she says to me.

"Thank you, Maman."

"Be good, my darling." My mother can't hide her concern about me, and I know that her red eyes are for me as well as Tata.

"I'll be all right, Maman. Don't worry about me."

"The pain will pass," she says as she kisses me. "Give it time."

THE CHARMING COUNTRYSIDE of the Île-de-France passes by as I gaze out the train windows, but I hardly notice its beauty. My nose is running, so I open my suitcase to get a handkerchief. Inside, a brown paper parcel is taking up most of the space. There is a letter from my mother sitting on top of it.

My Dear Pierre,
I found this parcel for you in Tata's apartment. I could not bring myself to give it to you in person. Please do with it what it was intended for by her.

I love you.
Your loving mother

Then I see another note in Tata's handwriting, which simply says,

For my Pierre, with love.

Tata

My hands are trembling as I open the package. Inside are lots of delicacies, including *touron*, a delicious sweet Spanish candy made with almond paste.

Aurora used to give me the best touron that could be found in Spain. Aurora and now Tata—gone.

For the first time in two years I am not hungry. I haven't eaten since yesterday at noon. Without tasting anything, I close the suitcase and put it on the overhead rack.

In the crowded compartment, most people are dozing, lulled to sleep by the train's rolling rhythm. I look out the window and begin to cry. Once I start, I can't stop. My whole body is shaking from the uncontrollable sobs.

"Young man, are you all right?" an old man asks me.

"Can I help you?" a woman with a baby in her lap says.

Now I am crying loudly. I have to get out of here. I stand up and move erratically, like I am losing my mind, trying to find my way to the lavatory. I lock the door behind me and cry even louder. People are banging on the door.

"Open up! Do you need help?"

I splash some water on my face to wash away my tears, and I walk out.

"Let me help you to your compartment," a kind old woman offers, taking me by the hand. "Everything will be all right."

Once we are seated, she says, "Did you lose someone, dear?"

I nod as the tears come back.

"It'll be all right," she says to comfort me, her hand on my wrist. She sits with me for the rest of the journey.

I CRY AFTER I get off the train, walking from the station to the Chateau. In the dormitory, I muffle my sobs with my pillow.

The next day, exhausted, I go to work and then wake up in the infirmary. I had been found unconscious in the field where I was gathering grass for the rabbits. I am suffering from an acute case of jaundice. Three weeks later, Maman is at my bedside.

"My poor Bunny Rabbit. What's happened to you, my darling?"

It feels good to have my mother here, but I know she has her own problems, and I am just one more of them.

"I was sick, Maman."

"The doctor told me that you are well enough to convalesce in Paris with me," Maman says, smiling. "He feels that this would help you heal, Pierre."

"When are we leaving?"

"Today. And you won't be coming back. You have been expelled for misconduct," she says matter-of-factly.

Somehow the Chateau authority has discovered my food chiseling operation. I wonder why they picked on me because everybody else is doing it too. We are all hungry and need food one way or another. But it doesn't matter. I am freed from this detestable place.

"Good," I tell her. "I can't stand it here."

FOR NOW I AM staying with my parents at the Clamart apartment. After almost a year apart, the four of us are together again: Papa, Maman, Gérard, and me. The question is, what are we going to do with me? Maman confides that the real reason I cannot return to the Chateau is because I am notorious for my past activities and pose a danger to the school by being there.

My parents are constantly quarreling, but I don't have any idea what they are fighting about. Maybe it's me, who knows? The war continues to take its toll on our family.

Will it ever stop? Last year the Allied forces landed in North Africa, and a few months ago they invaded Italy. On the eastern front, the Russians are beating the Boches soundly. There are rumors of an imminent Allied landing on the west coast of France. Normandy should be a prime candidate for such an operation, so it looks like the action could come back to France soon.

Paris is bombed lightly, but often, by the Allies, now that it is occupied. The Boches are getting more difficult. Massive arrests of civilians suspected of sabotage or subversive activities occur daily in and around Paris. Some are sent to Germany for forced labor, while others have been executed.

ONE DAY MAMAN ANNOUNCES, "Pierre, I've found you a job as a printer's apprentice."

"Good!" I say. "Where is this job?"

"In Montrouge. Théo Schmied, a friend of mine, has a printing shop there, and he has agreed to take you on. He specializes in fine rare books, limited and numbered editions. You'll like it because the books are very artistically done."

Work! Something new. Books! Instantly, I like it. Books make me feel close to Tata. My mind is finally coming out of its hopeless stupor.

"When do I start?"

"Soon, but first you have to move again," Maman says.

"From now on, Pierre, you are going to have to live by yourself. It is becoming too difficult and too dangerous for all of us to stay together," Papa adds.

MAMAN AND I wait until after the curfew to begin moving me to my new home two miles away. As we walk, Maman tells me a little more about where I will be living. "You are going to like Monsieur and Madame Rateaux. They have a son, Jules, who is a couple of years older than you and studies at the Sorbonne."

We enter a comfortable house in Issy-les-Moulineaux. Madame Rateaux meets us at the door and lets her husband know that we have arrived.

"Speak louder," he roars. "I can't hear you!"

"He was in the artillery during the last war," she explains to me as her husband enters the room. "The big gun explosions ruined his ears."

Maman and I greet Monsieur Rateaux and quickly fall into conversation.

"I was just released from jail yesterday," he tells me.

"What for?" I ask, curious what kind of trouble he got himself into.

"What?"

"What for, Monsieur Rateaux?" I repeat loudly.

"I stole from the Boches and got one year," he declares proudly.

"Stole what?"

"Everything I could from these disgusting Krauts. I specialize in everything that is against them."

"You are lucky that they didn't shoot you," my mother admonishes him.

"I hope that you have learned your lesson and that you are going to behave now," his wife says.

"I'm going to be an angel," he says, laughing and flapping his arms.

"And you, my friend, welcome to the riffraff outfit," he says to me with a twinkle in his eye. "I'm going to teach you to steal without being caught." He gives me a strong tap on the back and laughs again.

Madame Rateaux shakes her head. "He'll never change," she confides to Maman.

It takes us three trips and the better part of the night to move a mattress and a few minimal pieces of furniture that belong to Maman and Tata to the Rateauxes' home, making a small first-floor room relatively comfortable for me.

"I like Monsieur Rateaux," Maman says to me. "Overall, he is a very good man."

"I think I'm going to like him, too, Maman."

"I'm glad. But, please, stay out of his dangerous schemes," she advises.

On our last trip to the Rateauxes', I am carrying a bag full of miscellaneous things, and Maman has a small cardboard box containing some books. All of a sudden, a flashlight is aimed in my face.

"What are you doing here at this hour?" a sour French voice asks. Two French policemen are blocking our way.

"We are moving, and we are late," my mother replies.

"There is a curfew, Madame. You are lucky that we are not a German patrol."

Maman thanks them, and we finish our business quickly.

A day or two later, Maman takes me to the print shop and introduces me to Théo Schmied, my new boss.

MY WORKDAY begins at six o'clock in the morning after I've eaten a small breakfast prepared by Madame Rateaux. Next, I walk a half hour to the subway, which I ride to Montrouge, and then walk another half hour to the print shop. I work until five or sometimes six in the evening, without anything to eat.

Twice a week after work, I take the subway to Montparnasse, where I attend les Cours du Soir de la Ville de Paris, free adult art classes. On Saturdays, I spend the entire day at l'Académie de la Grande Chaumière, studying drawing. I eat my meager midday lunch while I draw.

I am learning the intricacies of anatomical classical art by drawing a live model. I learn by doing, but almost as much by discreetly watching older, talented artists creating masterpieces around me. Many famous artists, such as Marc Chagall, have sat on these very benches. By nine o'clock in the evening, I am back in my room at Issy-les-Moulineaux, just before curfew.

This routine goes from Monday to Saturday. I never see the daylight during the week. On Sunday, weather permitting, I treat myself by taking the subway at Les Invalides and head to Versailles. There, I recharge my creative batteries in its magnificent gardens. I study the sculptures and architecture and fill my sketch pad with drawings.

Sometimes, when I can't make it to Versailles, I spend time in Notre Dame Cathedral, which is much closer to where I live. I slip inside and draw the sculptures and the intricate carved woodwork.

I want to learn as much as I can and do it as fast as possible to earn money and be totally independent after the war. I study the basics of photography, engraving, illustration, decoration, and antique furniture at l'Académie de la Grande Chaumière. Learning and work restore my sanity.

I am not allowed to go to our family's apartment. If someone wants to see me, arrangements are made. Once when I meet Papa in Paris, he seems glad to see me, and after looking me over, he says kindly, "A button is missing on your coat, Pierre. You should wax your shoes. Look at your collar. Don't you think that you could wash it?"

"Yes, Papa."

His words are kind and concerned, not critical. I believe that he wants to help me, but he doesn't know how.

We don't talk about any of his underground activities, so I don't know if he is still active or not. I guess we are all still at risk from the Antibes business.

I WORK AND STUDY and am tormented by hunger again. Every week, I use my whole pay, minus my subway fare, to indulge once or twice at a black market restaurant. I buy two meals each time, stuffing myself silly. For the rest of the week, I mostly starve. There are a few exceptions. On the way to the print shop, I pass Tata's apartment building, and from time to time, the concierge invites me in for a bowl of soup. Other times I find a note on my bed that my mother has left for me, saying to meet her at such a place and such a time so that she might pass some food on to me.

I wait an hour, then another. Sometimes she comes, sometimes she doesn't. When she makes it, she usually gives me a loaf of bread, a pot of jam, a saucisson (dry sausage), a can of sardines, and sweetened condensed milk.

A few times when I have a little money and am lucky, I buy a black market potato or a smoked herring in the subway. At Montrouge's town hall, the Red Cross sometimes distributes vitamin cookies to the J3s, donated by American Quakers. I go there a couple of times and wait in line for hours, only to be told that the last box has been given to the person just before me.

I am getting taller and skinnier. My clothes are a hodgepodge of hand-me-downs from my family: My pants, shirts, and jacket belonged to Tata's father, who lived under Napoleon III; my coat is Grandfather Milhau's, which I have turned inside out to give it a new lease on life. My dress style is circa middle of the last century. My shoes worry me the most. They are starting to fall apart because of all the walking I do.

I ENJOY WORKING in the print shop, and six to eight weeks after I start, I find out just how interesting this business is. We have fake plates and ink to make forged "official" documents, and I become a specialist in forging official signatures. There is one problem: the availability of paper.

The Vichy government, in partnership with the Boches, prints all the official documents and passes here in Paris. I know the place well because I have passed it many times. The entrance is guarded by two German sentinels armed with menacing MP 40 Schmeisser submachine guns. Not far from the government printing house is a small bistro where the Frenchmen who work for the Boches take their coffee breaks.

I have been asked by one of Monsieur Schmied's master printers, Monsieur Adventure, to join him in solving our paper problem. He has visited the bistro to see if one of the Frenchmen could perhaps smuggle a few sheets of paper here or there. Monsieur Adventure reminds me of my father, and I am happy to help.

Finally, Monsieur Adventure receives word to be at the government printing house on such and such a day, at this exact time and location, with the biggest cart that two men can handle. The specified location is right in front of the two Boche sentinels!

When the two of us arrive with the cart, the sentinels look at us and we look at them. They say nothing, we say nothing. All the time I am screaming in my head, *Act natural! Act natural!* A few agonizing minutes later, two French workers come out, carrying a stretcher full of paper that they load onto our cart. Later, Monsieur Adventure is informed that this was a onetime deal and is warned not to show up at the bistro ever again.

AT THE PRINT SHOP, Monsieur Schmied seems to be pleased with my work. One day he asks, "Would you like to do some extra work for me on speculation? It could be a challenge."

"I'd love it," I reply.

"I would like you to design a cover for an illustration for the opening page of a book of Arab poems called *L'Agneau du Moghreb* (*The Moghreb's Lamb*)."

When my cover illustration is accepted, I proudly show it to everybody I know, including Monsieur Rateaux.

He seems genuinely impressed, then says, "I understand that you are learning engraving."

"Oh, yes," I say at full volume, "and I am getting pretty good at it."

A little time passes, and one Sunday when Madame Rateaux is out and the bad weather is keeping me from my usual trip to Versailles, Monsieur Rateaux says he has an interesting proposition for me.

"What is it?" I ask.

"Do you recognize this paper, Pierre?" With an exaggerated theatrical flourish, he hands me a few sheets of colored paper.

My eyes widen. "It looks like alimentation paper, Monsieur Rateaux." This special paper is used for all of the Boches' official documents.

"If it looks like alimentation paper, it is alimentation paper," he says with that certain air that only a true conspirator knows.

"Yes, but the color is wrong. Besides, they change the color every month," I reply.

"Let's assume that I can obtain the right color paper," he says. "Could you do a little discreet engraving, say, um . . . printing a few food coupons?"

"Food coupons would be nice. I can try," I reply enthusiastically.

"Wonderful. What can I do to help, Pierre?" he asks seriously.

"What about finding some heavy paper, the type that the Boches use for IDs?"

"Ausweis? Yes, I have connections. I think that I can get that." My partner's eyes are twinkling.

"We could sell those on the black market for extended leaves from the obligatory work in Germany."

"Make doctor certificates too," Monsieur Rateaux adds.

"Yes, and train station certificates with missed connection excuses to get back late, signed by the stationmaster." The possibilities seem endless.

"Good! Good! We'll set up shop in the basement right away, Pierre. My son, Jules, has some friends who can use some of those extended leave passes as soon as possible to escape being sent to Germany for work detail."

We are in business—monkey business.

FOR THE TIME BEING, my leisure time at Versailles and La Grande Chaumière is put on hold. But my newly acquired skills are paying off like gold. I engrave official stamps, forge high dignitaries' signatures, print false papers—any kind of official documents you are looking for, we have them all. I particularly enjoy reproducing high-ranking Boche signatures for passes and goods for Frenchmen. It makes me feel like I am more active in the cause. I requisition the ink from my job at Monsieur

Schmied's and deliver it to Monsieur Rateaux's private printing shop. I don't feel guilty because we all have the same goal.

After a while, Madame Rateaux discovers what we are doing. "This time you are going to get us shot," she shouts at her husband.

"Alice, can you detect the official coupon from the fake one?" he asks.

"This is false; any idiot can see that!" she says, waving one of the coupons in his face.

"Alice, which one of these passes is an imitation?" *Monsieur Rateaux would be an excellent poker player*, I think.

"Only a fool would accept these," she replies, holding up a handful of passes.

"So, my dear, you are both an idiot and a fool because you have chosen the real ones as fakes."

Madame Rateaux is flabbergasted.

"They sell like hotcakes," my business partner tells her.

"The police are going to find out, Albert."

"Alice, the police aren't going to do a thing about it because we supply them with all kinds of fake papers for their own use—free of charge. They are some of our best customers!"

"Be careful," his wife warns.

After a few days, even Madame Rateaux gets into the act by using some fake food coupons at the store. We eat a little bit better, but not by much. The food situation in Paris is getting so bad that even with the coupons we can't get what we need.

One day, my partner surprises me with a pair of new leather shoes. I am astounded and grateful, especially since I need them so desperately. My feet are growing fast as I sprout up. Monsieur Rateaux confides that he did business with a German soldier who was about to head to the Russian front, exchanging an extended leave of absence pass for two pairs of leather shoes—one for me and one for his son. Yes, even some of the Boches were thankful for our operation.

AT NIGHT THE AIR RAIDS keep me awake. The Allies have intensified the bombing in the Paris suburbs, where they know French factories and repair shops are under German control.

I don't see Maman often, despite the fact that she is working on her pottery at the Matisse estate, which is not very far away. One day I receive a note to meet her at one of our usual rendezvous places.

As usual, I see the worry on her face. "Pierre, the conditions in Paris are getting worse. It is not safe for you here."

"I'm all right, Maman. Besides, I have no other place to go!"

She hesitates, then says, "Pierre, there is something that I've never told you. You have grandparents living in Normandy whom I have contacted. It's possible that they'll consider helping you." I should have been surprised by this news, but by this time nothing about my family surprises me.

"I'm doing what I think is best for you. Next Thursday, be here at eight o'clock to meet Grandfather Leroy," Maman says hurriedly. Maman has always been in a hurry, even before the war.

The mention of that name sends a bolt down my spine. As much as I don't want to say it, I reply, "I'll be here, Maman."

THE FOLLOWING THURSDAY is gloomy with a steady cold drizzle. I wait in the hallway of a friend's building. The time is exactly eight thirty. I am on time, but I know that the air raids have been disrupting the already mediocre transportation system so I am waiting a little longer, at least until Maman arrives.

The door opens. "Ah! Maman. I am so glad you are here."

She hugs me and then begins giving me some background on my out-of-the-blue grandfather.

"Your grandfather was an attorney, but he got mixed up in a few bad cases that turned sour and got him disbarred, so he is retired now."

An hour later, the door opens and a gentleman enters the hallway. I estimate he is probably in his early seventies and is impeccably dressed in an expensive three-piece suit.

"Louise, I'm glad to see you," he says, taking my mother in his arms and kissing her on both cheeks. "How are things with you, my dear?"

He talks to her, but he avoids looking at me.

"Not too bad, except for the war problems. How is it in Normandy, Louis?" she asks.

"We're surviving, but it's getting worse. The Boches are turning the screws a little tighter every day."

Suddenly, to get to the point of things, Maman pushes me under the only lamp in the dimly lit hallway. "This is your grandson, Pierre."

Grandfather Leroy gives me a strange look.

Maman says nothing. The silence is embarrassing, and I want to run out.

She reads my mind. "Please, Pierre. Stay put," she says quietly.

Monsieur Leroy is now slowly walking around me, sizing me up from head to toe.

"Hum!" he says, appearing to be clearing both his throat and his mind.

He is now walking around me a second time. I glance at my mother imploringly, who looks like she has had enough, too. At that moment Monsieur Leroy's eyes meet hers.

"He's my grandson, Louise," he states simply.

I didn't hear anyone asking me my opinion, I think angrily.

Then he turns and hands me a piece of paper.

"I am your grandfather, and this is my address. Write to me and your grandmother. Her name is Mathilde."

"I am so pleased," Maman says happily.

"Mathilde is another story, Louise! Mathilde is going to have to be convinced."

Why does she need to be convinced? I am starting to get suspicious.

"What if Pierre and I come for a visit?" my mother suggests.

"Good idea, Louise. What about next week? Would you come with Pierre to see us?"

"Yes, Louis, I'd like that."

Maman seems relieved, but I can't say the same for myself. Still, I will keep my mouth shut. She has too much on her mind these days.

The well-dressed gentleman gives me another curious look and says to my mother, "Yes, he is my grandson."

He shakes my hand, kisses my mother, and leaves. The whole episode lasts maybe fifteen to twenty minutes.

I don't know if I like him or not. Now I have three grandfathers. I have an affinity with my first two. But this one?

Maman interrupts my thoughts. "Pierre, you are going to have to be nice to them. They can help you."

"I don't want to go to Normandy."

"If they invite you, you'll have to go, Pierre. There is no other solution for you."

The detailed inspection my "grandfather" gave me and the hesitant tone of his voice when he said, "Yes, he is my grandson," tells every fiber of my body that there is something strange going on here that I don't want to know about.

Pierre H. Matisse

21

GOOD-BYE, PARIS; HELLO, NORMANDY

Nothing is worth doing unless the consequences may be serious.

GEORGE BERNARD SHAW

THE DAY OF THE VISIT ARRIVES. After a three-hour train journey from Paris, Maman and I get off in Rugles and begin a two-mile walk to the Leroys' home. We are in the heart of Normandy. Apple orchards and cow pastures alternate between numerous cultivated fields as far as one can see. The smell of cow manure is pungent. I notice a trace of snow slowly melting on the ground under the pale winter sun. It must have fallen yesterday.

A German bus full of soldiers drives by us, and one Boche sitting on the roof shoots into a flock of pigeons, killing a few. The bus doesn't stop for the quarry. I guess he was just doing it for fun. I go into the field and pick up three fat pigeons. "A gift for the grandfather," I say to Maman and she nods.

We finally arrive at the Leroy estate, enclosed by a thick, squarely trimmed six-foot hedge. The entrance to the property is through a wooden gate with a bell attached, hung between two red brick pillars. Inside is a charming Normand-style house of red brick and white stucco with huge brown oak beams crisscrossing the exterior. There are light brown wooden shutters on every window, and the roof is covered with small dark red clay tiles. On the side, close to the road, is a wooden clapboard garage, and behind the house is a small barn in the same style as the house.

The weather has given the old home that very special patina that adds to its charm. It is a perfect picture for a Normandy postcard, suggesting coziness and country living at its best. In the back there is a large apple orchard, a vegetable garden, and a small pond.

Maman and I are met at the door by Monsieur Leroy, whom I barely recognize. He is dressed in horse-riding attire and fits the country gentleman image well. "Welcome to Normandy, Pierre. Come in and meet your grandmother, Mathilde."

She is a good-looking woman probably in her early fifties, but the way she looks at me makes me uneasy. She is neatly but simply dressed. She is not colorful, but extremely proper.

"He is quite a tall boy," Mathilde remarks to my mother, after having looked me up and down twice.

"Yes, he has grown up all of a sudden," Maman answers.

"On my side of the family, everyone is short. Louis's family members are all short, too. Strong, but not tall. Where do you suppose this one gets his height from?" Mathilde prods.

I am squirming inside, but I remain stock-still.

"Mathilde, kids are getting taller these days," Grandfather Leroy interjects.

"Really?" She draws out the word, while looking straight at my mother.

There is an awkward silence, like something is about to happen. Then she suddenly turns and smiles at me. "Are you hungry, Pierre?"

I exhale in relief. "Yes, Madame."

"Don't call me Madame. Have a glass of my homemade apple cider," she says, before busying herself at the enormous cast-iron stove. I am waiting for a cue from Maman and Grandfather Leroy, but they are talking.

"How was the train trip?" Grandfather asks.

"Slow, like everything else these days," Maman says, adding, "Apparently the Allies bombed a train last night."

"The underground blew up the track between here and Paris last week, Louise." It was one more way to slow down the Germans making their way to Normandy.

"Do you like rabbit stew, Pierre?" the lady of the house wants to know.

"Yes!" I answer, but hesitate. *How should I address her?*

"You can call me Grand-mère, Pierre. That'll do for now."

Suddenly I realize how silly I must look standing here with dead birds in my hands all this time. "I have some pigeons for you. They were shot by a German."

"Nice of you. Thank you. The Boches are robbing Normandy of everything," she says, taking the birds and then continuing to set the table with white-and-blue china.

During the meal, the three of them talk about trivial things. The main room, where we are seated, is a typical gigantic farm kitchen, dining room, and living room all in one. From my chair, I take in the surroundings: There are interesting knickknacks, oil paintings and a watercolor, small sculptures, colorful decorative plates, and bookshelves full of books. Every door is extensively carved. The whole place looks like an antique shop or museum.

In a corner, an old longcase clock dominates the room with its massive brass pendulum swinging back and forth. When the conversation quiets down, the clock takes over with its reassuring ticktock. This is the home of a country lord.

Grandfather is seated on an extravagant armchair, more like a throne, with a monstrous fireplace behind him. Mounted above the mantel are four deer heads with majestic antlers. I notice the gun rack is empty. Grandfather follows my eyes and says, "The Boches took my hunting rifles."

I continue scanning the room. There is a Singer treadle sewing machine by a window. My inquisitive look gets Madame Leroy's attention.

"I sew for the farmers living around here, which keeps us supplied with food."

"And I barter legal advice for food, when some overly creative

Normand gets caught chiseling the system. The war has made these Normand farmers rich, Louise," Grandfather says.

His wife's expression suddenly turns stern. She looks piercingly at Maman and says, "I'd like to know why Pierre is so tall, Louise. My son is short."

"Please, Mathilde, who cares?" Grandfather wants to end this discussion quickly.

"I do," she states firmly, as she cleans the table.

"It's late," Maman says, motioning me to stand. "We have to leave and catch our train."

Maman wants to get out of here quickly, before she is interrogated any more. Despite the good food, so do I.

Grandfather walks us to the gate, and as we bid him good-bye, he takes me aside.

"Do you have a watch, Pierre?"

"No, but I manage quite well without one. There are clocks everywhere in Paris."

He hands me a well-worn silver pocket watch with a chain. "This belonged to my father. You take it."

"I don't know what to say," I say, surprised by the gesture.

"It's very simple. You only have to say thank you," he replies, smiling.

"Thank you."

"No, you say thank you, *Grandfather*."

When I did, he smiled even more.

On the train, Maman and I don't talk very much. I know that she loves me, but because I have lived with her for only short periods of time in recent years, we have never had the opportunity to get as close as I had been with Tata. When I was first sent away to Paris, I believe Maman and Papa had hoped to become successful enough so they could support us and put our family back together.

But when Maman saw that I had virtually accepted Tata as a surrogate mother, she probably became concerned that I would forget who my parents really were, having me come home again. Unfortunately, Maman's relationship with Papa seems to become rocky when I am living in the Matisse family. I know I have been an impossible kid, getting into all kinds of trouble, but there is something else that I cannot quite put my finger on. I had tried to bring up this subject with Tata the last time we were together, just before she died. But now it is too late.

BACK IN PARIS, work at the print shop is getting more difficult. There is a shortage of ink, even of poor quality, and many supplies are getting harder to find. Limited electricity forces us to turn to primitive hand printing presses, which are slow and laborious. Alternative products to clean the machines stink to high heaven and make me sick, while the food situation is getting almost intolerable. Like every other Parisian, I am starving.

I am corresponding regularly with my Normand grandfather to build some kind of relationship. In one letter, he explains that his son, Camille Leroy, is my father and teaches art in Algeria. "He is a jerk," he notes plainly. "But his mother thinks that he is a genius." I am confused about this piece of information and have my doubts that it is true. Yet being taken into Grandfather Leroy's confidence makes me feel good and I tell him so.

A couple of times, Grandfather Leroy invites me to spend a weekend in Normandy, and I go, eating until I feel like I will burst from all the potatoes, rabbit, eggs, bowls of heavy cream soup, and fresh salads from the garden. During these visits, Mathilde is reserved, but she appears to like me. I am growing closer to Grandfather Leroy, who shares his books and enjoys talking about any and all subjects with me.

When the print shop is closed temporarily due to lack of paper, I have a holiday from work. On Sunday I go to Versailles, which I haven't visited for quite a while. The streets are almost deserted, but on a broad avenue a German infantry unit is training. These are not soldiers; they are German boys my age who are learning the art of killing. In no time at all, a sizable group of French teenagers gathers to watch.

The Boche corporal in charge doesn't seem to mind his young French audience. I can see by his uniform that he has served four years, and to me, he appears tired. By the end of the day's free course in the art of warfare, I have learned to operate a Schmeisser submachine gun, a Mauser rifle, and a full-size machine gun, as well as how to launch hand grenades. *Das gut!*

The war seems to be taking a bad turn for the Nazis. The Germans are getting increasingly nervous, arresting large numbers of people just to check their IDs. We call these German fishing operations "raffles."

The Boches know what they are doing. At this time, Paris is totally infested with "terrorists" (the resistance fighters) and spies from all interested parties. The Boches are absolutely right. There is so much activity against them that all they have to do is cast a net anywhere in a group of people, and they are bound to catch a few prize fish.

ONE DAY I AM working in the basement when Monsieur Rateaux comes home in a panic. "Pierre! We have to destroy everything," he says, quite agitated.

"What happened?"

"The guy in front of me got it." He is struggling to catch his breath. "I have run . . . all the way . . . from the subway station." He is still puffing and wheezing and sounds like a steam engine going uphill.

"What about the guy in front of you?"

"He put a pocket twenty-five automatic pistol in his scarf and then tied it around his neck."

"Gutsy fellow!" I wish I had been there.

"There was a raffle in the subway. He got caught directly in front of me!"

"So? You are safe."

"No, the Germans started shoving everyone around, and they caught me, too."

"But you are here."

"Can't you understand? *Sacre bleu!* The Boches took all my papers."

"What papers were there?"

"A complete assortment of our fake documents."

"Why didn't they arrest you then and there?"

"Because Mister Twenty-Five Caliber Pistol escaped, and they went after him."

My heart is racing now. "Did they catch him?"

"Yes, they shot him dead on the spot. In the confusion, I managed to escape. But they have the papers—phony ausweis, fake food coupons, look alike IDs, the works."

"Were any of them the finished ones with this address?"

"I don't think so." Monsieur Rateaux was frowning, trying to remember.

"Did you get the fake papers from this pile or that one?" I ask him anxiously.

He points to a pile. "This one."

"Are you certain?"

"What?"

"Are you certain?" I scream back.

"Yes, positively sure."

I exhale in relief.

"Then we are safe. Those had no address on them."

"If the Boches don't have your address or ID, there is no problem. You do have your personal ID, don't you?"

Monsieur Rateaux has stopped huffing and puffing, but now he is sweating . . . and so am I.

"I always carry it in this pocket," he says, patting his breast pocket, then frantically checking his pants pockets, too.

By the third pocket, there is still no ID. And there are no more pockets.

"They have my ID. I am doomed!" he says in a shaky voice, throwing his hands up in the air.

Now I'm alarmed too. "We've got to run."

"Alice!" he screams. "Where is Jules?"

She hurries into the basement. "At the Sorbonne. Why?"

"I have lost my ID, and the Boches are after me. We have to run."

"What have you done?"

"I told you. I lost my ID."

"Look at you, you old fool. Your ID is there in your shirt pocket, right under your idiotic nose." She pulls it out and waves it in front of him.

We all burst out laughing, genuinely relieved.

THERE ARE MORE TROUBLES when I discover that an employee at the print shop who has befriended me is an informant. He is gung ho for the Third Reich, a dangerous character. One day he shows me his Luger pistol and his official permit to carry it, bragging about his disgusting activities. *Does he suspect me of anything?* I wonder. Fortunately, thanks to Papa's early training, I have always been extra careful with my tongue.

Then a good friend of mine François gets caught moving weapons from one place to another. He is a year older than me. When his father goes to visit him at the jail, the Germans give him a small parcel with a few personal things—all that is left of his son. He had been shot by the Nazis.

Maman is aware of the escalating crackdown by the Germans, and the next time she visits me, she says, "Pierre, you need to go to your grandparents in Normandy."

"No! Maman, I want to stay in Paris."

Madame Rateaux has had enough too. The incident in the subway station was too close for comfort. She wants us to shut down our basement business immediately.

Obviously, she is right. So Rateaux & Pierre, Inc., Official Documents Unlimited, closes its doors. It is a shame because, for the first time, my artistic genius has been put to good use.

If this abominable war doesn't end soon, I really don't know what's going to happen to us. It is a question that plagues me, with no answer.

And then I become sick, covered with nasty boils. They are everywhere from my armpits to my crotch—gross, infectious, and painful.

When I see a doctor, he asks, "Do you have a relative or friend in the country?"

"Perhaps . . . in Normandy."

"Then, my friend, it's time for you to get out of Paris. You are in bad shape. At least in Normandy, you will be able to eat dandelion greens and breathe fresh air."

When I let Grandfather Leroy know about my situation, he kindly invites me to move in with them permanently. I appreciate the gesture, but I am reluctant to say yes because to me it would almost be like betraying Papa. The Leroys are nice people and seem to want me. But I want to believe that Jean Matisse is my father. I *need* to believe that Jean Matisse is my father. Deep inside, I know this to be true!

No, I will stay in Paris. I don't want to hurt Papa's feelings. I love him and I need him in my life. I will wait awhile to write Grandfather Leroy and tell him my decision.

22

JUNE 6, 1944: NORMANDIE

*The truth is not simply what you think it is; it is also the circumstances
in which it is said, and to whom, why, and how it is said.*

VÁCLAV HAVEL

IT IS DAWN and I am the first one to arrive at the print shop. I start the
woodstove to keep the ink from freezing. As I clean up and prepare everything for the day's work, I glance out the window just as a German patrol
passes by. Suddenly there is a blast. Someone must have thrown a grenade
or a homemade Molotov cocktail. I duck down and wait, listening for
any retaliation. Nothing.

I quickly go to the door and step outside. French gendarmes are pouring out of their station. I slip back inside the print shop to make sure
that nothing suspicious is out in the open. I have a couple of sets of
my homemade papers on me, but before I have time to hide them, the
Boches burst through the front door. I stand still and make no attempt
to run, but they grab me and begin roughing me up.

"We got you!" one of them says, trying to pin the grenade attack on me.

"It's not me," I respond in French as I am being dragged into the supply room.

"We know it is you. You might as well confess," another soldier shouts. He is holding my hand on the doorjamb and is about to slam the door on it. *How will I be able to create art with crushed fingers?* I wonder. I pray for courage or a quick end. At that moment, one of the printers arrives and surprises us. I am thrown to the floor, and when I attempt to stand back up, a soldier punches me hard in the stomach, then kicks me over and over—in my back and ribs until my head is spinning from the pain. The Boche officer says to the printer, "There is no use pretending. The kid told us everything."

The printer knows better. "You're crazy," he says defiantly. "There is nothing to tell." They beat him up and repeat the process with the second master printer when he arrives. We are all hurting badly, but I don't move to prevent more beatings to myself and the others. A few minutes later, another Boche arrives and announces they have caught the guilty party and are taking him for interrogation. The man who had thrown the grenade had another grenade on him.

As long as we fight for our freedom we are alive. Papa had told me on the night we were waiting for the submarine that retaining our independence daily in both thought and deed is the key to freedom. Those words have been imprinted on my heart.

The Boches jerk us to our feet and collect our papers. I give them one set of mine. We must report the next day to an address where we will be questioned further before our papers are returned to us.

When Théo Schmied arrives, I wait for things to quiet down, then ask to speak with him privately. I tell him it is evident that we have an informant in our midst.

"My papers will never pass the Gestapo inspection," I tell him honestly.

Monsieur Schmied is quiet for a moment, then he advises, "You need to get out of Paris for a while, until things cool down." He motions me to follow him, takes money from a drawer, and puts it in my hand. "Here's your pay. It is best that you leave now."

I leave immediately, hesitating for a moment outside the print shop. Where should I go? To my parents or Monsieur Rateaux? I decide my business partner would be the best option.

It is noontime. Monsieur Rateaux intercepts me on the way. He hands me a backpack and says the car with the "leather coats" (Gestapo) has been to the house looking for me.

"Thank you, Monsieur Rateaux. Please tell Maman that I am going to visit Grandfather Leroy. She will understand."

It's time to move to Normandy. I don't want to attract any unnecessary attention, so I am only carrying the backpack. When I enter the railroad station, it is packed solid with people, which is not unusual.

What is not normal is that there are French police everywhere, accompanied by German soldiers. *They must be after more terrorists*, I think. As I head to the ticket office, I notice the soldiers are checking everyone's papers. Mine are certainly not impeccable. Let's just say I'd rather that they don't look at them too closely. I know that while it's not likely I am the person they are looking for at the moment, I have climbed a few numbers up their wanted list, both for my past and my current resistance activities. *Time to think up another plan.*

Every exit of the station is blocked by either German patrols or Gestapo. I know better than to tangle with them. I go into the train station's restroom, hoping the heat will eventually cool down. When a French railroad employee comes in, I take a chance, hoping that he, like most railroad workers, is one of us.

"I need to take a train to Normandy—now. I don't want the Boches to look at my papers. Can you help me get on a train?"

"Where in Normandy?" he asks, matter-of-factly.

"Rugles?"

"Impossible. That track has been bombed by the Allies."

"What about any trains going in that general direction, passenger or freight?" I am sick, scared, and frustrated.

"The freight trains are all controlled by the Boches. But there is the train to Caen; you could get off at Évreux. Then you'll have to walk to Rugles at night. It's a long way to walk, almost thirty-one miles."

"That's fine. I've got to get out of Paris today."

"Come with me."

We leave the restroom and disappear behind a door marked *Personnel Only*. We walk through one office, into a corridor, and finally into a tool shop.

"Wait for me and, for heaven's sake, don't panic and run out. Stay out of sight!"

I wait almost an hour. This is not going fast enough for my taste. He comes back with two railroad mechanics.

"My friends are going to get you on the train to Caen."

"Thank you!" He nods and leaves hurriedly.

"You don't know us. We don't know you. Understood?" a mechanic says.

"Yes!"

"Follow us," the shorter one says.

"It's going to be dangerous," the other adds.

"No problem. I've got to get to Normandy."

"The train leaves in four hours. It'll be night by then."

We have been walking as we've been talking and enter an immense barn full of steam locomotives being repaired. Near a side door, two armed German guards are playing cards on a grease-stained table. When I see them, I start getting nervous and want to turn back.

"Not to worry. Those Fritzes are inoffensive," the shorter one says.

We enter another room full of rusted machinery. One of my escorts points to a pile of discarded items, and says, "Make yourself comfortable on this tarp until we come to get you."

"When did you have your last meal?" the other one asks.

"This morning."

"We'll get you something to eat before we ship you to the Normandy cows," he says, smiling. "Normandy has lots of milk."

IT HAS BEEN QUITE an adventurous day, and I fall asleep on the tarp. Two hours later I am awakened by a stranger.

"How about a bowl of bean soup, young fellow?" he says quietly. It is the best-tasting soup I have ever had.

After devouring it like a wolf, I thank him. "That was delicious," I say appreciatively.

"Compliments of my wife. Would you like another serving?"

"Yes! That would be nice." The stranger comes back with another full bowl and a little cloth pouch with a string strap.

"Put this around your neck. There's food inside for your trip. Your train leaves in twenty minutes. This is a map showing where to get off and the best route from Évreux to Rugles by the back roads. Take this canteen, too. It's water with a touch of wine."

It's now pitch dark. I follow my skinny guide closely, walking among a jungle of intertwined rails. I wonder how he can find his way in this huge railroad yard, holding just a flickering oil lamp set so low it barely casts any light. In his other hand, he is carrying a long steel tool. We are surrounded by steam locomotives, exhaling smoke and steam and making other strange noises. I trip on a rail and nearly fall, but my guide catches me just in time.

"Be careful not to put your feet inside a switching rail," he says quietly.

A German patrol walks by.

"*Bonsoir*," my guide says casually.

"*Gutenacht*," one of the Boches says without even looking at us.

"We are almost there. Are you all right?" my companion asks.

"I'm fine." A steel monster pushing a flatbed freight train loaded with German tanks is passing just a few yards from us, shaking the ground under our feet. Another one with closed wooden freight cars follows it.

"Here is your train. You will travel first class—in between two wagons on a small platform. The train will slow down before Évreux, and that's where you jump off."

The train is approaching. Slowly, the puffing locomotive passes us. I can see a few people bracing themselves on the platforms as best as they can. With my friend's help, I'm boosted onto a platform occupied by two men.

"*Bon voyage* and *bonne chance!*"

"Hello!" A voice with a strong Mediterranean accent welcomes me.

"Hello!" I reply uneasily.

"Hello! Don't worry. Once we get through these confounded switching rails, it's a piece of cake," a second voice with a Parisian argot accent adds.

As we go over the switch rails, the car goes sideways and shakes terribly. A thick black smoke, full of coal cinders, chokes me, and a hot cinder flies into my eye. I blink away the pain while I hang on for dear life.

"We are lucky this train has a Boche flak station on the last wagon," Monsieur Argot says.

Monsieur Mediterranean elaborates, "The flak station is a four barrel, anti-aircraft gun set on a flatbed wagon. If we are attacked by the English, they'll shoot back. We should have a better chance to reach Caen."

"Yes, but I'd prefer that they shot this train with its Boches into many small pieces," Monsieur Argot responds, then turns to me. "Where are you going?"

"Somewhere. I am not too certain where exactly," I reply, remembering one of Papa's rules: In wartime, one should never volunteer more information than necessary.

"Where are you going?" I ask. Question for question is only fair.

"Caen," they answer in unison.

"Business?"

Papa's rule number two: If you ask questions, you won't have to answer so many.

"Black market," the two say, laughing in unison.

I have cautiously slid down so I am sitting on the platform instead of standing.

As the train rushes on, I get lost in my thoughts, remembering my past adventures with Papa, relying on what he has taught me to keep safe.

The train slows down to pass a burning freight train.

"Adolf isn't going to like this," Monsieur Argot chuckles.

ANOTHER HOUR PASSES, and we come to the place where I had been instructed to get off. The train is slowing down to a walking pace here because the track has been damaged by either sabotage or Allied bombs. I leap off the platform and roll.

I am on my own, hoping to find my way to the Leroys. My backpack is becoming heavy, feeling like it weighs a ton or two. I start getting anxious and light a match to look at the map. I do this sparingly because I don't want to attract a Boche patrol. Finally, I come upon a stone marker: Breteuil 22 km (nearly fourteen miles). I am headed in the right direction!

Suddenly, I hear a terrible racket behind me. Instinctively, I jump into the ditch. A German half-track, with its headlights off, is passing by at full speed. I hold my breath, listening. But thankfully, the Boches disappear into the night. I get up cautiously and start walking again.

A thunderous noise startles me, and I hit the ditch again. It's a convoy of Tiger tanks. I don't know how many pass me, but they slow down and stop close to me! I hear German voices. One is walking close by and stops to relieve himself. *I am dead*, I think. Even though it feels like hours, a few minutes later the convoy is gone.

BY DAWN I AM OFF AGAIN, walking through a dense forest. My feet hurt and I'm as hungry as a skinny wolf. It's time to take a break. I sit behind some big oaks and open the pouch. There is a feast before me— bread, raisins, dried prunes, an onion, and a small can of corned beef. Bless you, my railroad friends! It is a meal fit for a king, washed down with the watered-down wine in the canteen.

The full belly makes me drowsy, and I curl up under the tree, sleeping until around noon. Back on the road, the next sign indicates that Rugles is only twelve and a half miles away. My grandparents' villa is located outside of Rugles, so I am almost there. That promise keeps me going.

I arrive late in the afternoon, completely exhausted, just able to drag myself to the gate and ring the bell.

"Pierre!" Mathilde covers her mouth with her hand, horrified at my condition. For the next few weeks, it is difficult for me to even stand up. I can see my feet, but they seem so far from my head and they don't seem to work. My days are spent eating and sleeping, and when I am finally able to go outside, I lie in the grass, soaking up the sunshine.

FINALLY, ONE DAY I AM feeling strong enough to walk to a nearby farm. "Do you like milk, Pierre?" the farmer asks me.

"Sure do!"

"Take that with you." He hands me a bucket full of fresh milk from the cow.

"Bring the bucket tomorrow morning, and I'll give you another full one. We can't ship anything, so we have to milk the cows and throw the milk away."

"What a pity!" I mutter to myself, thinking about the children in Paris who are starving.

I sit under a tree and gulp down a gallon of milk. An hour later, I drink another gallon. Maybe I'm exaggerating the amount, but I do empty the bucket! I return the following day, and the farmer has a bucket of milk waiting for me. I still remember the half-inch of cream lying on the surface of that fresh milk. A few weeks of this diet, and I am strong as a bull. That farmer saved my life.

Grandfather Leroy has obtained local government papers legitimizing my presence in the village, including real alimentation coupons. The mayor of the village has made me promise that there will be no resistance activities while I am staying there. It seems the Boches have taken to shooting the mayors, city council members, and teachers in these villages if the underground activities get too intense for their liking.

As I continue to recuperate, Mathilde and I are becoming close friends. I start doing a few chores—gardening, caring for the rabbits, and constructing a couple of beehives.

ONE DAY I have a surprise visitor. Théo Schmied's wife is standing at the gate with a bicycle. Three medium suitcases are tied to the back luggage rack, and a bigger one is lashed up front across the handlebars. She looks completely exhausted.

"Madame Schmied, I'm so glad to see you. Please come in."

"Pierre, I thought I'd never make it! I'm so tired."

Before I can finish introducing her to my grandparents, she begins to cry.

"I'm so ashamed to intrude like this but . . ." She buries her head in her hands, unable to control her sobs. Finally she is calmed down enough to continue. "In Paris, my son and husband are starving. I've come here in hopes of finding some food." She begins to cry again, and her next words are phrases, not complete sentences. "My child is ill . . . any kind of food . . . anything edible . . . at any price." She brushes the tears from her cheeks. "I have money to pay you."

Mathilde places a glass of fresh cider in front of Madame Schmied, and after a drink, she explains that because the trains have been taken over by the Germans, her only option was to ride her bicycle from Paris to Normandy—150 kilometers (approximately ninety miles). Even my journey doesn't compare to hers on a rickety bicycle held together with chicken wire, the tires filled with cork since the inner tubes are missing. Besides, I had some food to keep me going. But nothing was going to stop her from trying to complete her mission for her family. Her undaunted courage makes my grandparents and me begin to cry too.

Madame Schmied recuperates for a week at my grandparents' house, enjoying the same wonderful milk that had brought me back to life. Once she feels strong enough, there is no delay—she wants to get back to her family as quickly as possible with her four suitcases, now containing beans, potatoes, lentils, salted pork, a small smoked ham, carrots, cabbages, flour, and butter melting in glass containers. It is such a heavy load for her on a wobbly bicycle. I am moved by her sacrifice, bravery, and love for her family.

As soon as she leaves, I go into the woods and speak out loud and clear. "God, it's me, Pierre. Please look after Madame Schmied. Keep her child alive and see that she makes it safely to Paris with her suitcases. Please!" Looking up, I see the pure sky through the trees. I hope He is listening to me up there. "Thank You in advance. Thank You a million times."

It's not much, but it's all I can do to help her. (Thankfully, I will learn much later that she did make it back safely to her family with the food.)

THE GERMANS ARE increasingly taking over everything. Now we have no train, no gazogène bus, no mail, no electricity, no newspaper, and no private radios.

One day when Grandfather Leroy is visiting friends, I finish my usual chores, spend time studying my English, then join Mathilde at the table for lunch. As we are eating, she says, "Pierre! I have to tell you something important."

"Did I do something wrong?" I ask.

"No! No, not at all," she assures me, smiling faintly. "What I'm about to say is going to be very difficult for you, but I think that you should know." There is a long silence. She takes a long deep breath and then exhales, setting herself to a hard task.

"This is strictly between you and me. Your grandfather disagrees with me. But I know. I was there."

There is another silence as she searches for her words.

"You are not our grandson, Pierre," she states firmly, but kindly.

I have come to admire Mathilde during these months together. To me she is 80 percent Paris concierge, 10 percent Aurora, 10 percent Tata, and, for good measure, an extra 100 percent honest Mathilde.

By now I am used to the surprises of my dysfunctional family, so even though I am taken aback at her pronouncement, I recover fast.

"How do you know that?"

My tone is as straightforward as hers. *Finally, someone with the answers who is willing to talk!* I think.

"I was there when you were born on rue Lecuirot in Paris. My son, Camille, and Louise were no longer living together. He was working on an art project in Nice at the time. Jean Matisse was one of Louise's neighbors in the apartment building where she lived." Mathilde stops to take a sip of cider.

I lean forward. I am all ears.

"We had heard rumors that your mother and Jean were more than friends. But the way he was pacing back and forth was almost as if he were going to give birth himself. When he and your mother chose your names together, I realized that this was more than a friendship. They were obviously in love—even a fool could see it."

She pauses to look at me.

"Camille and Louise's marriage had been stormy from the start. Right after your birth, your mother filed for divorce against my son. As soon as she was free, she married Jean Matisse."

"How do you know for sure?" I ask. I want this matter settled right here, once and for all.

"After your birth, your mother confided to me . . ." She stops halfway through the sentence.

"What exactly did my mother confide to you?" I want to know. I *have* to know.

"Louise said, 'How sad that this child is born of true love, yet he is the shame of my life.'"

Cet enfant est la honte de ma vie. I am the shame of my mother's life.

"I'm not surprised," I say quietly. Somehow, I truly am not surprised. Nothing surprises me anymore.

"Surely someone must have remarked on how much you look like Jean Matisse. You must have noticed the similarities yourself. You're a bright enough boy." Mathilde pauses and waits, but I cannot speak.

"That was why it was so awkward when I first met you. When I saw you, I had no doubt in my mind that your mother was right. She knew who your father was—her lover, Jean Matisse."

It was a lot to take in, but I knew I loved Maman and Papa. They must have had their reasons to keep this from me. I know Papa loves me. *He is the only father I've ever known*, I think to myself. Inside, I know he loves me as his son and has never doubted it.

"My mother must have hated such dishonesty and deception," I say to Mathilde.

"I am quite sure she did, Pierre. I have nothing against your mother. She is a decent person who found herself in a bad situation. Jean, too. They clearly loved each other, but I believe that Jean's circumstances were controlled by the Matisse family. Mostly Jean's mother, I would guess. But please know you were loved from the moment you came into the world."

"Did Tata know?"

"She did. But she never wanted to interfere in her niece's affairs."

"Before she died, I sensed that Tata had something she wanted to tell me," I say, almost to myself. "Perhaps that was it."

"She probably would have in time." Mathilde nods.

"Pierre, you are a wonderful grandson, and I am happy to call you my own. However, it is precisely because I have come to love you that I cannot remain silent. I don't want to be part of a deception that robs you of the truth. Now that you know, it never needs to be spoken of again. You can be ours, with no secrets. The choice is yours."

I don't know what to say.

"You are welcome here for as long as you want to stay, for the rest of your life if you'd like."

I am still speechless.

"Camille is our only child, and he has no children. We have had no news of him since the Americans landed in Algeria."

Mathilde stares out the window. "Pierre, this war complicates everything," she says. "Soon, Normandy might find herself in the middle of a battlefield. Who knows what will happen next or who will survive to see the end? I thought that you had a right to know who your real father is. Maybe I am not the one who should have told you this. All I know is that now you know the truth, and it's yours to keep."

She looks squarely at me, her eyes shining with kindness and concern.

Finally, I find my voice. She has given me the truth, a gift I can never repay. I stand up and take her small weather-worn hand in mine, and returning her honest gaze, I reply, "Thank you. You were right to tell me the truth."

At that moment, Grandfather bursts through the door and says excitedly, "This morning, the Allies landed on our beaches and are only forty-four miles away. The Boches have declared martial law in Normandy. We are now on the battlefield."

It is June 6, 1944.

For now, surviving the war takes priority over everything else, even this new revelation about my identity. Still, numerous questions swirl inside my head. I know Mathilde wouldn't lie or have an ax to grind. I need to pull myself together. At the proper time, I will tackle this delicate subject about my father head-on with my mother.

Now more than ever, I vow to go to America, leaving all these bad memories behind me forever.

23

SPITFIRES, SHRAPNEL, AND ALL THAT JAZZ

To live is the rarest thing in all the world. Most people exist, that is all.

OSCAR WILDE

TWO DAYS AFTER D-DAY, there is no immediate change for us because the fighting is still on our doorstep. The Germans are moving east, but there are more of them every day, and it's a risk to go out.

"We might have to evacuate," Grandfather Leroy reports.

"Evacuate? Are you crazy?" Mathilde is going to have none of that. "Walking for days and being targets for exploding bombs and machine-gun fire. Never! Don't you remember what it was like in 1940 when the Germans first overran us? You hear me, old fool? Never!"

"But what's going to happen to us when we find ourselves in the middle of a war zone, Mathilde?" he replies, the worry lines on his forehead deepening.

"We'll survive as best we can in our own home." This lady knows exactly what she wants.

"Or die in our own home." Grandfather could be right.

"Right, or die in our own home, Louis. What do you think, Pierre?"

"I know that the exodus from Paris to Bordeaux in 1940 was horrible for Maman, Gérard, and me. I prefer to stick it out here. At least it's more comfortable."

"Pierre is right, Louis."

"That settles it then. We stay," Grandfather Leroy decides.

Mathilde flashes a beaming smile at me.

WE ARE ON the back lines of the Normandy battle, still under German occupation. For the most part, the German army hides during the day and moves their troops and equipment at night.

Twenty-four hours a day, there is a humming drone overhead from British and American planes, which have supremacy in the air. The Luftwaffe had been driven out of the clouds a month or two before. We are used to the sound. In fact, we really only notice when things are quiet, which is rare.

We try our best to ignore the war and live as normally as possible. For me, that means gathering grass for the rabbits, my regular chores, and continuing to polish my English. When I can, I take long walks in the woods and fields, in hopes of seeing what the Boches are up to.

I am sketching a landscape by the roadside one afternoon when I notice an odd-looking Normand with a trumpet under his arm. He stops and looks over my shoulder for a few minutes.

"Never put people in your drawings. They are nothing but trouble. Put more trees in this one. I like trees."

Then, with a salute, he introduces himself as "Désiré Lambert Against the Prussians."

Taking his well-polished trumpet, he blows me a lively military tune. I shake his hand. "I'm Pierre Against the Boches, and I prefer jazz."

"What did you say your name was?"

"Pierre."

"Peter the Great," he proclaims with a theatrical flourish.

"No, my name is Pierre," I try to correct the funny fellow.

"Look here, you! For me, you are Peter the Great," he commands.

No use arguing. For Désiré, that's who I am.

To the sound of an imaginary orchestra, he dances for a moment or two. He looks to be in his late fifties, a stocky fellow of average weight and height. He is dirty as can be and stinks to high heaven. A childish, mischievous smile lights up his face, which seems to have weathered a million storms. Désiré displays such total childlike abandon and kindness that he immediately puts me at ease. He could be a little crazy, or he could be a genius—it's hard to know.

"Now you can tell me if I'm wrong, Peter the Great, but I believe this is one of your favorite songs. Listen!"

A moment later he is playing "Stormy Weather." Since the Boches confiscated all the radios in Normandy, I have not heard music for ages. The melodious notes go right to my heart and bring tears to my eyes.

"How did you know it was my favorite song?"

"I am the village idiot, Peter the Great. We know these things."

"Get down!" I push Désiré to the ground and roll next to him.

Shee . . . shee . . . boom! Boom! The bombs seem to be falling directly above our heads.

A quarter of a mile away, a huge cloud of smoke mushrooms and obstructs the sun. Two small German cars speed past us.

"They got them. Hip, hip, hooray!" Désiré is jumping and pointing his horn at the passing vehicles, making machine-gun sounds.

"*Tac-tac-tac.* I'll kill you!" he screams.

One of the German soldiers catches Désiré's theatrics and shakes a menacing fist in our direction.

"What do you do for a living, Désiré?"

"I'm a carpenter. But in the last war I was a general. I had pigeons that sent love poems to my wife in Paris."

Odd, he doesn't look the general type.

"So you were living in Paris?" I inquire politely.

"Yes, until I returned from the war to my beautiful wife."

"How did you end up in Normandy?" I ask, curious.

"My wife left me for an admiral. After that, Paris was never the same.

Normandy is not the same either. Nothing is the same. Something is wrong, Peter the Great. Something is very, very wrong, but I don't know exactly what it is."

He turns his horn in his hands, wipes a tear from his cheek, and says, "Now I'm the village idiot, but I'm not as stupid as they think."

"I don't think you're an idiot, Désiré."

"Thank you. That's awfully nice of you to say, Peter the Great."

I like him, and I know Papa would like him too. Later I learn that he had been terribly shell-shocked in World War I and has been battling the demons ever since.

BECAUSE THE BOCHES use the power lines for their telephone communication, we have no electricity. The Nazis have taken total control. This means no telephone, no radio, no newspaper, no mail, no public transportation, nothing. We are cut off from the rest of the world. Worse, we have been ordered to keep all doors unlocked so that the German army can enter our homes at any time, day or night.

But how to get back at them? I explain a simple sabotage trick to my new friend, and he is a willing coconspirator. We place pins in the telephone lines to short them out. This can take days to detect, locate, and repair. Désiré enjoys asking the German soldiers what they are doing as they painfully check miles of wires. *If only they knew*, I think. But I'm thankful they don't.

One day I am by the roadside cutting tidbits of grass for the rabbits. I don't hear the amphibious car with two Boche soldiers inside until it stops next to me.

"Caen?" The driver gestures, asking for directions.

"What?" I answer, shrugging my shoulders.

"Caen!" the passenger repeats more loudly as he points his machine gun at my belly.

"Ah! Caen, why didn't you say so?" When machine gun is being spoken, I understand perfectly.

I use sign language and draw a little map in the dust, and they leave, heading in the wrong direction.

Later, when I am walking back home with my full burlap bag, I sense something is amiss. A quick look behind me confirms my premonition.

"Swine *Françouse!*" a Boche yells. The amphibious car is racing toward me, intent on running me over. The soldier with the machine gun is taking aim, but I am running in the ditch, and when the car goes off-road it bounces crazily. I hear the *tac-tac-tac* of the first gunfire, and out of the corner of my eye, I see specks of dirt popping up from the ground. Everything is rolling in slow motion, but I think fast. If I can make it to the woods, only a few yards away, I'm safe. They are catching up to me, but the field is bumpy. I know that Mister Schmeisser can't hit me easily under these conditions.

Between the forest edge and the field, there is a barbed-wire fence that I have to jump over. I'm running so hard that my heart wants to blow out of my chest. I jump, fall on the other side, and roll away. My legs are too weak to stand, so I begin to crawl. Suddenly I hear a bigger machine gun and the high-pitched sound of an airplane. *Tac-tac-tac.* A British Spitfire is above us.

The amphibious car is retreating, hugging the fence. It hits a heavy corner fence pole and then begins zigzagging to avoid the plane's bullets. A second Spitfire makes a pass, shooting at the vehicle. The car slows down and a Boche jumps out, disappearing over the fence into the woods. I can't see the driver, but suddenly the car is on fire and then flips over. I wait a few minutes to catch my breath and then take a detour back to where I dropped my bag of grass.

A neighboring farmer, who has witnessed everything, comes up to me. "That was a close one, Pierre."

My legs and hands are shaking, but I keep my composure. "Yes, it was."

It does feel good to be alive. I think of Papa and wonder if he would have been proud of the way I handled this crisis.

A WEEK LATER, I'm heading out of Rugles in luxury, pedaling a beat-up bicycle with only rims for tires. Apart from the Boches, the streets are deserted. A civilian gazogène truck sporting a white flag puffs uphill and passes me. I grab the side of the platform on the back to hitch a ride, although it's a bit uncomfortable and dangerous being so close to the smoky gazogène stove.

Even though I could have walked faster than the truck is going, I'm enjoying this. Suddenly, a lot of things happen very fast. The asphalt is breaking apart, then pieces of the truck begin flying off, and my bike folds underneath me. Merde! The next thing I know, I am flat on my belly kissing the road. A diving Spitfire is heading right for us.

That's when I see a ditch with a cement culvert. *Fantastique!* To this day, I still don't know how I managed to squeeze into that tight space.

The sound of the airplane fades away, and I can hear a woman screaming and a man swearing in German. A moment later, two planes make a second pass, but this time they don't fire. The woman is still screaming, but I don't hear the man's voice anymore.

Why does my left foot hurt? My hand is pressed against my left leg, and I can feel that it is sticky with blood.

"I lost my shoe," I say out loud.

I am jammed in this culvert, and I don't want it to be my coffin. It takes all my effort to twist and turn my way out, but I finally free myself.

Flames are coming from the engine of the truck, and the woman, one of three passengers, is still in hysterics. The driver is lying by the side of the road with his right arm in shreds. The German soldier is trying to calm the woman down. My bike is useless, and I can't find my shoe. I look at my leg and realize I have been hit by shrapnel, and there is a nasty wound on the sole of my foot.

As I search for my shoe, I notice ammunition boxes and food supplies in the back of the burning truck. The Boches are using civilian trucks to move their supplies, protected by white flags. When I see a German command car approaching, I decide it's wise to get out of here. This is not the time for introductions or tea. Using a large branch as a temporary walking stick, I limp to the doctor in Rugles.

"YOU'RE LUCKY," the doctor says, extracting small pieces of metal from my foot and knee and cleaning the wounds. "Nothing more than some superficial scratches and a little metal to remember your escapades today."

He hands me a roll of heavy cloth. "Wrap up your foot with this."

"Thanks, Doctor."

I know the less time I spend here, the safer it is for him.

He smiles. "In the last war, we used to call these Russian shoes. Now, go directly to your grandparents and stay out of trouble."

Before I go home, I need to make a stop. I recall there's a grave close to a destroyed Boche half-track. The reason I noticed the grave at all was because of the boot tips sticking out of the dirt. I need shoes, and the boots are made of heavy-duty leather.

I find the grave, thankful that the boots are still there, and improvise a shovel with a scrap of metal. The rotting body in the shallow hole smells horrible, and I turn away to vomit. I feel faint, but I only need to shovel a little more around the boots to pull them off.

"Sorry to disturb you, soldier. I don't mean any disrespect," I say. "I just need something on my feet." I hope he understands. Besides, like Papa used to say, a man has to do what he has to do, period.

It's almost dark when I finally finish. The boots are almost new, with hardly any mileage on them. Clutching my reward, I make my way home, hiding a few times from German vehicles passing on the road. I don't tell my grandparents any of the details of my adventure because it could potentially put them in danger. Papa has taught me well.

I clean the boots well, but until my foot heals I have to wear wooden clogs. Clogs are not the best for long-distance running, so I will need to stay put for a while and not plan any adventures that might need a quick getaway

Finally the day arrives for me to try on the boots. They fit perfectly. I don't know it yet, but I will wear those boots for the next four years.

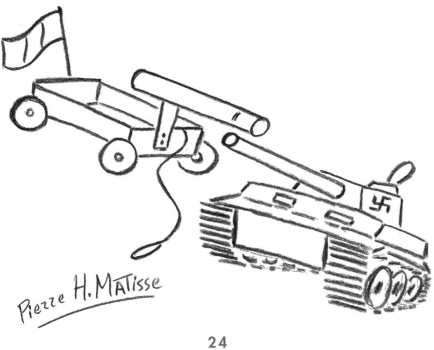

Pierre H. Matisse

24

KAPUT

Freedom lies in being bold.

ROBERT FROST

IT IS A CLEAR DAY, and Désiré is teaching me the fine art of finding escargots near Bois-Arnault's cemetery. As we search, my mouth is watering. I can already taste this French gourmet specialty. A quarter of a mile away to the west in a small field, a plane cuts its engine and, with landing gear retracted, force lands on its belly. We don't hear anything until the propeller hits an apple tree, which gets our attention.

I can tell from the markings that the plane is American, and as we are about to rush to the pilot's assistance, I see two German cars on the road.

"Désiré, look! Boches."

"Merde!" he says, spitting disgustedly.

"We have to get out of here. It's too late to help the pilot anyway."

"No, Peter the Great, we are going to help the pilot!" he answers firmly.

"Désiré, we are going to get shot."

The cars have stopped, and German soldiers are running toward the wounded bird. We hide behind a tall hedgerow to watch what happens. The pilot is slowly getting out of the cockpit, and I can see some blood on his arm. In no time at all, the Boches surprise him and brutally yank him out of the plane.

"The war is finished for him. He is now a prisoner," I explain to Désiré.

"No! They are going to shoot him," Désiré declares.

"They can't. It's against the Geneva Convention, Désiré," I argue.

"The Prussians do not care about convention. Any convention," Désiré says, making one of his peculiar facial expressions. "We'll have to stay close and hope for an opportunity to help him escape."

The Boches drag the pilot to one of the cars and then drive right by us to the nearest farm. Désiré and I follow at a safe distance and lie low near the farm all night, waiting for an opportunity to possibly rescue the pilot. It doesn't come.

Early the next morning, the Boches come out of the farmhouse with the pilot. They drive a few miles away and make him dig his own grave. We arrive just in time to see one of the soldiers empty a Schmeisser magazine into his body. *Killed in cold blood.*

"God will get them, Peter the Great," Désiré says with tears in his eyes and fists clenched. "They won't get away with it forever. He sees all their deeds."

"I'll volunteer to help Him if I get the chance," I solemnly vow as we silently slip away.

LATER THAT DAY, we return to the huge plane—a P-47 Thunderbolt— which did not sustain much damage.

"I want the tailwheel to put on my wheelbarrow, Peter the Great," Désiré says, ready to scavenge.

"I need the radio and the earphones to get some news," I add.

Though the mayor of Rugles initially made me promise to have no part in the resistance, he recently had a change of heart and asked if I knew how to rig radios. When I answered yes, I was given a new dual role—the official installer of illegal antennas and concocter of radios made from anything and everything I can find. I have built a number of crystal radios that operate without electricity. If I can put my hand on the plane batteries and radio, I can just imagine the mayor's delight when I present him with the real thing!

"Let's go for it," we utter in unison, making plans to return in two days.

IT IS A RAINY MORNING when we set out, armed with a hammer, wrench, and chisel. We carelessly walk out in the open, and about ten feet from the plane, a voice calls loudly, "Halt!"

The ominous sound of a rifle bolt loading a round freezes our blood and our movements.

Désiré and I slowly hold up a hand as we turn toward the voice. Our other hands are clutching the burlap sacks over our shoulders. Mine has two German grenades and a British Sten gun in it. Désiré has the tools, his trumpet, and a pistol. *This is the end of the line.* Two Boches are standing there, a young one about my age, the other possibly in his early sixties. The young one is pointing his Mauser straight at us, ready to fire.

"Terrorists!" he tells his companion.

"*Nein!*" the old one answers, pushing Junior's rifle up so the shot goes above our heads.

"Nein! Nein!" says Senior Boche.

Désiré is talking fast in German. Senior answers with a smile, and the tension eases. We are still holding our bags, and amazingly, they don't grab and search them. Junior has closed his mouth, but he is still pointing his gun directly at my belly. I don't understand a word of what is being said. Désiré opens his bag and pulls out his horn. *Is he going to play a tune?*

"Nein!"

They don't seem to appreciate music.

After a few minutes, Désiré's perfume must get to them, and they let us go. Slowly we walk away. I expect to be shot in the back at any moment, but it doesn't happen. *Whew!*

As soon as we are out of earshot of the Boches, Désiré says, "We'll come back tomorrow."

"Are you crazy?" I ask . . . and then remember who I'm talking to!

"The old one told me they are retreating this evening. Tomorrow will be safe. Are you afraid, Peter the Great?"

"Me, afraid? You must be kidding, Désiré. I am only slightly petrified."

My instinct is to take care of my friend, but he is an adult and I'm a kid. Granted, he is a loony adult, but I think that works to his advantage.

SENIOR BOCHE WAS telling the truth. When we return to the plane the next morning with our burlap bags, the Germans are gone. It's time for us to get to work.

The Thunderbolt has the pilot's name written on the fuselage: Lt. Lloyd. I utter a silent prayer for this dead pilot. (I've never forgotten his name. I thought maybe someday I would be able to tell his family what had happened to him. How naive that seems now, considering the millions of lives lost during the war. Yet I felt, in some way, a sense of responsibility because I had witnessed his unlawful murder at the hands of the Nazis.)

After inspecting the plane, I grumble. "I can't see any earphones, and getting to the radio isn't going to be a piece of cake either," I mutter to Désiré.

"Help me with the tailwheel first," he pleads.

I start to hammer at the mechanism.

"Amazing! Look at the quality of this stuff, Désiré. How can we get it out?"

"You go inside the fuselage, and I'll work from the outside."

"There's a big steel plate in the back of the cockpit. Impossible!"

"We'll chisel a hole in the fuselage, Peter the Great."

I work my way inside the fuselage, which is a tight space even for me, and I see the shiny cylinder attached to the rear wheel. Just then, I have a feeling that something is not quite right. *Am I getting claustrophobic?* I have the jitters and try my best to calm down.

Boom . . . boom . . . What is that?

"Get out! Get out!" Désiré screams.

I abandon the tools and scramble to get out of the plane. My shirt gets caught and Désiré tears it to free me. On the way out, I scratch my side against a piece of twisted aluminum.

"Planes!" Désiré shouts.

We run as fast and as far as we can, then flatten ourselves on the ground.

Tac-tac-tac . . . *boom* . . . *shee* . . . Once. Twice. And then another time. Three American planes are destroying *our* plane. The Thunderbolt is in flames.

As we watch the fire, Désiré laments. "My wheelbarrow wheel is gone!"

WE COME BACK again the next day. The only part of the plane left intact is the tail end. It takes us the whole day to chisel Désiré's tailwheel out, but we do. At least one of us is happy.

On our way back to the village, we come across civilian war refugees. An old man is pushing a wheelbarrow full of his belongings, with a little boy around six or seven walking next to him. I can see they are tired. The old man sings an old French song to keep the boy's spirits up. "The oil painting, / That is beautiful. / But it's more difficult, / Than watercolor painting."

Désiré takes out his horn and plays the tune. The old man smiles, and the boy seems absolutely charmed.

We all sing the song together.

"The war is a few miles to our back. Our house has been destroyed," the old man explains as they continue on.

Désiré is wiping tears from his eyes, and so am I.

THE NEXT MORNING, a German Red Cross bus loaded with British and American wounded prisoners drives slowly by the house. *Are we losing the war?* It's hard to know for sure. In the afternoon, I see hundreds of German soldiers on foot retreating east.

"That's it. *They* are losing the war. We should be liberated at any moment," I tell Grandfather with confidence.

It must be about midnight when a plane's engine wakes me up. When I hear the engine being cut, I immediately think that the plane has been hit. Suddenly a parachute flare lights up the whole countryside.

What's going on? I wonder, hopping around on one foot trying to get my pants on. I climb out the window and down into the yard to enjoy the show.

By the flare's eerie light, I can see the plane gliding down. The pilot makes a pass over the road, then guns his engine to climb, and disappears in the dark night.

A moment later, I hear a tank, probably a German Tiger, about a mile up the road. *Only one tank? That's odd.* Usually they travel in convoys, covering one another. An isolated tank is a sitting duck.

The mechanical rattle is coming closer. I can't help but smile with satisfaction when I hear that the motor is quacking irregularly. *That's why he's alone—a straggler with engine trouble!* The plane must have been looking for him to finish him off. The tank backfires loudly; then there is silence.

Perfect. He must be stranded between me and the forest, smack-dab in the open. It will soon be daybreak, and the Allied planes will fry him for their breakfast.

"Kaput, Mister Tiger," I say to myself.

Merde! The blasted machine restarts, although it doesn't sound good. I am hiding behind a big bush, and now I can see the Tiger and smell the dying machine's oily fumes. *If only the plane would come back. One pass, and the Tiger would be dead.* I can see the silhouette of the Boche commander standing in the tank's turret, swearing like a madman. If I had a flashlight, I could signal the plane. But unfortunately I don't.

The infernal war monster turns off the road a hundred yards from me, taking cover under four big trees shading a wayside cross. *The Boches will stay here until they fix the engine.* I sneak back home and peer out my bedroom window. I can see the tank clearly. It's difficult to go back to sleep because I'm anxious to see what will happen next.

AS SOON AS I WAKE UP, I am back in my hiding place to peek at the Tiger, which is covered with tree branches. Only the menacing long gun is sticking out. The Boches are up early too, and judging from their efforts to hide the massive machine, perhaps they never went to sleep. Other than the noise of clanking tools accompanied by lots of swearing, the morning passes in relative quiet.

The disabled tank is situated between our estate and a neighboring farm, where the Rouville family lives. Madame Rouville is pure Gypsy, and her Normand husband is quite a character. Over time we have become good friends. I especially enjoy their two boys, about five and eight years old, because they are a second and third edition of Pierrot Tatiou the Terrible.

Like the Jews, Gypsies are being hunted down by the Nazis for annihilation. But there is a big difference. The Jews cannot believe this is really happening to them and remain an easy target. If the Nazis arrest a Gypsy, all the others immediately disappear, making sure to take Adolf's wallet with them. Stealing from the Germans is one of their pleasures.

From my vantage point, I see the older Rouville brother sneak up a couple of times to look at the tank. I am tempted to reveal myself, but I know it is safer for both of us to stay hidden. Still, I am certain that his reconnaissance means he is up to something. In the early afternoon, I watch the escapade begin. Actually, I hear it before I see it. Something is being dragged in this direction.

Moments later, a mini-tank made of old crates and camouflaged with some branches appears, pulled with a rope by a young infantryman— the older Rouville—wearing a kitchen pot helmet. *Ah, almost like the one I had for my short aviation career.* The baby Tiger has a nasty-looking gun fashioned from a rusted stovepipe, pointing straight toward the enemy.

The tank commander is the younger brother, banging on an empty tin can to skillfully imitate the backfiring engine of its larger counterpart, and swearing in a guttural German voice. I can't help but smile, admiring their creativity and attention to detail.

The subversive tank passes near the Tiger. The Boches are too busy with their own troubles to notice the small intruders. The boys turn around and make another pass. No reaction. Next, the kids take out a few tools and proceed to bang on their tank with a chorus of swear words. Still nothing happens. That's when Désiré appears around the corner with his horn tucked under his arm. I can see that he likes the setup immensely.

In a panic, I run from my hiding place to get the kids out of harm's way before all hell breaks loose. But just then, loud and clear, Désiré announces his presence and sounds the charge. Now the Boches are paying attention.

"Swine Françouse!"

With my hands up and facing the Germans, I stand between the two tanks.

"Désiré, get the hell out of here. Run, Désiré! Run!" I scream, expecting a deadly burst from a machine gun.

Behind my back, I can hear the two boys imitating the *tac-tac* of machine-gun fire. They seem to think that it's all a wonderful game. Since the boys believe I'm attacking the Boches openly by standing between them and the enemy, they decide to cover me.

"Village idiot! Not dangerous," I try to explain to the stupefied Germans, making a circle with my finger near my head to indicate craziness.

The kids are throwing all kinds of trash at the real tank, and I get caught in the cross fire, hit in the back of the head with an empty can. Ow! The Germans start laughing and give me time to get the kids out of harm's way. Désiré salutes me and disappears.

A few weeks later, the same boys are in the nearby forest when they come upon three German soldiers, who have gotten separated from their retreating army. The soldiers are ready to surrender and put their hands up high over their head. These lost German soldiers prefer this minor humiliation rather than retreating with their defeated army. It is quite a sight seeing the boys proudly march their prisoners through the main street of the village.

A month later, when things quiet down temporarily, I find the same Tiger by the roadside, miles away from where it had first broken down. It has a five-inch hole in it, compliments of a plane rocket. Just behind the massive steel wreck are four shallow graves.

ONE NIGHT AS I AM lying in bed, I can hear big guns firing in the distance. The next thing I hear is a German ammunition train being blown up, lighting up the sky. The wreckage burns for days.

A few nights later, I wake to somebody shaking me and shining a flashlight in my eyes. A German, waving a pistol barrel right under my nose, is ordering me to do something.

I get out of bed and quickly put my pants on. A thick-chested German sergeant pushes me into the main room, where my terrified grandparents are seated in a corner, with two young soldiers pointing rifles at them. One guard looks plump like a pumpkin, while the other one looks like a student, totally out of place.

Thick Chest, an ugly brute, sits in Grandfather's armchair. Even on this throne, he'll never pass for royalty. He proceeds with his intimidation by slamming his handgun on the table, explaining to me in poor French that he can't get anything sensible out of the elders because they are stupid. I decide not to say what I am thinking, since he has the gun.

It's now between him and me, if the three of us are going to live or die.

"*Essen und trinken,*" Thick Chest declares flatly.

"*Verstehe nicht,*" I reply. "I don't understand."

He picks up his pistol and waves it at me.

"Verstehe," I say. The pistol goes back on the tabletop.

"Gut! Food. Drinks," he demands.

Pumpkin escorts me to the larder outside the kitchen, where I pretend to forage for a few minutes, knowing full well that we have nothing to eat.

"Nothing to eat," I try to explain to him. He pokes me hard in the ribs with the butt of his rifle. I have to find something for the Boches to eat, or they will kill all of us. Then I spot a big cast-iron pot and remove the heavy lid. It holds what looks like some kind of stew, but it doesn't smell too appetizing.

"Gut!" Pumpkin says.

I bring the pot inside with a pitcher of rancid cider that Mathilde has been saving to make vinegar. I've decided to serve only the best to our guests. Thick Chest motions that he wants to be served. While Grandfather and Mathilde, guarded by Student, watch silently, I put three glasses and three plates on the table with forks and spoons. Student and Pumpkin decline and ask for only water.

All the more for Thick Chest, who stuffs himself with cold stew washed down with rancid cider. After mopping up the cold gravy with a slightly mildewed piece of bread, he burps loudly a few times.

When I take a seat, Thick Chest barks an order, and Pumpkin hits me hard in the side with his rifle butt again, telling me to stand up.

"Fix tires," Thick Chest commands.

"With what?" I ask.

"Garage! Tires." Thick Chest is pointing his pistol at me, and he and Pumpkin push me outside.

Their big French four-door sedan, sitting outside the gate, has two flat tires. Once we go into the empty garage, I explain as best as I can, "Your troops stole our car in 1940. We have no car and nothing to fix your tires."

Thick Chest slaps my face, and at this moment, something clicks inside me. *I can be as much of a jerk as he is.* Obviously, I can't use violence, but I can be defiant and arrogant.

"*Allez en enfer*," I tell them. "Go to hell."

They both understand. Thick Chest can't believe what he has heard and shoves his menacing pistol in my face so hard that he cuts my upper lip.

"Go ahead! Kill me if you want, you rotten sausage," I reply calmly.

Pumpkin laughs, and Thick Chest tells him something that I don't understand, but it definitely doesn't seem to be flattering. Pumpkin goes back inside to Student and the grandparents. I am now alone with the brute.

"I need a horse to tow the car under the trees," he says gruffly in pig German and French, motioning with his hand.

"Horse?" I repeat.

"Yah! Horse."

He almost smiles, pleased that I understand him.

"Follow me." I gesture, and we go into the dark night. He needs me, and I am grinning from ear to ear.

"Shortcut," I say.

He stays behind me, occasionally poking his pistol in my back.

"Horse," he repeats over and over, becoming impatient.

"Yah! *Verstehe*. Horse," I answer.

Now I've got him where I want him. In a couple of apple orchards, I have made a few turns, and I know that he is completely lost in the dark.

"Horse!" he demands angrily.

By now, even this dumb Boche figures out that he has been had. So he throws a tantrum, swearing like the devil and gives me a little thrashing. I have to save my hide, so I point to a farm nearby.

"Gut!" Thick Chest exclaims.

When we get to the farmhouse, I knock on the door, with Thick Chest breathing down my neck.

A few minutes later, the farmer opens the door a crack, and I say, "The Boche wants your horse to tow his car off the road."

"Tell him to get lost," the farmer replies, slamming the door in my face. *No, I've already tried that line, and it doesn't work*, I think.

I try to explain to Thick Chest that the farmer's horse is sick. "We go to another farm," I suggest.

"Nein!" Thick says furiously, walking to a window and breaking the glass with the butt of his pistol. Then he shoots a round inside the dark room.

"Swine Françouse, come here now," he screams.

"Come right away, or the German is going to kill us both," I implore the farmer.

The door opens, and the farmer is shaking plenty while he puts on his trousers.

"Gut!" Thick Chest says, satisfied.

Over the next few hours, the car is towed off the road, parked under a large tree, and covered with branches. Since I cooperated, I hope that Thick Chest is going to let me go. Not a chance! He wants me to stay with him and makes it clear when he pulls out a machine gun. We begin walking away from the house.

Occasionally, we encounter a retreating German truck overloaded with soldiers that drives by slowly with its lights out. Thick Chest tries to flag them down, but he is waved off. No one has room for more soldiers.

As I continue walking with Thick Chest down the road, I am glad Papa is not here tonight. I am certain that one of us would have been killed. On second thought, we might have killed the three Boches between us.

My mind wanders back to a similar scenario at our home on l'avenue de Clamart. There was an air-raid alert, and I was on the sixth-floor balcony of the apartment with Papa. Maman and Gérard had gone to the basement shelter, but we wanted to watch the show.

A bus full of German soldiers had stopped in front of the building, and as they got out of the bus to get inside the building for shelter, Papa threw a lit cigarette butt over the balcony, which landed close to the bus driver. The driver looked up, and Papa saluted him. The Boche driver saluted back.

Suddenly, flak guns opened fire, and shrapnel fell all around us. The Boche driver nonchalantly looked up at us—he had no plans to run for shelter either.

Bombs began exploding, and the building was shaking. I was shaking. Only Papa and the lone Boche driver on the avenue were not shaking. The two adversaries were in a standoff, showing each other defiance and courage, very much like me and Thick Chest. *Yes! Papa would have loved this adventure tonight.*

A short burst from Thick Chest's machine gun shakes me out of my thoughts. He has shot a volley of bullets into the air to get the attention of a truck driver. He has had enough. Exasperated to the limit, Thick Chest is standing in the middle of the road, pointing his submachine gun at the truck driver as they trade insults. Finally, Thick Chest wins the argument.

The truck driver follows us in his vehicle to the hidden car, and I help Pumpkin and Student load the looted boxes and packages from the trunk of the car into the truck. Then Thick Chest gives me a swift kick and a less-than-complimentary good-bye. I reply in my best Italian sign language, adding, "Boches kaput!"

I can hear Pumpkin laughing and Thick Chest firing insults back at him as the truck pulls away.

When I arrive back home, my grandparents rush toward me, relieved that we are all still alive. As we hug one another and I sit down to catch my breath, Mathilde says, "Pierre, you fed the Boche the dog's food!"

We all burst out laughing.

Pierre H. Matisse

25

INTERLUDE

There are incalculable resources in the human spirit,
once it has been set free.

HUBERT H. HUMPHREY

IT IS MID-JULY 1944, and the war continues around us, with Allied planes being shot down by German anti-aircraft guns. Sometimes we see a parachute in the sky, and other times, only the smoke pouring out behind the disabled aircraft as it plummets to the ground. German soldiers, haggard and weary, are retreating east in trucks and on foot. The nights are lit up by flares, and the sounds of the big guns of the Allies' artillery divisions are coming closer.

A few days after my escapade with Thick Chest, a bomb falls near the village, and the call goes out to help a woman who is trapped in her house. She had been preparing lunch on the stove when the blast caused the roof of the house to cave in, pinning her underneath the rubble.

I join the rescue party and begin digging through the debris with everyone else. The woman is relatively calm, trying to direct us to her location. It seems like it takes hours to get her out, but in reality it is only a short time. She is badly burned on her face and arms from the stove but is grateful to be alive.

Lately, the Boches have been arresting civilians and making them perform temporary chores—unloading or loading trucks, digging graves, or patching up the craters in the road created by bombs. Whenever the German soldiers come too close for comfort, I choose to run. They have become unpredictable ever since the invasion. I have seen some senseless murders, including that of a child in the past week. Papa has told me on numerous occasions to stay out of the Boches' reach, and I have always placed great value in my father's wisdom and on my neck.

Still, I always want to know what's going on, so I never stray too far. I am careful not to walk on the road, usually following at a distance in the field alongside it. One beautiful summer morning, the road near the house is deserted, and everything is unusually quiet when I start out. No Boches, no planes, no gunfire—just silence.

After a while, I decide to cross the road. I drop down in the field and crawl to the ditch nearest me, checking carefully for any sign of anyone or anything. It looks safe, but as I begin to stand up to run across to the far ditch, I hear, "Stop!"

Did he say just say "stop"—in English? I raise my arms in front of a green hedge and watch as a big gun protruding from a bush comes from behind the hedge and runs straight toward me.

"I am a French civilian and speak English!" I scream at the running bush on wheels, which is actually a camouflaged small tank.

The bush stops and answers me. "Have you seen any German soldiers?" Then one of His Majesty George VI's soldiers jumps out from behind the leafy bush.

"None since yesterday morning," I answer.

"How were they?"

"Beat up, and headed toward Paris."

"You can put your arms down," another soldier says, approaching me.

"Gentlemen, I am glad to see you."

"Is there any German defense in the area that you know of?" The voice is clipped and authoritative.

"Maybe in the forest near Breteuil. In this immediate area, they always move in and out fast," I explain.

"We are only an advance patrol. We can't go farther than here," a lieutenant says.

"I hope that you aren't going to turn back!" I exclaim in alarm.

"Your English isn't bad, young fellow. What is your name?" he asks.

"Pierre."

I am surrounded by British soldiers now. "A cup of tea?" one of them asks.

"With pleasure."

The tea is delicious and even has powdered milk and just a touch of sugar. I am literally tasting freedom. To this day, I have never tasted anything as good as this liberation day cup of tea.

I hear a radio crackling in the rolling bush.

"Could you do something for us?" the one in charge asks. He is dressed in a battle uniform, standing tall with dark, intense eyes that could bore right through you.

"Anything! I'll do anything to get the Boches out. And . . . it won't be the first time," I assure him.

"Not so fast, my good fellow," he says, laughing. "Who is the person in authority in the nearby village?"

"Captain Vion. He's not the mayor, but he was in World War I."

"Where does he live?"

"A couple of miles away, toward the Germans."

"Could you go and ask him to meet us here?"

"Yes," I say, always up for an adventure.

"Good! You are now our official emissary."

I proudly walk to Captain Vion's cottage, not caring if I catch a bullet at the last minute. I am in no-man's-land between the Boches and the British, and this is my heroic moment. Everyone is hiding, except me. Maybe Désiré isn't the only crazy one! *Wait until I brag about this to Papa.* Freedom! Perhaps now we can all be a family again.

The village seems deserted, and when I arrive at Captain Vion's

cottage, I ring the gate bell as hard as I can. "Captain Vion. We are liberated. The English are here. Come out!" There is no answer, but I know
he is there. I open the gate and knock on the front door. Silence. This is
important, so I enter the house.

"Monsieur Vion, an English officer wants to talk to you."

"Close the door, idiot! Are you trying to get us shot?" Captain Vion
emerges from a dark room armed with a huge revolver.

"The English want to see you—immediately."

"How many are there?"

"A dozen or so!" I reply.

He frowns. "That's only an advance patrol. The Boches can launch
a counterattack at any moment. It's too dangerous," he says, not liking
the odds.

"It's not possible. The Boches are too busy running with their tails
between their legs," I declare with the flamboyant attitude of a hero who
knows his stuff. "Besides, I walked here in the open without any trouble
whatsoever."

"Fool! Then why can't your British officer come here?"

"The lieutenant told me their orders are not to advance any farther.
You were in the last war. Surely a soldier following orders makes perfect
sense to you, Monsieur Vion."

"I don't like it," he mutters. "But let's go. Heroes die young, so you
walk behind me."

As he slides his revolver under his belt, Monsieur Vion gives me a
friendly tap on the back. The veteran had seen hell in World War I, so
he knows the true reality of war. A little while later, we join the English
patrol.

I begin to translate to Captain Vion what the officer is saying, and as
we are talking, more small tanks and armed vehicles begin to approach.
A Jeep pulls up beside us, and an English captain in the passenger seat
has a map unfolded on his knees. After introductions, he says, "Explain
to Mister Vion that we want to occupy this field, this one, and this one
out there," pointing to the map.

I translate the captain's message and the answer from Monsieur Vion.

"That will be fine. I'll make the arrangements with the farmers to get their cows out," he promises.

The captain puts Monsieur Vion's mind at ease when he adds, "We will not enter nor occupy any house in this village. Our camp will be in the surrounding apple orchards."

Now lots of military trucks are coming, and eventually a regiment of 150 men sets up camp. Monsieur Vion and I are invited to ride in the Jeep with the captain for the liberation announcement. Bois-Arnault, with a population of about five hundred French souls, is liberated. We are free! The war will rage on brutally for almost another year, but not in our backyard, not under our noses. For us, the war is over.

No more shooting.

No more bombing.

No more Nazis.

No more fear for our lives.

Rapidly, I make friends with the English soldiers, who give me a pair of pants and a shirt, almost making me look like a regular limey soldier. I have a new position as the interpreter for our Allied friends.

The English soldiers give me tea, biscuits, and canned meat, which I bring home to my grandparents. They rejoice at the news and enjoy the liberation meal.

IN RUGLES, a few farms away from our village, late-to-the-game French resistants are arresting the women who have slept with the Boches. These disgraceful men, whom I haven't seen anywhere near danger for the last few months, are now busy shaving the heads of these unfortunate women, painting swastikas on them, and parading them through town. It reminds me of *The Scarlet Letter*.

If that isn't enough, these after-the-fact buffoons wearing armbands arrest anyone suspected of being collaborators or black-market business-men. I want to tear their armbands off and bend their arms back until they break! The true resistance patriots quietly continue to deal with those who have sold out their country when necessary. These French collaborators had been getting supplies for the French people and were taking great risks doing so. I have only praise for their activities. However,

I despise these fools who suddenly appear when the danger is gone and strut around like they are the heroes.

I am mystified by a man who won't stand up for his country and family, who is not willing to face an armed enemy invader. Even more mystifying is the one who has the audacity to pop up and place blame on other war victims after his hide has been saved by the real patriots.

"What fools! Women are for poems, love, and peace," Désiré declares in disgust.

"Yes, and the black-market merchants don't shoot back," I add.

(It will be the last time I ever see Désiré. But in my mind I will always hear him playing "Stormy Weather" just for me.)

I'm not surprised when the after-the-fact fighters ask me to join them.

"No," I reply. "But I'll give you a gift of a German grenade and my Sten gun. The gun will look good on you. With the Boches gone, I don't have any more use for it."

I also politely decline to participate in their hairstyling activities.

"You disappoint us" is their last word to me. Not as much as they disappoint me.

AS REGIMENT AFTER REGIMENT arrives every day, the fields surrounding the village of Bois-Arnault become a tent city for thousands of troops, camped for miles in each direction. The traffic on the road is unbelievable. Day and night, nonstop, vehicles are moving soldiers, ammunition, guns, and tanks of all sizes. Huge trucks are carrying pontoons to be used as portable bridges across rivers.

I travel with the English captain in the immediate area and quickly realize how fortunate our village is—the destruction around us is extensive. Mile after mile, there are burned German convoys destroyed by Allied planes and dead bodies rotting in the summer sun. German prisoners are put to work digging the graves.

Grandfather Leroy and Mathilde accommodate some of the civilian refugees who have been pushed out of their homes by the bombings and the senseless horrors of war. I have not forgotten when I was a refugee and how the Marrots opened their home to Maman, Gérard, and me. However, we had been evacuated in luxury, with a car and a chauffeur.

As I watch loaded trucks heading east toward the front lines and empty ones returning to the Normandy beaches to reload war supplies, an idea forms.

"Captain, is there any way that we can fill those empty trucks with refugees?"

"It's a good idea. However, I'm not sure that the transport command will approve."

"Can I try?" I ask.

The captain smiles and says, "Here's a pass and a recommendation from me that you can show the transport command. You can use my Jeep and driver, but I can only spare it once in a while for a morning."

I get right to work, contacting the transport command. I didn't have to persuade them to implement the plan, but they did have one condition: I must get the civilians to a refueling pit stop. With the daily convoy schedule in hand, I am in business . . . except for one small problem. I need a truck, rather than a Jeep, to get the refugees there in time.

I approach my captain friend again.

"First, you borrow my Jeep, and now you want a truck! Are you never satisfied, young fellow?" he says, teasingly, but with a smile that says yes.

The repatriation operation gets under way. On the way to the front, the truck drivers tell me which villages are intact and which ones have been destroyed, and I pass on the information to the refugees. Then I organize transport for the ones who have a home to return to.

At one pit stop, someone calls my name. A woman ready to board a truck says, "My grandmother wants to kiss you."

The grandmother is being carried by two soldiers because she can't walk. I fight to hold back my tears, for the frail woman reminds me of Tata.

Helping the refugees makes me feel good about life again. Finally I have a remnant of hope for the future and something to distract me from worrying about the fate of my family in Paris. Are they still alive? It has been weeks since our village has been liberated, and we still have no communications in or out of the area.

IN LATE AUGUST 1944, with the last refugees safely on their way, I hitch a ride to Paris, which has finally been liberated.

As we enter the city I see bullet holes in walls and bouquets of flowers or ribbons marking where a French person fell. When I reach the apartment, I anxiously knock on the door.

"Maman, Maman," I call out, hoping against hope that she will answer. Immediately, the door flies open, and Maman is standing there with tears in her eyes. We share a long embrace until we are pulled apart by Papa and Gérard, who embrace me too. Everyone is safe.

I only have a short time to be with them, but what a precious time it is. The four of us can't stop hugging one another, and we all talk at once. We share stories of how we survived and savor the wonder that we are together after so many close calls. We have no way of knowing what tomorrow will bring, but we are here today. It is a day full of laughter and tears as we reminisce about old times and loved ones who have been saved or lost.

Late that evening, on the ride back to Normandy, I reflect on how blessed I am to have found my parents and my brother alive and well. Silently, I give thanks to God.

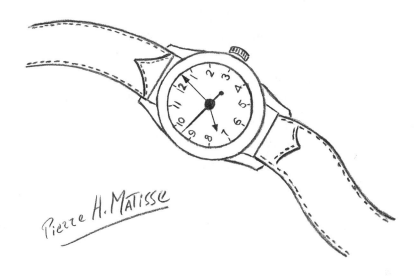

Pierre H. Matisse

26
RITE OF PASSAGE

I haven't got it yet, but I'm hunting it and fighting for it, I want something
serious, something fresh—something with soul in it! Onward, onward.
VINCENT VAN GOGH

A FEW WEEKS LATER, the Leroys receive a card from the Red Cross with
news about their son, Camille—the person who is supposedly my father,
but, according to Mathilde, is not. He is alive and serving somewhere in
Charles de Gaulle's Free French Army.

Before we know it, this same stranger shows up at the gate, dressed
in an American uniform. He knocks at the door, and Grandfather Leroy
lets him in. Mathilde is delighted to see her son and introduces Camille
to me. I recognize him from photographs I have seen around the house,
and although I am respectful, I'm not friendly, and neither is he. Mostly
we are embarrassed.

We have nothing in common, neither looks nor otherwise. His eyes
are clear blue, while mine are dark brown like Papa's. I am much taller

than he is, something the grandparents had noticed years ago when I first met them. It is fairly obvious to me that we are not father and son.

The next day, during a meal, the grandfather quarrels bitterly with his son. Mathilde tries to put water on the fire, but it doesn't work. I have no idea what the two men are arguing about, and I could not care less. I feel nothing for this man, and his coldness makes it abundantly clear that he has no use for me, either. A few days later, he leaves for Algiers. When the war ends, he plans to resume teaching art there.

We don't say good-bye to each other. I am glad that this visit is over and done with and that we'll never meet again.

NOW THAT THE WAR IS OVER IN NORMANDY, I have to decide what to do next. It is green and peaceful here, and I love being able to take long solitary walks in the forest. The truth is, I am tired and need the serenity of the Normandy countryside and have no desire to return to Paris. I am a man and will find a job here. The Leroys are thrilled that I have decided to stay, but I insist on paying rent for my room when I start working. I am no longer a guest but a man who is on his own.

Because of the war, many businesses are short on manpower, and I easily find work as an apprentice in three different antique restoration shops—in Rugles, L'Aigle, and Breteuil. I have been approved by the French government to become an accredited *ébéniste*, an artisan skilled in rare woods and in design and sculpture, studying under these master craftsmen. I work from 8 a.m. to 6 p.m., six days a week. Each payday, I hand my check to Mathilde for room and board, and she gives me a little spending money. She also makes me a sandwich for lunch to take to work each day.

At first, I travel back and forth on a bicycle—legitimately purchased!— but eventually I upgrade to a recycled German army motorcycle, minus the sidecar with its attached machine gun. I leave that on the battlefield for someone else to find.

For the next three years, beginning in 1944, I work and become skilled with the special tools of this trade, completing my ébéniste degree early. I am a specialist in the Louis XIII, XIV, and XV periods and register with the French government as someone who is authorized to restore antiquities.

Now I can actually begin to make repairs on buildings, such as churches, that were damaged during the war. In my spare time, I begin sketching again and keep studying English. I still plan to find myself a place in the sun in America someday.

Occasionally my restoration work brings me to Paris for research in the Louvre or other art archives. If time permits, I stop and see my parents for a brief visit. These are always at a moment's notice and last an hour at the most.

One time when I am at the Louvre, I attend an art exhibit featuring paintings and sculptures created by the disabled. I cannot believe my eyes—the Normand woman I had helped pull out of the caved-in house was one of the featured artists. Her face was scarred from the burns, yet she radiated such inner beauty. Even though her arms had been amputated, that didn't stop her—she painted with a brush held between her teeth. I could not have done any better with my two hands. What an inspiration!

IN 1945, World War II officially ends worldwide. Hitler commits suicide in April, the same month that Mussolini is executed with his lover and strung up in the streets of Milan, and Germany surrenders in May. Cities in Japan are leveled by the atomic bomb in August, and the Japanese surrender on September 2. Civilians all over the world are starving and homeless. Only Spain's dictator, Francisco Franco, continues an iron-fisted control of his country.

Sixty million people (or possibly millions more) have died during this war. Eleven million of these are men, women, and children murdered by the Nazis in their death camps—six million Jews and five million Russians, Gypsies, mentally ill civilians, and prisoners of war. Cities throughout Europe are completely destroyed, bombed beyond recognition. It will take decades to restore the physical damage and lifetimes to recover the rest.

EVENTUALLY, MY GERMAN BOOTS give up completely, just in time for me to join the French army and be issued new ones. Military service is mandatory in France, and young men must be on active duty for two to three years. In December 1947, I am in Paris to tell Maman that I'm joining the army.

"Pierre, the Matisse family has connections," Maman says. "Grandfather Henri can arrange for you to serve your military obligation here in Paris in the geographic office. Surely you have had enough of war."

I think for a moment, trying to find words to explain what I'm feeling.

"I don't want to upset you, Maman, but I don't want any privileges or favors from anyone."

Her face is pale, and I feel terrible that I am causing Maman more worry and pain. But I need to do this. She looks down at her hands and then walks to the open balcony that looks out over Paris.

"Promise me you won't go to Indochina." We have heard that Ho Chi Minh's soldiers are butchering the French army there.

"If possible, I will promise. Maman, remember. I am a man, and I want to be treated the same as anyone else. No special privileges."

I RETURN TO NORMANDY, and the French government offers me a deal. If I volunteer for a real man's regiment, a commando outfit, I will get to choose the place to sweat it out. The catch? It has to be outside of France, for a period between twelve and eighteen months. The recruiting officer in Rugles makes it sound like a dream come true.

I am rested now and restless for adventure. A vacation would be nice, and travel sounds even better. So I volunteer for a French commando paratrooper outfit in North Africa, keeping my promise to Maman to stay out of Indochina.

I bid the Leroy grandparents good-bye. Though we do not speak of it, I am and will be forever grateful to Mathilde for explaining and confirming the truth about my father as I set off on my new adventure.

ON MY WAY TO MARSEILLE, where the unit will embark for Algeria, I make a short stop at my parents' home. All of us are together and we have a wonderful dinner.

Papa could not have been kinder to me. We reminisce for the entire evening about my memorable mischievous acts as a child, and we all have a good laugh.

I tell Papa about Désiré, and Papa agrees that he would have liked him. As I entertain my family with my wartime adventures in Normandy, Papa comments over and over, "Those escapades were great!"

"No, Jean, they were *not* great. It was foolishness!" my mother corrects him.

"And now you are going to be a parachutist. That's something I would like to try," Papa says, ignoring Maman's last remark.

"Men! What fools!" Maman replies.

Papa offers all kinds of advice on how to conduct myself in the army, but one piece especially sticks with me.

"You have to watch out for the women," he tells me quite seriously. "Women of questionable virtue."

"I will."

"Good! Do you have a wristwatch?"

"No."

"You need a wristwatch to pass the time on long nights of guard duty. Take mine," he says, handing it to me.

"Thank you," I say, touched by his parting gift. Then I quietly thank him again, with one additional word, "Thank you, *Papa*."

Papa reaches out and hugs me. We linger in silent accord, two souls hungry for each other, clinging to what has been taken away from us.

I have only one father, and I want to bring the whole packet of dirty linen out in the open right here and now. But I can't, not now. I am not sure quite how to handle it—yet. However, one thing I know for sure—the first dinner we share as a family in four years, just before I leave for possibly another year and a half, is not the time. When I come back. *That's right*, I promise myself, *when I come back.*

Seeing that Papa is proud of me is enough for now.

"I want to accompany you to the railway station," Maman says as she begins to make her way to the door.

"No, Maman. I want to go alone."

"Louise, let him go like a man," Papa says with a smile and a wink at me, and one last big hug.

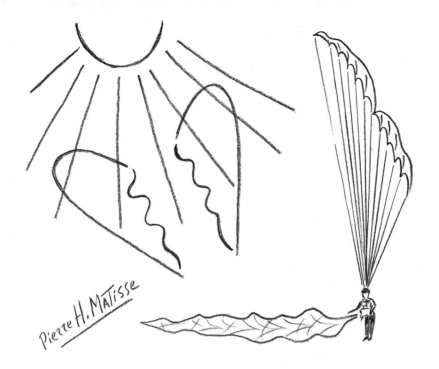

Pierre H. Matisse

27
ALGERIAN HOLIDAY

"I'm very brave generally," he went on in a low voice:
"only today I happen to have a headache."

TWEEDLEDUM, IN *THROUGH THE LOOKING GLASS* BY LEWIS CARROLL

THE JOURNEY FROM FRANCE TO ALGERIA is a sailor's nightmare. Not long after we set out—eight hundred men strong and transporting a herd of cows—we are caught in a torrential storm. Rather than being squeezed like a sardine in a can with men and seasick cows, I decide to stay on deck. I wrap myself in a tarpaulin and rope, tying myself to a handle on the cap of the hold. I will wait out the storm, hoping my adventure doesn't end before it begins! The voyage takes three days, twice as long as usual.

In 1948, when I arrive in Algeria, France is trying to hold on to a crumbling colonial empire with a handful of soldiers who are underarmed and outnumbered, yet expected to cover a territory twenty times larger than their home country.

It is more like being at the epicenter of a hurricane, where it is calm yet surrounded by menacing clouds of war ready to hit at any moment. This conflict, which will eventually escalate into all-out war, is based on hatred characterized by guerilla warfare, maquis fighting, terrorism against civilians, the use and abuse of torture on both sides, and counter-terrorism operations by the French army.

I find myself in the city of Bougie (present-day Béjaïa) in the region of Kabylia where the fighting is the toughest. This small town has two populations: the French colonists, who consider themselves the elite, and the Arabs living in the casbah, who are considered second-class citizens in their own country.

My home for eighteen months is Fort Barral, an imposing hilltop fortress that dominates the entire area. The location is a beautiful place to be stationed, with the city at our feet, sloping down gracefully like an Oriental carpet to the blue Mediterranean. This area used to be a stronghold for Barbary pirates, and I can understand why. There are some fabulous beaches bordering the Mediterranean, and when I can, I love swimming there. In the surrounding countryside, there are also Roman ruins to explore.

From the fort's parapet, I look south and can see the snow glistening on the tops of the Atlas Mountains, and beyond those peaks is the expansive and mysterious Sahara Desert. The sunsets are stunning here, and the night sky sparkles with what looks like millions of stars.

As a member of the commando unit, I wear a steel helmet on my head that is American, while the small 7.65 mm grease gun in my hands is French. This weapon is not as good as the American made Thompson we had in Antibes during the underground days with Papa. My uniform is a military hodgepodge, with pants courtesy of the English and the rest of my wardrobe American.

We are equipped with the remains of what every army left on the European battlefield, which means everything is outdated, in bad shape, or sometimes plain useless. The parachutes we are using have holes, marked by a circle drawn around them. Small holes don't matter much, but when the holes get too large, they need to be patched. Our planes are three-motor Junkers from the German Luftwaffe.

Our mission is to keep the lid on this powder keg and make everyone play nice together. France conquered Algeria more than one hundred years ago, and prior to World War II, nearly 700,000 French citizens had settled in the colony. But the Muslim population also increased dramatically during the same time period, and Algerian nationalism has since been on the rise. Now the situation is ready to explode into a nightmare of hatred between the Arabs quarreling with the colonials, who maintain authority, as well as other opposing tribes. France is flexing her muscles, hoping to keep her prized colony under control.

I am relaxing in my quarters with a group of former J3s, each one of us living through our own consequences of war at a tender age. Many of us were active in the French underground during the war. We don't need extensive training since we already know how to shoot, throw a grenade, and handle explosives. Above all, we know when to hit the dust at the slightest sign of danger.

"This reminds me of the Boches in Lyons," says my partner, a tall, skinny fellow born in Alsace. We naturally nickname him Alsace. He and I first met at the Don Bosco school, so my moniker of Mister Cran from my time there is mine here, too.

"Except now we are the Boches," another member of our group says, with a pronounced Parisian accent. In civilian life, he works with his parents, who own a delicatessen shop in Paris. This short fellow with red hair we call Delicatessen.

"I wonder if they have an underground movement fighting against us?" asks another Algerian occupation force member armed with a paratrooper folding rifle. This soldier is just slightly under the maximum weight accepted in this fighting outfit, and we give him a fitting name—Babar, after the famous French elephant of children's storybooks.

"Right. The Boches did this to us from 1940 until 1944," I say.

"Yes, but we have been doing it to the Arabs since 1848," Alsace replies.

I can't help but bristle at his words. "We are not the French Boches because we are not persecuting anybody like the Nazis did, and we are not putting the ones who oppose our political ideology in concentration camps. Besides, the Muslims have been invading and trying to take over Europe for centuries."

"Mister Cran is right. We conquered Algeria militarily, but we took them out of their barbaric Middle Ages and gave them access to French culture, education, a superb infrastructure, hospital health care, and much more," Alsace proclaims, giving me a quick nod.

"However, it seems because of their Islamic teaching, they reject any and all progress on any level," Babar adds.

"The recipe for social troubles is all here. The French have the best jobs, the best farms, the best of everything. Opportunity galore for the French and none for the Arabs," Alsace replies.

"They have no options other than to revolt," Babar deduces logically.

"Also there is this tricky religious problem—Muslims versus Christians to add spice to the whole scenario," Alsace concludes.

"Muslims versus everyone, including each other," Delicatessen says. "In France they say, 'France to the French.' I wonder what will happen when the Arabs finally say, 'Algeria to the Algerians'?"

"The same thing that always happens. The Arabs will kill as many of us as they can and eventually kick us out of North Africa," Alsace replies.

"Then they will return to their barbaric way of life, torturing and killing each other. A real friendly source they are," Babar says.

"History has a way of repeating itself," I explain, thinking back to Tata, who taught me this lesson when World War II was just on the horizon.

We are with our sergeant, behind a big machine gun mounted on a heavy tripod, in full view of everyone passing the Bougie street corner.

"I couldn't shoot an elephant at two meters in a tunnel with this folding piece of junk that you call a gun," Delicatessen informs the sergeant.

"Wait until you see the holes in the parachutes," a two-year veteran says, giving us a heads-up.

I realize this is the same setup we had with the Nazis in France. However, this time I am standing on the trigger end of the mean barrel.

I had arrived in North Africa with a little suitcase prepared for a relaxing vacation from my childhood war years. At least, that was what I was led to believe from the recruiter. I have five sketch pads and an assortment of pencils, ready to draw everything of interest in Algeria. I've also packed three books to prepare for my baccalaureate exams: an advanced English textbook with grammar lessons and literature selections, a good math textbook, and a philosophical French classic to learn what makes people tick.

Although I do have a good amount of free time over the next year and a half, I find out pretty quickly that a vacation is not exactly what the French army has in mind for me.

TODAY WE ARE on our way to Philippeville, a charming harbor city with one of the best grass-strip airfields in the area, for another parachute jump.

We take off in the German Junker, an aluminum corrugated beast with nonretractable landing gear, a Luftwaffe workhorse that saw Adolf Hitler rise up and go down.

"The main parachute is on your back. And just in case, the safety parachute is on your belly," our instructor points out.

"The main parachute is for you. The belly one is for your big ego," Babar wisecracks to Delicatessen.

The plane's engine fills the space with stinking oil fumes. I am slightly sick, or am I scared? Probably both. Besides, I don't trust this beat-up German bird.

"What if one of those Arabs has done a little personal adjustment of his own to the plane?" Delicatessen asks.

"That's what you have a para . . . para . . . chute for, clown," Babar answers with chattering teeth.

"Are you scared?" a cool and collected Alsace asks.

"Me! Sca . . . scared? Are you crazy?"

"They say it isn't any more dangerous than crossing a street in Paris," I mention casually.

Privately, I'm debating which is greater—my stupidity for trusting the French army recruiter and buying into the idea that this time of service is not dangerous or my stupidity for not taking Grandfather Henri's offer to help me get assigned to the geographic service in Paris.

Delicatessen peers out the window. "What are those ambu . . . bu . . . lances with red crosses waiting underneath us for?"

"Just in case," Alsace shouts.

"Yes, just in case," I yell in agreement. Although I try to control my fear, it's the "just in case" that concerns me.

"Go!" the instructor shouts, and one man dives out.

"I'm getting out of this flying outhouse," Babar screams, jumping out of the plane as if the tin bird is on fire.

I'm next. I clip my static line from the parachute to the cable that runs the length of the plane. As you jump, the static line tears open the parachute to free it. I've done this many times, and nothing seems different this time . . . until I jump.

That's strange. Usually I feel a strong pull when the parachute opens, but this feels different. I look up and can see that my parachute is only partially opened. One set of suspension cords has gotten draped over the back of the chute, and with my weight, the cords are cutting into the fabric. Half a canopy won't do.

"No time to even curse," I hear a voice say in my head.

I am going down fast. The safety parachute! I must open the safety parachute—right now!

"Calm down, or you are dead," the same voice says. "As you were instructed, make a nice little coffee table with your thighs. Don't panic, and don't look down."

The voice continues to tell me what to do.

"Good, now put your left hand on the belly parachute. Looking good. With your right hand, pull the rip cord's steel handle, and save the handle in your jacket pocket as you were instructed." *Who said anything about that?* The only thing I'm interested in saving is myself! I throw the blasted handle away.

"You shouldn't have done that. It's against the rules." This internal instructor is getting on my nerves.

"Damn the rules!" I scream. I know I will have to fill out a report explaining why I don't have the handle, but I'll worry about that if I survive. If I die, it's one less thing to do!

In order to save my neck, I have to get the safety parachute positioned so that it will catch the wind and balloon out. I look down, and the ground is coming closer fast. The parachute is not cooperating.

In a move that is a combination of temper and desperation, I throw the safety chute out in front of me. The parachute becomes an inviting queen-size bed. Flat and white, it lies there doing nothing. This isn't going to save my life. Then it collapses, and I can't see it anymore. The main chute rips in two.

Suddenly, my left leg is jerked up, and I'm tilted at an angle. Wincing in pain, I look up. The safety parachute has opened next to the half-opened main chute. Suspended by one leg, I suddenly am not careening anymore. I'm floating like a daisy in the wind, and seconds later, my backside hits the ground with a thud.

I lie there for a moment, thinking the worst, until I realize that I'm alive, and nothing is broken! I breathe a deep sigh of relief and whisper my thanks to God while collecting my wits and shaking off my fear. Thankfully, no one else has a problem with their parachute. In practice rounds, there have been times when we have laughed at each other, especially if someone lands in a tree and can't get down. But in the backs of our minds we know this is serious and could get us killed.

That night in the barracks, I think back to when I said good-bye to my parents and remember the look of envy on Papa's face when he told me, "I'd give ten years of my life to go parachuting out of planes with you in North Africa."

Yes, Papa, I would have loved to have you by my side today.

HALFWAY THROUGH MY TIME IN BOUGIE, it is national election day for the Algerians. I am patrolling the streets along with others, armed with submachine guns aimed at the citizens. Apparently, the election process is so crooked that the French government expects a lot of trouble. We only get some nasty looks and a few insults. There are no major incidents, and Algeria remains under French rule. The violence and war will come later when I am out of harm's way.

Soon after, I am on a different mission. At Mathilde's request, I set off to visit her son, Camille. I don't look forward to this visit and simply go to please Mathilde. I have a terrible time just getting a pass, not to mention trying to find his apartment from the address I had been given. His home is in a nice complex of condominiums in the upper-class section of Algiers.

I ring the bell for the concierge at his building and ask for Monsieur Leroy's apartment number. "Monsieur Camille Leroy is spending some time at his country villa," she says and kindly explains how to get there.

Once again, I am lost for a while, zigzagging up and down streets and being turned around several times before finally arriving at his residence. It is a lovely hillside villa with a spectacular view of the Bay of Algiers.

I ring the bell, and my "father on paper" opens the door a crack. Like an idiot, I stand there proudly, resplendent in my soldier uniform. The door is now half-open, and I can see him standing there, silent.

Then he says, "Ha! I see you have a parachutist decoration."

"Yes," I reply.

More silence. The door doesn't move.

"Listen," I say, trying to get out of this awkward situation, "I was just passing by, and I didn't want to leave the area without paying you a courtesy visit. Now that I have done so, I should probably go. Perhaps this is not a convenient time."

"Thank you. Good-bye" are the words I hear from the doorway. Before I can get out my good-bye, he closes the door. I have no trouble walking away.

ONE NIGHT WHEN WE ARE OFF DUTY, four of my buddies and I somehow get hold of a Jeep to do a little joyriding outside of Bougie, heading toward Constantine. We aren't out long before trouble comes. *Boom!* The Jeep hits a mine, and everyone but the driver is thrown out of the vehicle before it smashes into a wall. When I awaken, I am in the Constantine military hospital with a serious head wound, along with three of the joyriders, whose injuries were minor. Fortunately, the mine we hit was a small homemade explosive, not powerful enough to blow us sky-high.

At the hospital I see the consequences of the war raging in French Indochina, with the wounded being transported here from across the world, as well as the casualties coming from Algeria day in and day out by ambulance. Around me are young men, bandaged and writhing in pain from burns and wounds, some close to death. I see plenty of French foreign legionnaires, many with strong German accents, one whom I recognize from an encounter in Normandy from what seems like a lifetime ago.

When I am discharged from the hospital a couple of weeks later, the only way to get back to Bougie is to travel alone by train through Arab country. But before I leave, I take the day off, against doctor's orders, to explore the ancient city of Constantine on foot.

I cross the iconic suspension bridge Sidi M'Cid that spans the deep Rhumel Gorge carved out by the river of the same name below. I wander through the Arab marketplace and the casbah—noisy and colorful and aromatic. What a sight! The city has been a trading center since it was founded by the Phoenicians, and everyone wants you to buy their wares. It's hard to believe that I am in the twentieth century and not in the first.

Finally, I must bid the city adieu. The train, as usual, is packed solid with Arabs and Berbers, the corridor full of fatimas with their children, as well as some goats and a multitude of clucking chickens in woven cages. Cumbersome packages wrapped in colorful rags are everywhere.

As the train rolls out of the station, I offer the kids some of my sardines and bread. When I give them my entire chocolate ration, they scream with joy. A plump fatima with intricately tattooed feet smiles at me and gives me dates stuffed with almond paste, and the men sitting nearby offer me hashish. I have a difficult time explaining to them without hurting their feelings that, unlike Papa, I don't smoke anything.

At the first stop, some Arab teenagers on the platform are peddling delicious fried pastries, a kind of pretzel dipped in honey. I get off the train and buy a whole basket of them to share with the children in my car. We resume our journey, and I let one of the boys try on my paratrooper beret. Before I know it, they all want to try it on! The beret is passed up and down the aisle, finally returned to me after one of the mothers puts a few drops of perfume on it.

Arab kids, like children all over the world, have something special. They possess an innocence or *joie de vivre* that I find totally enchanting.

Night comes, and one by one, the children fall asleep, followed then by their mothers. The men wrap themselves in burnouses, long woolen cloaks, but they don't fall asleep. Like them, I keep an eye open.

In the corridor, a man sets up a small charcoal stove. A few minutes later he passes around cups of mint tea. I am offered one, which I gratefully accept.

Slowly, the Sahara Desert rolls by the window like a panoramic movie on a screen. Even though I am tired, I am too excited to sleep, taking in the exotic landscape. The Sahara sky is like no other. A city's sky is crowded by buildings. A forest has some degree of light but little sky to speak of because of the canopy of trees. The sky above the sea is unique unto itself, almost as if there is no difference between them.

But there are no appropriate words to describe the awe you feel when standing under the glorious heavens over the desert. Breathtaking is an understatement.

IN THE MIDDLE OF THE NIGHT, we stop at a station that looks more like a camel camp than a railway station. I feel like a time traveler again, just like in the casbah. Bedouin tents are scattered everywhere, and fires burning camel dung create small pools of light in the sand. A few dogs are roaming around, and through my open window on the train, I catch the pungent musk of the camels, which I find surprisingly pleasant.

An Arab is tending to his camels, and when he passes closer to the train, the band of cartridges crossing his chest gleams in the moonlight. Up close, I can see the rifle hanging by a strap on his back. He looks fierce but not menacing.

"Tuaregs and Berbers, desert pirates," one of my Arab companions explains.

One by one, the stars fade as the dark blue firmament lightens on the eastern horizon. It is the glorious moment of a new day, a sunrise like no other, an extravagant gift dressed in yellow, red, and orange flames.

"It's going to be a good day," I say to myself out loud. An Arab nods in agreement.

When we reach Bougie, the sun is high and burning hot like it only does in Africa. Intoxicated with beauty but aching with pangs of hunger, I check into my regiment just in time for lunch.

My days pass with doing what a soldier does: When I am not out on commando missions, I am guarding this and guarding that, always with an uneasy feeling that an uprising may occur at any moment.

But my inner battle rages on too. In the French army, roll call is done by last name. All day long, call for chores, call for guard, call for mail, call for patrol, call for inspection, call, and call, and call. Leroy, Leroy, Leroy. I hate it when I hear that name again and again, but I have no choice except to answer, "Present." I only want to answer to the name I've known since birth. Matisse—like my father, mother, and brother, period!

I have decided to confront my mother alone with what Mathilde has told me once I return to France. It is much too tricky to make a frontal attack on Papa and Maman at the same time. Besides, it would not be fair to Maman. When I am alone, I rehearse my delicate speech to my mother, trying different approaches.

Once this name business is settled, I will set off for America.

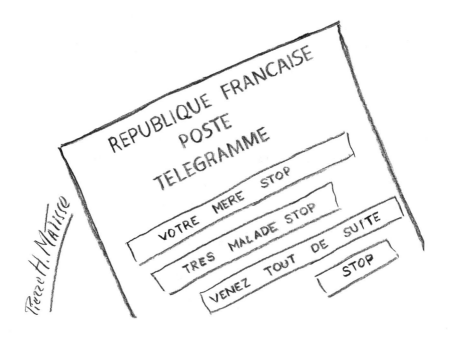

28
ONLY A MOTHER'S HEART

*Mothers never die; they live forever in places you never
knew existed, deep inside your heart and soul.*

PIERRE H. MATISSE

I LOOK AT THE WRISTWATCH Papa gave me and can't help but think of
him and Maman. I have been doing a lot of thinking here in Algeria.

I didn't volunteer for an overseas post without reason. It was all part of
a plan to accumulate an enormous quantity of courage, like others amass
large amounts of money. I am certain that belonging to a commando
paratrooper outfit will prove my courage to Papa.

I remember that night in Paris when I told my parents what I had
decided to do. I could see that Papa was proud that I had volunteered
for this "regiment of fools," as Maman referred to it. Maybe fools, but
brave ones nevertheless. Papa knew I would fight and work hard for what
I believed in.

I want Papa to be proud of me, and I want to be worthy of him. I want to return to France a true hero. My visions are grandiose at age twenty.

I have been writing once a week to Maman since I first arrived in Algeria, and I eagerly await each letter from her. My letters are full of details about the people living in this exotic place, my studies, the antics of my temporary pet chimpanzee, and some of my future plans. She doesn't need to know about any of the dangerous situations I've been in. Her responses are few and far between, and each one is only a few lines long. A few months after I arrive in Algeria, she writes to tell me her father, Grandfather Milhau, has died—another family member I loved. Still, even a few lines is a connection to Maman, and when I receive a letter, I find a place where I can be alone with her.

One afternoon, a letter comes, and when I read the words, I am in shock. Maman has left Papa. I'm in disbelief. How can this be possible? I know they truly love each other. What could have happened to destroy their loving relationship? Of course, Maman gives no personal details in the letter, other than to say she has moved to a one-bedroom apartment, and Gérard is with Papa.

It's difficult to sit down and reply to her, but I write back, expressing my sadness and concern for her. I do not ask for further details other than the few she has given already. An absent son has no right to ask these questions.

AS MY SERVICE in the army comes to a close in October 1948, I contract malaria. But when I am discharged, I head straight to Maman's new address in Paris, even though I am suffering. As soon as I arrive, I can see she looks worn out, but she takes me in her arms and wipes away a few tears. It feels good to be with her. Still, it disturbs me that she and Papa aren't together.

"Gérard hasn't been good to me," she mentions. I don't know what to say. But here, now, what can I say? She is frantically busy.

"I'm sorry I don't have much time to visit, Pierre. I have an appointment with a night club owner regarding some redecorating," she explains. "And then, a very important business meeting at one o'clock. But I did want to give you a gift from your grandfather."

Maman hands me a copy of Grandfather Henri's book *Jazz*. I sit down and admire each of the twenty colorful cutout collages, which seem to come alive and dance on the pages. Grandfather has written an inscription to me in the front of the book and also has written me a separate letter, which makes me feel like he is here. I leave both of the items with Maman for safekeeping.

"Listen, Maman, I have a little touch of malaria," I say. This is putting it mildly, but I don't want to worry her. "I will go to Normandy, put myself back together, and sort out my affairs. Then, in about fifteen days or so, I will come back to spend some time with you in Paris. Perhaps I can be of some help. What do you think?"

"Wonderful idea, Pierre. That would be perfect," she answers with a faint smile.

I AM WELCOMED WARMLY by my grandparents in Normandy and know that I will soon be back on my feet. A couple of weeks after I arrive, I receive a telegram.

> *Pierre. Your mother is gravely ill. Stop.*
> *Come as soon as possible. Stop.*
> *Signed: A friend of your mother. Stop.*

I HURRY BACK TO PARIS even though I'm still weak, feverish, and fighting the chills from malaria. There I am met by two of Maman's friends, whose names I've long forgotten. They were so good to me that in my memory they are forever Monsieur and Madame Good.

Madame Good takes me to the hospital, and when we walk in, I can't believe my eyes. *This must be a mistake. Maman can't be here.* There are hundreds of beds that go on forever. My mother, Madame Louise Milhau Matisse, married for twenty years to Jean Matisse, the son of world-renowned painter Henri Matisse, is in a huge common room—a ward—that reminds me of a second-rate military barracks. My hospital room in Constantine was the Ritz in comparison. Once, when my brother had a bad injury, he was taken to the American hospital in Paris, the best one in the city. But now, I am seeing something straight out of the Middle Ages.

This hospital has to be a million years old, I think, *a place for Paris's poor and destitute.*

I am so heartbroken, I can barely move or see or hear. As Madame Good takes my arm and leads me down the aisle, questions flood my mind. *How can the Matisse family have allowed this to happen to one of their family members? Where are Papa and Gérard?*

Madame Good stops and says softly, "We're here, Pierre." I am afraid to look at the person in the bed, and when I do, I hardly recognize her. Maman looks like she has aged two hundred years since I saw her just a few weeks ago. My anger builds inside. *This is outrageous! Why isn't my mother in her own home, her own bed, with Papa and other loved ones there to comfort her?*

Maybe this is a nightmare that I will wake up from soon. It can't be true. What has happened to her?

I sit on the bed and take her hand, which looks so small in mine. At first, she does not know who I am.

Then she says weakly, "Pierre?"

"Yes, Maman, I'm right here." I squeeze her hand, but a moment later she lapses into a coma.

I can't bear it. "I want to see a doctor," I shout to the first nurse I see.

"It is not possible," a nurse answers.

"I want my mother out of here, now. Right now! Immediately! Do you understand me?" I scream in despair.

"It is not possible," the nurse repeats.

"My mother is going to the American hospital with me. Now!"

Madame Good kindly puts her hand on my wrist and softly says, "Pierre, it's too late. Your mother is dying."

No, I haven't had enough time with her. I want to talk to her, to know her and love her like I did Tata. I want to give her what I could not give to Tata. She could come with me to America, to live a long life and die happy.

While I was in Algeria, I fantasized what it would be like for me, as an adult, to have a relationship with Maman. In her letters, brief as they were, Maman seemed hungry for my attention, to possibly reclaim the lost years when I was at boarding school or living with Tata and the

Leroys. And yes, I had been going over and over again how I would bring up *the* question, the question that has tormented me for years. I want to hear what she has to say about it.

I want. I want. I just want so much. I am a man, but like a baby, I want my mother. I need my maman.

But I have come too late. As I sit at her bedside, Maman takes her last breath. I don't want to leave her here alone, so Madame Good and I sit there for a little while longer as she comforts me.

I CRY ALL THE WAY from Paris to Normandy. I think of that train journey years ago after Tata died when I couldn't stop crying. Then I realized that I would never have a chance to take care of Tata. Now I will never have a chance to take care of Maman.

I want life to be right, to be fair. But it isn't right or fair.

Once in Normandy, I cry for days, grieving for Tata, Grandfather Milhau, and now my mother. I am only twenty-one. Where are my loved ones? Where is my family?

Malaria hits me harder, and in the midst of that, I receive the invitation for Maman's funeral. She will be buried next to her parents in Saint-Georges-de-Didonne. I'm too ill, and I don't have the money to travel that far. Coming out of the army, I'm flat broke.

To add insult to injury, the invitation lists all the family members—the Matisses, and then *Pierre Leroy*. It cuts me through the heart to see it.

It's probably best that I cannot attend. I was the only one there with Maman at the end. I am seething with anger toward the Matisse family, especially Papa. How could he let my mother die in such abject conditions, abandoned and alone? Maman loved him with all her heart and soul. I love him, but I am deeply hurt by what has happened and how he did nothing to stop it.

I eventually write to Gérard, telling him how sorry I am. After all, he has lost his mother too. I never receive a response.

The items from Grandfather Henri that I left with Maman are never returned to me either.

Now everything in my mind is blurry and confused. Only one thing is clear to me. I hate the abominable name I carry. I am alone, without a family, and I don't want to hear about it any longer. I will do what I have to in order to survive. Whenever I get to America, I am never looking back.

29
O CANADA

There are two kinds of adventurers: those who go truly hoping to
find adventure and those who go secretly hoping they won't.

WILLIAM LEAST HEAT MOON IN *BLUE HIGHWAYS*

DURING THE WAR, my adventures did not include young women. But
now that I have recovered somewhat from malaria and the loss of Maman,
I turn to a new folly. Her name is Anna De Wever, and we have known
each other since I moved to Normandy.

Her father, George, is a Belgian farmer who lives a half-mile from the
Leroys on a huge estate. Over the years, I ran to their farm nearly every
day to buy something that either Mathilde or the craftsmen needed, so I
naturally became friends with Anna, along with her two sisters and three
brothers.

Anna is twenty, a tall, good-looking girl, and I fall for her. Such lovely
sirens have a tendency to get us sailors venturing into dangerous waters,
mostly into deeper trouble than we can handle.

We get married on April 1, 1950, and in December 1951 our first child, Patrick, is born. I adore him, and like most fathers, I work hard to support my family but steal every moment I can to hold him and play with him. I am concerned for his future here in France. The country is becoming socialist and communist, which is not what the good men and women fought and died for in World War II.

We have been married for about a year and a half, but Anna and I have not grown as close as I thought we would. I hope that she will come to trust me and will share with me more freely over time.

One day I tell Anna, "I'm tired of France and the direction this country is heading. I want to see the world and spend our lives in America. Right now, it's easier to emigrate to Canada. What do you think?"

I expect some resistance, but Anna agrees to the move. After bidding her family and the Leroys good-bye, our family of three flies out of Paris's Le Bourget Airport in an Air France Constellation, heading to a new adventure in Montreal, Quebec.

Since Quebec is a French-speaking province, it will be less of a culture shock for Anna, who speaks only French. She will have time to learn English before we move to the United States. However, when we arrive in 1952, Montreal is experiencing a chronic unemployment problem. Wages are desperately low, and I take as many temporary jobs as I can. The savings that we brought with us from France melts faster than the snow.

I need to find steady work. So after only a month in Montreal, I buy a 1941 Dodge sedan that has seen better days. We leave Montreal in mid-March, heading nearly three hundred miles north to Chicoutimi in the Quebec wilderness, where I've heard there is work. At forty miles an hour, the car is sliding all over the icy road while passing eighteen-wheelers stranded in the ditch.

We arrive in Quebec City safely—only 130 miles of desolate wilderness to go. The snow has stopped and the roads look clear ahead.

"Don't you think that you are going a little too fast, Pierre? I'm getting queasy," Anna says with concern.

"Relax. There is nobody on the road. Look out the window, Anna. It's the great Canadian North—so beautiful and wild. Chicoutimi, here we . . ." Before I can finish my sentence, the car is doing fancy figure eights. I turn the wheel like a madman, hoping to avoid hitting the snowbank at full force. We don't hit it, just do another pirouette. This car can really skate.

I make an abrupt left turn, then right turn. Anna is screaming. Finally, the car stops spinning, right in the middle of the road.

I am dizzy, but I get out of the car to steady myself. As soon as I put my foot down on the road, my feet fly up in the air and I fall on the icy surface.

Somehow, we make it to Chicoutimi, where we learn the road's nickname: the Boulevard of Death.

THERE IS NO WORK in Chicoutimi, so we continue to Saint Joseph D'Alma. We find a room at a primitive hotel, and while we are having dinner, a tall man approaches our table.

He holds out his hand. "Bonjour, my name is John La Rivière."

I guess we look a little out of place in our city clothes, sitting in a roomful of locals dressed in boots, heavy wool shirts, and fur-lined parkas.

After the introductions, I ask the important question: Is there work here?

John, a Plains Cree Indian from Saskatchewan, actually served with the Canadian army in France so we become fast friends.

"The work is farther north, in La Chute du Diable."

It's always a little bit north.

What is a little bit north is the construction of a hydro-electric dam project, so John and I team up as carpenters. As we get to know each other, John learns that I have handled explosives in Algeria. Soon, John says, "Follow my lead," as we enter the command shack.

"This is Pierre, the Frenchman who knows all about explosives," John says to the crew foreman.

The foreman looks at me. "You can handle dynamite?"

"Sure," says John with a smile that says trust me.

"Very well. However," the foreman's expression turns serious, "I must tell you that the last few dynamite jockeys died on the job."

"No problem," John answers, and we leave to meet our crew.

Once again, John makes the introductions. "Hello, this is Pierre, your new crew chief, and I am his assistant."

One man steps forward, offering his hand. "My name is Paulo. Welcome, Boss," he says with a big grin and a thick Italian accent.

"So, what are we trying to do?" I ask.

Once I see what needs to be blown up, I begin calculating how much dynamite to use. I carefully check and double check myself, then tell John, who relays the information to Paulo. "We will need three and a half sticks of dynamite."

As I check once again, I turn just in time to see one of the workers take out his knife to cut the stick of dynamite in half. "No!" I scream, startling everyone and just about knocking John over to get to Mister Knife and snatch the stick from his hand.

Now that I have the men's attention, I wait for my heart to stop hammering in my chest and then show them how to whittle a piece of wood into a knife. "You have to use this to cut dynamite," I explain, "to avoid any static friction from the metal that could ignite the dynamite and blow us to kingdom come!" The crew appreciates the valuable information.

"John, we do this gig only for three months and then we quit. And not a word to Anna that I've been handling explosives. Agreed?"

"Agreed!" he answers without any hesitation.

They say God watches over fools and children—I know we fit at least one category.

ANNA, PATRICK, AND I live in a rented log cabin on a small river, which we call home until the fall. Each evening, when I get home, a lone owl welcomes me with its hoo-hoo. Anna likes seeing the occasional moose and black bear, and Patrick is lulled to sleep by wolves' choruses.

My budding photography skills are coupled with my love of aviation when I am hired to take aerial photographs of the construction as it progresses. That's how I come to know a bush pilot whom I quickly nickname Flying Circus.

His plane is a beat-up Piper Cub that looks more like a kite than a plane. I can tell he has had more than a few beers just by the way he is navigating himself toward me.

"What's your name? You ever flown before?"

"I'm Pierre. Yes, in German Junkers, but I was only parachuting out of them."

"I don't like parachutes. They make me feel that flying isn't safe." From that moment on, he calls me Frenchy Parachute.

I show him on the map where we need to go for the photographs. As we get in the plane, I tighten my seatbelt as much as I can—the door has been removed on my side.

Flying Circus makes the first pass, but the plane is too high and has drifted off target. On the second pass, my eyes are glued to the camera viewfinder. This time I know I got the picture, in all probability . . . posthumously.

For whatever reason, Flying Circus can't pull up, and we keep on going down. The menacing Devil's Fall Dam construction site is coming at us so fast, I feel I can touch the rocks and taste the cold water.

"That blasted down draft almost did us in," says Flying Circus calmly, after he miraculously lands us on the ground safely. "I need a beer. How about you, Frenchy Parachute?"

I am just glad that I have the photo I need and didn't lose my lunch during the flight.

IN MY FREE TIME, I return to my art studies, making plans for the future, and I dream. Hopefully, I can become as good a creative artist as Grandfather Henri and, with success, support my family.

What an ambition! Well, if one dreams, why not dream big? Cheap dreams are for the timid. Besides, whether dreams are small or big, the cost is the same—nothing. Dreams are about the only free thing in this world.

I remember well what Grandfather Henri told me many times: "Pierre, you have to have more than one string to your bow. What is your second string, Pierre?"

Without any hesitation I would answer, "I will be a famous painter like you and a great writer like Hemingway."

Grandfather Henri thought for a moment, gave me a nod of approval, and logically concluded, "First you will have to get a regular job to support yourself, then work at your art on the side."

AT AUTUMN'S END, John leaves for Saskatchewan. Anna and I have decided to winter in Chicoutimi, and I find some odd small construction jobs to keep us going. When the work dries up, who shows up at our door? Flying Circus! I'm surprised he is still in one piece.

"How about a little photo flying, Parachute?"

"Does it pay?" I ask, not sure this is a good idea.

"Danger always pays well."

"What am I photographing?"

"We're surveying wolf packs and a few other scenic shots."

"All right, but no drinking before flying!" I say firmly.

"Only one small Molson before takeoff or no deal, Parachute."

I reluctantly agree.

We are dressed for a polar expedition and with our bulky outerwear, we barely fit in the plane. Fortunately, the air is smooth. Half an hour later, we see only ice-covered lakes and snow-packed woods.

"Take the controls while I read the map. I think I'm lost!" screams Flying Circus above the loud propeller.

"I don't know how to fly this thing!"

"Nothing to it, Parachute. Grab the stick. Pull it toward you, and we climb. Push it away from you, and we go down. Left, we bank and turn left. Do the opposite to go right. If you need power, the gas control is on your left."

We bump up and down while I desperately fiddle with the stick.

"Parachute, you're all over the sky. Keep her steady, will you?" Finally, my fear begins to subside.

"Much better, but watch your air speed. You're a natural, Parachute. I know where we are. Get your camera out. I'll take over from here."

I pass my first lesson with flying colors. After a few more of these outings, I am landing the plane and taking off too.

WE ARE IN the initial weeks of the Canadian winter when Anna and I welcome our second baby, Louise Henriette Victoria, into the world. I have been making a hand-carved, wall-mounted table for a friend, Monsieur Mallard, and when he mentions that he is going to France to purchase some antique furniture, I give him names of dealers in Normandy. After his business is finished, he plans to visit the Leroys for me.

When Monsieur Mallard returns to Canada, he has a surprise for me from Grandfather Leroy. As soon as he leaves, I open the box and cannot believe my eyes. Inside are the impromptu ink sketches that Grandfather Henri did while attending my mother's exhibit of her figurines in 1942, as well as the finished composition pieces of the same sketches that he completed in his studio. I fall silent, overcome with emotion. It's as if Maman and Grandfather Matisse are in the room with me. When my mother died, I was too traumatized to take care of the succession formalities and asked Grandfather Leroy to do it on my behalf. My inheritance from Maman was these valuable drawings that Grandfather Leroy had put away and forgotten about.

After I show Anna the drawings, I put them in a safe place. It is a comfort to know they are here in my possession now. However, shortly after, Anna develops a serious health problem requiring surgery.

I have no option except to get as much cash as possible for dear Anna.

But what do I have of value? Only the Matisse sketches. With a heavy heart, I contact the local art dealer to show him the original impromptu sketches by my grandfather.

I will not let the other drawings out of my hands, the cherished composition drawings Grandfather made of Maman's ceramic figurines. They are all I have of her. When the art dealer offers me the shameful amount of ninety Canadian dollars for the drawings, I take it. What else can I do when adversity rocks my boat but survive as best as I can?

I WORRY about our little family's future, and say yes to one more lucrative adventure with Flying Circus. Off we go, in the middle of winter, to what looks like a wild, forsaken place. We complete our job and land for the night. Flying Circus sets the plane down as close as he can to the only inn for more than a hundred miles.

We put on snowshoes and tramp through the drifts. Parked outside the inn are a few dogsleds, some with barking dogs still harnessed to them.

Flying Circus kicks the door open. The big room is packed solid, and the smoke from pipes, cigars, and cigarettes is so thick I can barely see or breathe. My partner strides to the service desk with a tough air of importance.

"We need a room," he demands rudely.

"You're lucky. It's the last one," says the fellow behind the desk.

"What's for dinner?" asks Flying Circus.

"Moose stew." We find a table and sit down.

Suddenly, a man the size of a mountain in a black bearskin coat enters the inn. He goes straight to the desk, takes a hand as big as a shovel out of his fur mitten, and pounds it for service. The whole place shakes. He appears to have consumed too much "caribou," the local moonshine, and can barely stand.

"I want a room!" The drunken Giant roars.

"We don't have any." The clerk pauses, then looks at us. "Those two fellows took the last one."

I believe the Giant could kill me with his breath alone, so I am ready to duck under a table. The Giant grunts, burps loudly, growls, and gives us a dirty look. Then, rolling from side to side, like a vessel in a stormy sea, he heads straight to the wall and turns around. Backing up, he reaches for the collar of his coat, and hangs himself on a couple of big pegs like an abstract painting, immediately falling asleep and snoring. I am having a hard time keeping the cork on my laughter, but I hold it in, just in case the Giant wakes up and takes offense.

Eventually, I get a few hours of sleep, but not in our room. Flying Circus needed some privacy for a romantic interlude. So I stretch out on one of the tables in the big room. What a trip—thankfully, the last one.

NEXT, I WORK HARD painting billboards for an advertising company, and for a while everything goes well. But then, an unwelcome intruder shows up in my life. I had no idea this troublemaker existed until he began complaining once in a while. I tell him to shut up, but he doesn't listen. It turns out I have a serious back problem, and I need someone to fix it.

The X-ray results are not a surprise—my villain looks like a snake! At times, the pain is so excruciating that I'm forced to stay flat in bed for a full week before I can go back to work. When I don't work, there is no money. The Boches were easier to beat than the menacing Back. We are sinking financially, and our plans to move to the United States are being trampled by rising medical expenses and lost wages.

EVERY TIME I look too closely at Anna, she gives birth to another child. Next comes Peter in November 1954, two years after Louise. At twenty-six years old, I have three wonderful children, whom I love with all my heart. I teach all of them English, and we speak it at home.

Finally, the last week of November, I see a famous Chicoutimi ortho-pedist, who examines me, looks at the X-rays, and says, "Here's the bad news: You need a serious operation. Without it, you will die." Then he gives me the good news. "If you survive, you have a chance of not only living many more years, but regaining mobility. The surgery involves taking a piece of tibia bone and fusing it to your lower spine, then fus-ing two vertebrae together. I would surmise that this deterioration of your spine is a combination of malnutrition during the war, physical stress, as well as that fall you had on your back in that parachute jump you described to me."

"Operate? No way!" I reply. "I chicken out at the sight of a needle. I have a family to take care of. I must have time to prepare."

"Your sacro-lumbar area is a mess. You have waited too long, and now you're in serious danger."

"What about an alternative?" I'm open to all suggestions, except this one.

"Pierre, you don't realize the extent of your injuries," the doctor says. "We are not talking about being crippled—this is life threatening."

"Nothing to it, eh! You take my leg and stuff it up my behind," I reply bitterly.

"I understand," he replies kindly. "If all goes well, in two months you'll be back home, in a cast for four weeks, and then, I believe you'll be on the mend and headed in the right direction."

ON DECEMBER 15, 1954, I kiss Anna and my three children good-bye and catch the bus for the hospital that is four miles away. I stop at Sears & Roebuck on the way to order Christmas toys and clothes on credit for my children. Regardless of the surgery's outcome, I make sure they will have presents under the tree.

I arrive at the hospital, and as I'm being prepped for the surgery, I feel so alone. If only I could truly connect with Anna and have her here. When I wake up again, every bone in my body aches, and all I want to do is sleep. I drift in and out of consciousness for days, from both the pain and the pain medication.

When I finally am alert, my doctor gives me a progress report. "So far so good, although it is too early to be sure that it worked. I brought you some reading material to help pass the time." He hands me a copy of *Paris Match* magazine, thinking I will enjoy reading something in French.

He has no idea of my past or my family in France, but there on the front cover is Grandfather Matisse with scissors in hand, creating colorful paper foliage cutouts that fill the wall behind him. A paragraph in the corner contains the news: Henri Matisse died November 3, 1954. The magazine is over a month old. News comes late to this part of the world.

Alone in my hospital bed, I read the magazine cover to cover. The entire issue has been dedicated to my grandfather, and I can't help but feel proud to have known this man. No matter our family's problems, he was always nice and welcoming to my mother and me. But now he is gone too. I leaf through the pages and study all the photos that accompany the articles. Papa, Uncle Pierre, and Marguerite are pictured together at the funeral. There is a blurry photo of Papa, looking like he is running away from the reporters. I stare at the photo for a long time. How I wish there were some way to reach out and let Papa know that I send my love and prayers. We are separated by events in the past and are now worlds apart. We are no longer a family in any sense of the word. Our family died with Maman.

Months go by, and the surgery does not eliminate the pain. The vicious cycle of trying to work while in the throes of pain continues. Our youngest daughter, Nellie, is born two and a half years after my surgery, and now I am the proud papa of four good kids—actually, *great* kids.

Whenever my back gives me a break, I rent a place in the Canadian wilderness for a family getaway. The children and I explore and play out-side as much as we can, just as I did as a child. During the long winter months, they enjoy sledding and skiing. On the bitter-cold days, they play with toys and create art indoors. Patrick likes to shape figurines out of clay, Louise and Nellie enjoy watercolors, and Peter is interested in mechanics, specifically how the washing machine works. That is, until he catches his finger in the wrong place and has to be taken to the hospital for stitches.

In the middle of my struggle to work and provide for my family, Gérard writes me and asks if he can stay with us in Canada, where he is hoping to find work. Except for the war years, Gérard has been pampered his entire life, so he is not prepared for the lack of amenities in the wilder-ness. Although I try to help him find work, he isn't able to keep a steady job for long. With my back flaring up, my patience is running short. I love him, but we hardly know each other. We share some memories but little else.

Every once in a while when we are alone, Gérard's tongue slips, and he calls me Papa. *Is he calling me Papa because he goofed or because I look like our father, or is it because I am trying to make him shape up like a man?* All kinds of questions come to mind, related to the same one I've had for years. *Who am I?*

After about eight months, Gérard leaves Canada. We part cordially, although a gulf remains between us.

ONE DAY, WHILE RUMMAGING through an old drawing portfolio, I find a business card from my antique restoration business in Normandy with a note from Grandfather Matisse. It goes like this:

Pierre,
Congratulations on your business and card. Glad you are a man
standing on his own two feet. Your success is already within you.
                                                              Henri Matisse

This note from my grandfather was in response to a letter I had written to him, thanking him for the kindness and friendship he had always shown my mother when she was alive. I had enclosed my business card.

Somehow this letter brings an inner strength and peace to my ravaged body and soul. I carry these words of encouragement—the last from my family. He seemed to be proud of me then. Would he be proud of me today? In these hours of despair, I need his support.

I can't sleep that night with the torturous pain in my back, and I pray to God for courage to endure. As I look out the window and watch a beautiful aurora borealis dancing across the sky, I start a one-sided conversation with my grandfather.

"I have done something very bad. I've sold your wonderful sketches," I confess, feeling the guilt.

There is no answer. He was always so busy in his studio when I was a child that I imagine he's still busy now. Nevertheless, I continue, "The point is, Grand-père, that today I can't stand on my own two feet for very long without falling apart."

Just then I hear a voice. "I can relate to that, Pierre. I was in a wheelchair for years."

Though the shame I feel for having to sell his art has consumed me, I have an idea of how to alleviate my remorse and keep his presence in my life. I will create beautiful drawings and fill the world with joy like he did.

I explain the project to Grandfather. "What you share with me, artist-to-artist, will help me. It will be all I have left of my family."

"Your idea makes sense," he says kindly. "Let's get started."

Grandfather Henri was always a man of action.

So I begin to draw slowly. He visits me in my dreams—day and night—and I ask him many questions, which he patiently answers.

"Purity of line is everything, Pierre," he repeats over and over again, pensively stroking his beard.

"I got that."

"Restraint is gold. Less is more. Simplicity is the difficult part, but it is the key, Pierre." I think back to my very first lesson with him when he took away my precious box of paint tubes and left me with only four colors, instructing me never to use more than those four.

"I'll try my best," I say.

"Trying is not good enough. Only excellence will do."

Perfection, always perfection, and nothing less than perfection. It is enough to drive anyone crazy.

On another night, Grandfather demonstrates the point he is trying to make by moving his hands slowly apart. "Subtle economy of effect is of paramount importance. Do you understand what I'm saying, Pierre?"

"Yes, I do. Less is more."

"Let the viewers use their imaginations to fill in your carefully placed, mysterious blanks. It's a way for them to participate."

"Of course," I say. "It's all very clear to me now."

"Good! Repeat everything you've learned if you can."

"Purity of lines, less is more, simplicity is difficult, shoot for excellence, economy of effect. Finally, let the viewers participate. I especially like that last one."

A MONTH LATER, my preliminary drawings still don't look anywhere close to Grandfather's standards. It's been two weeks since he has visited me in dreams. But then he comes rolling back in his wheelchair again. In his hand is a long wooden stick with a piece of charcoal attached to the end.

"How are you making out with those drawings of ours?" he asks.

I show him my clumsy sketches. "Not very well."

"You're right. This looks like something Picasso would do." Satisfied with a dig at his old competitor and friend, he continues, "However, I discern a certain promising element of form showing up here and there. Don't give up; you're on your way. Let me show you."

I wake up in a sweat in the middle of the night. Anna and the children are sound asleep. The music I had been listening to when I was working is still playing in my mind, the vibrant notes dancing in my head.

In my sleeplike trance, I walk over to the white sheets on the table and pick up the charcoal. I draw a few little arabesques on a scrap of paper to loosen my fingers. The charcoal seems to come alive, and pure lines flow from it.

One drawing falls to the floor. A charming nude, if I say so myself. Done.

"Don't stop!" Grandfather directs.

My hand is bringing a floral design to life on the second sheet.

"Beautiful. You've got it, Pierre." Do I hear a smile from Grandfather? Does a smile make a sound?

Second drawing done.

"Who is doing this?" I ask myself. It can't be me.

"Not to worry," Grandfather answers. "A true artist eventually discovers exactly from where it comes."

The third sheet's statue in a garden tumbles to the floor.

An elegant lady with a stylish chapeau is looking at me from sheet number four. Done.

My back is hurting, but my hand is not tired. I have no time for my pain right now.

A tall ship at sea sails to the floor. Number five done.

Two more to go.

Within a short time, a reclining nude on sheet six now rests at my feet.

My hand tries to create the seventh drawing, but I can't do it. My back is killing me.

"I must rest," I say to Grandfather, wincing in pain.

"No, Pierre! You don't quit when you are inspired. Ignore your back. We don't have time for it."

"Hold on just another thirty minutes," I implore my blasted back. The monster answers by sending excruciating pain throughout my body, from my head to my toes. It makes me shake all over, except for my hand, which continues drawing.

Number seven, a detailed still life, flies onto the paper. It is one of my best! *Finis.*

"Didn't you forget something?" Grandfather says.

I scratch my head.

"The drawings have to be signed."

One by one, I carefully sign each drawing *Tatiou.*

30
ART, INTERPOL, AND UNCLE SAM

Hope is the word which God has written on the brow of every man.

VICTOR HUGO

IN EARLY FEBRUARY OF 1960, I move our family to Montreal, where both the work situation has improved and the schools are much better than in Chicoutimi. My back has waged war on me for six years, but it is not winning yet! I soon land a job with a publicity firm, where I draw gigantic road signs, which means I am standing on my feet all day long.

Two months into the job, I am taking my lunch break in my car and enjoying the warmth of the sun upon my tired and aching bones. Today, my wretched back is in charge, and I am so tired that I fall asleep.

"Pierre, it's ten minutes past one. Wake up!" My coworker is shaking me. "It's time to go back to work."

"Tell the boss I'm resigning," I reply. I cannot go on standing on my feet all day.

"Are you crazy?" he says, surprised at my response.

"Crazy as they come, my friend," I tell him, putting the car in gear and waving good-bye.

When I arrive home, I go straight to bed and sleep for three days. I visit the employment office, determined *not* to find a job. I plan to take two months to rest and then find employment.

After this hiatus, I become a Fuller Brush representative and enjoy the freedom that being a door-to-door salesman gives me. I get out of bed at ten in the morning, work at my own leisurely pace, and go home around four in the afternoon—contented and a few dollars richer. I take time to fix my car, which is falling apart. When my back begins acting up again, I take it easy and research other job opportunities, just in case.

When the leaves begin turning red and yellow, I am still pushing Fuller Brush products, but I do feel a little bit stronger. My back seems to be behaving, so I quit my sales job and find a full-time job as a graphic artist. Two weeks of demanding eight-hour workdays put me exactly where I was the previous winter—on my back. It does not want to hear anything about a steady job.

The dreaded Canadian winter is just around the corner. What am I going to do? I have an old beat-up 35 mm camera that I could use to take photographs. But I don't have any start-up money to build a business, so I quickly discard that idea.

IT IS A SUNNY SATURDAY in mid-November when someone rings the apartment doorbell. Anna and the children are in the kitchen eating lunch, so I get up to answer it.

When I open the door, a middle-aged woman is standing there. "Are you Mister Pierre Leroy?" she asks. "I'm Katherine, your children's teacher."

"What kind of trouble are they in?" I ask quietly, anxious to know the latest problem, even though I have enough already.

"No! Your children are wonderful. But I did want to talk to you about something else. Is there somewhere we could speak privately?" she says, looking a little ill at ease.

"Well, our apartment is small. How about going outside?" The two of us go down the stairs and out the front door.

We stand outside the building in the deserted street, and she seems to relax. "I'm here about Christmas. Your children are saying that they won't have a Christmas this year."

"They always have a good Christmas. Why should this year be any different?" I am annoyed that she would mention such a ridiculous thing and inwardly ashamed at how poor we are.

"Because the children know you haven't had much work the past few months and think there is no money for Christmas," she explains, looking embarrassed. After taking a deep breath, she says, "If that's the case, we can help your family."

Did somebody punch me below the belt? I react quickly with my most convincing smile.

"Katherine, our kids have had a special Christmas from the day they were born. This Christmas is going to be as good as any other. Yes, I have had some minor financial difficulties, but that is all over now. I just landed a very good job."

"Are you sure?" she insists. I guess my convincing smile didn't convince her.

"Absolutely. Thank you for your concern, Katherine."

"If you need anything for the children, please contact me," she says as she turns and leaves.

I have to hold back my tears, partially from the pain I'm feeling as I limp back upstairs, but mostly because I am just plain mad—at my circumstances and the problems my back has caused our family. After I have a little talk with God and send Him my pleas, I don't feel so alone. Settled at heart, I have the courage and vision to move forward and do what needs to be done. My children will have a Christmas.

IT IS A MISERABLE last day of November or first of December (I've since forgotten the exact date). It is a gray, drizzly day, and I can feel the icy dampness down to the marrow of my bones. And of course, the heater in our rusted jalopy has been broken for a while.

I arrive at my destination and park my piece of junk between two freshly waxed Rolls-Royces. One of the chauffeurs, sitting inside his luxury car, gives me a dirty look. I am on the street in Montreal where all the top art galleries, antique shops, and jewelry boutiques are located.

I get out of the car and glance at the window displays of the various galleries, evaluating my choices. Before my appearance attracts too much attention, I pick a promising one and am greeted by a chic saleswoman.

"Good morning, madame! May I please see the owner?" I ask with as much confidence as I can muster.

"May I inquire who wants to see him, sir?" She is looking me up and down. Obviously, I don't seem to fit the profile of the usual clientele. Maybe I should act like the poor genial artist.

She seems to read my mind. "Our gallery isn't taking on any new artists at this time, sir," she says with a pinched-nose tone of disgust.

"Listen," I say with a smile. "I want to see the owner about an important personal matter. Tell him that it's about some Matisses."

At last! I have her attention. Could it have been something I said? A magic word, perhaps? A faint smile appears on her lovely face as she disappears to find the gallery owner. I have brought all of the remaining drawings of my grandfather's. The sum total of my inheritance.

I have also included my recent drawings and paintings, hoping that Grandfather's art will be my drawing card and I can show and sell my own twenty-five pieces for five hundred dollars, which is all I need. I will certainly show the owner Grandfather's sketches, but my plan is to hold on to them if possible.

"I am Monsieur Artsmart. Whom do I have the pleasure of meeting?" he says. (Yes, I have forgotten his name!)

"My name is Pierre Leroy. I was wondering if you would be interested in acquiring some Matisse drawings." My words are difficult to say, and I am now sweating bullets.

"Perhaps we might be interested. Where can I see them?"

"I have them in my car and can bring them in right now." I have to make this deal for the kids and Anna. This may be my last chance to save my family.

"That will be fine," Monsieur Artsmart says.

The cold rain feels good on my face, which is burning up. I have to be running a three-hundred-degree fever with my heart beating out of my chest. But I have to get back to business.

I go inside the gallery and pull out twenty-five of my drawings, which are signed Tatiou. At first he shows interest in them, but when he sees the signature, he turns to walk away. I quickly place the Matisses on the counter next to my works, announcing, "And these are the Matisses."

He turns back around, clears his throat, and smiles. Monsieur Artsmart pushes my drawings aside and begins to carefully scrutinize Grandfather's works.

"I like them. But they will need to be authenticated by a fully accredited art expert before I consider any transaction. And I must have provenance."

"That is no problem," I assure him. I can write a statement of how they were given to my mother and then passed on to me. "I would expect nothing less," I continue, disappointed that the sale can't happen right here, right now. "It's perfectly agreeable with me."

"I'm going to New York next week," he says. "If you agree, I would like to take them with me for an expert evaluation."

"Yes, take them with you."

The die is cast once more. There is no other way. With any luck, he will go to my uncle Pierre, the prominent New York art dealer, and that should settle everything nicely.

All of this takes a half hour or so, and I leave with the drawings I did. Now I have to wait for what comes next. Waiting has never been my strong suit. Waiting eats up my nerves.

A FEW DAYS LATER, I am eating breakfast when I glance at the newspaper lying on the floor. My spoon falls out of my hand.

"What's wrong with you, Pierre?" Anna exclaims. "You look like you've seen a ghost!"

I don't answer. Instead, with shaking hands, I pick up the paper and read aloud that Interpol and FBI agents have uncovered a worldwide art forgery organization. Three suspects have been arrested in New York, with more arrests expected to follow in other countries. The news doesn't faze Anna, but I begin to panic.

What if the New York art experts decide that my Matisses are fakes? I don't trust the art experts. They have been proven wrong before. Now all the police departments of the world are going to be looking for art forgers. What if some zealous Interpol investigator decides to nail me as a criminal international art faker? Based on my past experiences with the Matisse family, I have learned to be ready for the shoe to fall whenever I am involved with them.

My fertile imagination is going wild, and I have gone from being concerned to being scared. The way my luck has been running lately, it's time to reconsider my strategy and do damage control right now.

I dial two wrong numbers before I finally connect with the everything-expensive art gallery. I'm shaking like a leaf. "Excuse me, may I talk to Monsieur Artsmart? It's rather urgent."

"Monsieur Artsmart is still in New York, Monsieur Leroy." It is the woman whom I first met at the gallery.

"I see. Could you tell him that I am sorry, but I have changed my mind? I do not—I repeat—I do not want to sell my Matisses."

"All right, Monsieur Leroy. As soon as he returns, I'll give him your message."

I HAVE TO WAIT some more, wondering if it will be the police or Monsieur Artsmart who will be contacting me.

I can't keep it a secret from Anna anymore, especially if the worst happens. I tell her the entire story and why I am nervous now.

"We know your Matisses are authentic, and the art experts know their business," she says reassuringly.

"I am not too confident about the art experts' expertise—that's what concerns me."

"Well, if you go to jail, I probably can get government assistance," Anna says.

And then a different catastrophe forms in my mind. *What if the art experts declare my dear Matisses to be fakes and they are destroyed?* That would be the worst possible scenario.

AN UNSETTLING WEEK PASSES at a snail's pace with no news. Every time I hear something loud—a police siren, the phone, the doorbell, an alarm clock, whatever—I totally lose my composure.

Finally, the call comes. "Allo! Monsieur Leroy, what do I hear? You don't want to sell your Matisses?"

"No, I mean, yes! I have changed my mind. I want to keep my Matisses."

"Well, that's a shame because we are very interested in acquiring them," Monsieur Artsmart says disappointedly. "The experts in New York have declared them authentic, and I could offer you a very generous price."

I want to believe him, but I hesitate. "No, thank you. I will come by tomorrow to pick them up," I say, hanging up the phone, still scared and unsure of what to do.

The next day is another day of drizzling icy rain. Not only has the heater given up in the car, but the windshield wipers have decided to quit too.

"Do you really want to take the drawings back?" Monsieur Artsmart asks me when I arrive. "At least let me make you an offer."

"How much do you think they're worth?" Slowly, I am skating toward thin ice.

"How about six hundred dollars?" he proposes, with an enticing smile.

I am thinking as fast as I can. I promised Grandfather no more bargain-basement art sales.

"Not a penny less than one thousand," I reply with the best poker face I can put on.

I have never seen such a huge sum in my entire life. Anna will be delighted. Perhaps this will be the Christmas when we become a real family. There will be money for the kids' Christmas presents. Maybe a used car to replace our jalopy. And certainly warm clothes for the winter.

"Did you say a thousand dollars, Monsieur Leroy?" he says, feigning doubt.

"Correct. I'll not part with these masterpieces for a penny less," I reply, thinking I won't let Maman and Grandfather down again.

"Deal!" Mister Artsmart says, with a large smile.

As he is preparing the check, he looks at the drawings spread out on his desk. "One can see the hand of the master," he says almost reverently.

"Unmistakably," I agree.

My hand is shaking, and my heart sinks as I write the letter of provenance. With check in hand, I stroll out of the gallery as calmly as my jagged nerves allow me. A shooting pain goes down my leg, and I sit in the car until it fades away.

Once again, my imagination begins to spin out of control with what-ifs. If Monsieur Artsmart saw my hand shaking, he may have misinterpreted the reason why. What if Uncle Pierre won't vouch for me? What if Monsieur Mallard has moved from Chicoutimi, and I can't get in touch with him?

I drive slowly to the bank, glancing often in the rearview mirror. I can't see any suspicious cars following me. I enter the bank lobby, walking straighter than I have in months, no doubt because I am scared stiff.

"Are you sure that you don't want traveler's checks?" the charming young teller asks me.

"No, thank you!" I answer too loud.

"It's not safe to carry large sums of money with all the crime around these days," she says with concern.

I relax and am about to reply, "Nothing to worry about, Miss. I could be the criminal, given this sum of money" but catch myself just in time.

"Nothing to be concerned about, Miss. I'll be careful."

When I get home, I hand all the money to Anna. "Give the kids the best Christmas they have ever had. Then hide the rest of the money in a safe place. I don't want to know where. If the Royal Canadian Police come poking around and asking questions, you are broke and know nothing."

"You sold your drawings?"

"Yes, some of them."

"We are rich, Pierre!"

"Don't be silly, Anna. Not so fast. I might go to jail. But no matter what, you have to promise me that you will not turn the money over to the authorities. It was my inheritance from Maman, and you and the children have a perfect right to the proceeds. If things get tricky, you and the children go back to your parents' farm in Normandy. Understand?"

Anna understands and agrees.

THE WEEKS PASS and nothing happens. Christmas comes, and the kids enjoy their best Christmas yet. At least if I go to jail, I'll have the memories of this last holiday with the children to take with me.

During these troubled days, strange visitors call on me in my dreams: the Royal Canadian Mounted Police, Interpol, the FBI. They all want to know everything.

Even the Gestapo shows up, accusing me loudly, "Forgery verboten, swine Françouse."

"Yes, I know. I fooled you before, didn't I?" I answer defiantly in a moment of rebellious courage.

"Hang him!" I hear someone screaming in the background.

"No! No! No! I am *not* selling them!"

"Pierre, what's the matter with you? You're kicking me like a crazy man!" Anna exclaims, shaking me awake.

"Sorry, dear. I was having a nightmare."

She turns over and goes back to sleep.

BY THE END OF JANUARY I realize my fears have been unfounded. I laugh harder than I have ever laughed in my life. I do hope that Grandfather is not too mad at me. I still detest what I have done, but I will keep working on my art as I promised Grandfather I would do.

"Tomorrow I am starting my own business, my dear," I tell Anna. She shakes her head and smiles.

Actually, my first thought is I want to make enough money to buy back my Matisse drawings—a hope that still remains unfulfilled.

I do get an antique restoration and appraisal business up and running in Montreal, and by 1965, I am doing well enough to put away a little savings. As the weather begins to turn colder, Uncle Sam seems to beckon even louder. The border is only fifty miles south of us.

My back has a better idea. Sunny Florida. I have secured immigration visas for Anna and myself, so I have what I need to fulfill my childhood dream.

AS WE PREPARE to leave Montreal, I receive a long letter from an unknown lady—Madame Annie Leroy. While we've been living in Canada, we hear through Anna's parents that both of the Leroy grandparents have died, two years apart. These two strangers had accepted me into their home and hearts, and I was forever grateful for their kindness and love. So when I see the last name Leroy on this letter, I am momentarily confused.

Dear Pierre, the letter begins.

It is Annie Leroy, the third wife of Camille Leroy, writing me. Actually, the way she describes her husband as a wonderful man, I think she must have him confused with someone else. Could there be two Camille Leroys?

Well, it seems that Grandfather Leroy has thrown a tricky curve in his will. He has given half of his Normandy property to his son and the other half to me. I am deeply touched by the old gentleman's gesture.

"Would you be so kind to contact the lawyer in France to sort things out?" she asks. "We can't get anything done without synchronizing with you."

Suddenly, Camille Leroy needs me. It's a good thing I am not his real son. If I were like him, he might really be in trouble right now.

I write the French lawyer and say that I don't want anything from the Leroys. Camille Leroy can have everything. I sign the necessary documents and turn over all my rights to Camille. Then I write Madame Leroy the third, telling her exactly what my position is in regard to the family, any family for that matter. I have no Leroy family, no Matisse family, and no father.

Finally, in mid-November 1965, our little family gets into a Pontiac station wagon, towing a small utility trailer with all our worldly possessions behind it. We are leaving Canada, never to return. I have a wife, four children, a broken back, and seven thousand hard-earned US dollars in my pocket.

What I need now is more courage, I think. Suddenly, courage comes from my youngest son, Peter, who says, "Uncle Sam, here we come!"

31

WHAT'S UP

What is life, but a series of inspired follies? The difficulty is to find them to do. Never lose a chance: it doesn't come every day.

GEORGE BERNARD SHAW

RIGHT AWAY, I implement phase one of my master plan to bring Anna and me closer together. We head to Florida for a couple of weeks of family vacation, during which I look for possible employment to resettle. Unfortunately, there is not much available. What attracts me to this location is it's the same latitude as the French Riviera, giving it the same light that Grandfather Matisse painted by. The right light is critical for any artist. This is where I feel at rest and want to remain. However, it's not to be just yet. I now have a job waiting for me in Texas.

We drive to Houston, where I have been contracted as a consulting ébéniste for the architectural reconstruction of a French castle. The castle had been bought by a rich Texan, taken apart piece by piece in Europe, and brought to the United States. For two months, I make sure it is put back together accurately. Now I launch phase two of my plan.

I have a surprise for Anna and the children—a two-week vacation to Normandy, when this job is completed. It will be a number of firsts for the children—their first time flying, their first time seeing Paris, their first time meeting their Normand grandparents and other family members from Anna's side. All in all, a great adventure for everyone.

While Anna and the children are enjoying Normandy, I fly to Algiers to finalize all the inheritance paperwork for Camille Leroy. Et voilà! I am glad that he is out of my life once and for all.

When we return to the United States, we land in New York and head to Boston, which will be our new home. I am going to start my job with Mass Motion Picture, as well as being a stock photographer in Boston, shooting landscapes, weddings, or whatever I'm asked to do.

My enemy, the Back, returns, and for two full months, I am in agony. I can only walk on all fours. Somehow I patch the back up for the thousandth time, but I know I need to slow down. As a photographer, I often have to stand for long hours and carry heavy electronic flashes and cameras, so my job is in jeopardy.

My marriage with Anna has been on the rocks for a long time. We never grow as close as I always hoped. Taking a turn for the worse, we first separate and eventually divorce.

Divorce is a failure, and I can't stand failure. But even more devastating is that I lose my children, and it's killing me. I leave them in God's care, often asking Him to protect them. These are very dark times for me, and some days I really must fight to go on.

I MARRY AGAIN—this time to a lovely Scottish lady named Christiane.

Finally, like it or not, I have to see a doctor for my back. I cannot survive with the trouble it's given me. His prescription? "Above all," he says, "you need rest, sun, and a lot of swimming to patch up your back."

"How about Florida, Doc?"

"Florida would be perfect, Pierre."

That settles it. I'm going back to Florida no matter what. Chris and I will work our way south from Boston in our Volkswagen. We'll take whatever jobs we can find along the way to move us toward the southern coast. In 1968, we go to a prestigious employment agency in New York City, and within an hour are on our way to the Waldorf Astoria in Manhattan for an interview with Madame Violette. She and her husband, retired Rear Admiral Violette, need a cook/maid and chauffeur/butler at their home in Annapolis, Maryland.

After we answer questions in person with Madame Violette, she calls her husband, who continues interviewing me on the phone. He is originally from Louisiana and speaks perfect Parisian French, having seen action in France and England during World War II. He asks me about my war experience and explains that the person he is looking to fill the position must also be an armed garde du corps—bodyguard. That sounds adventurous to me. Chris and I are offered the positions, and the next day we drive to the mansion, which overlooks Chesapeake Bay.

Among the rear admiral's personal pleasures are a seventy-foot yacht, a complete photo studio and lab in the house, a Minox spy camera, and a Rolls-Royce, his favorite car. In fact, he loves the car so much that he prefers driving it, which I learn immediately.

A few days after I start, I am the passenger instead of the chauffeur when the rear admiral decides I need a more appropriate wardrobe for my position. He drives us to a haberdashery in Washington, DC. When we pull up to the curb in the Rolls, a man immediately comes out of the store, graciously opens the door for me, and whisks me inside, leaving the rear admiral to park the car. Rear Admiral Violette is not amused, and from that time on, whenever we have somewhere to go, he pulls the car over a few blocks away from our intended destination and has me switch seats so he can be the one with the grand entrance.

As interesting as the job with the Violettes is, I still want to get to Florida, so after a few months, my wife and I find jobs in DC. Chris is a secretary, and I am an architectural draftsman. Unfortunately, my back problems put an end to this career and prevent me from accepting the Smithsonian's offer of a prime position in their antique furniture department that comes with a fabulous salary.

Chris and I finally arrive in the Sunshine State, after about a year on the road.

FOR WHATEVER REASON, I am always being blessed. When I go to the unemployment office to look for a job, I notice that the state of Florida has a posting for a cartographer. I can read a map and even draw one if necessary. I am confident that the job is mine.

The unemployment counselor doesn't agree. "You aren't qualified," he says, after reviewing my initial questionnaire.

"You're not qualified to judge whether or not I possess the skills for the job," I tell Mr. Know-It-All. "Just send me on the interview." A few minutes later, I leave the office with the information I need.

The job opening is in the property appraiser's office, located in the Orange County courthouse. When I sit down with the human resources person, once again I am about to be dismissed for not having the right credentials.

I am not giving up yet. "Do you think they would have sent me here if I was not qualified? Just let me speak with the manager of the department." I win round two and am introduced to George.

"George, I need this job. I am a good worker who learns fast."

"Pierre, you don't have the proper knowledge and skills for the job. But that's beside the point. I don't do the hiring. My boss, Mr. Ford Hausmann, does. He is not here today, but he is so ignorant about the job that if you come back on Monday, I am sure he will hire you." I follow George's advice and just as he predicted, I hit it off with Mr. Hausmann and am hired on the spot.

I am forty-one years old. The trick now is to hold on to this job and to heal my back with a good dose of sun and swimming. I apply to become a US citizen, pass the test, and am sworn in with a roomful of others, all of us proud to call ourselves Americans.

Florida in the early seventies is not as overdeveloped as it will become. The landscape is predominantly made up of orange and grapefruit groves and large agricultural fields that seem to go on forever. In some ways, it reminds me of rural France. There are incredible amounts of wildlife, especially birds, and lakes where I swim with snakes and alligators.

After a year, I am promoted to manager of the cadastral department. I record property boundaries, buildings, and other details. Mr. Hausman lets me work at my own pace. Over a period of four years, I help take an unorganized department and turn it into one of the top mapping teams in the country. When I am interviewing potential employees, I look for the same three qualities that have served me well: a desire to work, a good attitude, and the ability to learn.

In my leisure time, I begin painting Florida landscapes, detailing the rich ecological diversity around me. Coastal and inland terrains, swamps, marshes, sunrises, sunsets—there is always something interesting to capture. With a palette knife I spread thick coats of flamboyant colors on canvases, developing my bold and dashing style. When I'm concentrating on landscapes, it brings me an inner peace as I drink in the handiwork of the Master Artist.

IN 1976, I AM EXHIBITING some of my work at the Maitland Art Center when a fellow artist quietly takes me aside. "I saw that Jean Matisse died in Paris," she says. It is a shock to hear my father's name, let alone hear the news. Other than the obituary my friend gives me, I have no other information and hear nothing from anyone, not even Gérard.

Over the next few weeks, memories of Papa come flooding back. He was the one who taught me that I could do whatever I wanted if I put my mind to it. When I was developing some of my inventions, he never laughed or said that they were silly or wouldn't work.

When I assisted him in the studio, Papa would repeat his father's mantra: "Simplicity, Pierre. Simplicity is the most difficult." Unlike his fellow sculptor Maillol, Papa would work up a sweat, his beard full of stone chips, plaster, or clay, and he would muse, "We don't have to please everybody, Pierre. Just be true to yourself and your art."

Papa lived in the shadow of his father's fame and never achieved real acknowledgment in the art world. I know this was painful for him—after all, I'm an artist too. Yet he didn't give up. He had no choice because he was born an artist.

"Always roll with the punches, Pierre! One of these days your turn will come, my boy."

In the process of creating art and while exploring the inlets and waterways in my sailboat, I slowly bid Papa farewell. I always spend time in the boat when I need to work things out. Am I alone? Maybe.

Or maybe I am there with God. All I know is that I find some peace and solace at last.

MY JOB IS GOING EXTREMELY WELL. In 1982, Mr. Hausmann calls me into his office and announces, "Pierre, we have decided we would like to computerize your entire department. What do you know about computers?"

"Mr. Hausmann, I know next to nothing about computers and I don't want to learn."

"Pierre, you knew nothing about cartography when I hired you, but you learned that. You'll be grand at this new challenge."

Touché. He knows me too well.

NEARLY TWO YEARS GO BY. My office is located in the Orange County Courthouse and I am sometimes asked to be a translator for French speakers appearing before the judge. That is the case on January 10, 1984. The presiding judge asks me to explain to a young French woman arrested for hitchhiking how dangerous the practice is, and that she has twenty-four hours to leave Orlando. The two of us are dismissed and leave the courtroom, taking a seat on a bench just outside the door.

A few moments later, I hear a gunshot from inside the courtroom. People are screaming and when the door opens, a young bailiff runs out, rushing past us. "Get down!" I say instinctively, pushing the woman sideways on the bench while I lean forward. The shooter, Thomas Provenzano, runs out of the courtroom and fires again. The gun's flash is so close that I sustain powder burns to my face. Provenzano disappears in pursuit of the bailiff, and the French woman bolts in the other direction.

When Provenzano is caught and everything is over, one of my friends is dead, another is critically injured, and a third corrections officer is shot too. Even though Mr. Hausmann encourages me to take the rest of the day off, I prefer to stay.

That evening, when I go to the parking garage—surprise! There are police everywhere and yellow caution tape cordons off an area. My car is in one of the restricted spaces. When I approach an officer and ask if I can get to my vehicle, he says, "I'm sorry. The car next to yours belongs to the shooter. We found multiple weapons, ammunition, grenades, and pipe bombs in his vehicle, and he may have placed a pipe bomb in your car and the one on the other side. They are investigating right now."

It took a while before all three cars were checked thoroughly, and Provenzano's vehicle was towed away. I never did find out if the police found a bomb in mine or not. Good thing I didn't try to go home early. God had my back twice in one day. Once again, I thank Him for protecting me and so many others.

MY TEAM AND I are reaching the culmination of our computer challenge—to have the geographical information system (GIS) software ready to be sent into space on a satellite. That satellite launched by NASA will be sending information back, based on the interfacing with sensors that have been placed throughout the county. If it works, it could be the national standard for survey mapping.

On a cold morning in late January 1986, I am invited by NASA to be at the launch. Seventy-three seconds after liftoff, the Challenger shuttle explodes, obliterating the hopes, dreams, and lives of the seven crew members aboard.

I mourn the deaths of these fallen heroes, along with the rest of the country, and pray for their families. I remember President Ronald Reagan's words that night on television. "We will never forget them . . . as they prepared for their journey and waved good-bye and 'slipped the surly bonds of earth [to] touch the face of God.'"

The tragedy grounds US space missions for three years, pushing back our schedule for the computerized mapping. In due time, another satellite is launched and I can tell Mr. Hausmann that the project is finally working.

IN 1990, AFTER TWENTY YEARS in my quiet desk job, I retire to follow my dreams—I will be a full-time artist and pursue writing as well. Florida's sun and waters finally get the back patched up, for the most part.

Shortly after I retire, marriage number two falls apart. I have to face the fact that I have trouble communicating with the people I love and hold dear. Years ago, I couldn't talk to Maman to ask her the questions or say the words I wanted to say. The same is true with my children, even though I try.

But I do not have to wait long to fall in love again. The next charmer is pure French, a woman named Edmond. This marriage gets off to a rocky start because Chris is still in my life. I am helping Chris—there is no one else she can turn to.

IN 1992, I RECEIVE an unexpected letter from Camille Leroy, who is nearly ninety. He asks me to come to the French Riviera to sign some legal documents—again. On paper, I am still his son.

In France, there is a strict right of succession law concerning direct descendants and the inheritance of property. So Camille has cooked up a scheme. His wife is going to adopt me so that when Camille dies, she can inherit his property without having to share it with me.

I reassure him that I will not object. "You should know by now that I wouldn't take a speck of dust from the Leroy family," I write in response.

"Paper is always best. Better to be sure," he replies.

Over the next few months, we exchange several brief letters, coordinating the time when I can visit. Hopefully this trip will break my connection to him forever.

When I see him, I feel nothing—I have no affection for him. Even in his older years, he is certainly nothing like his father.

After the lawyer leaves with the official papers and we are alone, I decide to tackle the burning question that has been eating at my heart for years. Now that the property is forever his, he has no more reason to tell me anything but the truth.

"Your mother told me that you are not my father," I say.

He looks at me with his cold blue eyes. "She was right. It was never in question among those of us so intimately involved. It was an impossibility. But if asked, I will deny it to the world," he says, waiting for me to react.

I can feel the rage rising inside me, but I keep it inside. "Why didn't you clear this matter up long ago? It would have saved you a lot of trouble."

"Your mother was a wench, and your father, Jean, was a drunk. They used me and humiliated me. This is how I have gotten even with them all these years—through you." His face is expressionless and emotionless.

"You all made it so easy," he goes on. "Now, thanks to your stupid code of honor and pride, it is finished. I have it all, and more to the point, you have nothing from either side!"

I am at a loss for an answer but instinctively respond, "I loved my mother and father."

"That's visceral," he answers, not the slightest bit disturbed.

I am ready to strangle him. "What did this achieve?"

"I did not want you, but I did not want them to have you either. Don't you see? They had this son, but he could never really be their son." His eyes gleam with vengeance, even after all these years.

Camille continues. "Jean got Louise, but I withheld his firstborn son and disinherited you. You have been very helpful in my plan, and now I have my victory!"

Though I am supposed to stay in the French Riviera for two weeks, I leave the next morning and head for Paris to visit a friend and then head home. As I make myself comfortable in my seat for the transatlantic flight, I am relieved. This Leroy chapter is truly finished now.

Unfortunately, another relationship ends for me two years later, when Edmond and I divorce in 1994. As Edmond reminds me, Chris warned her that I wasn't good marriage material. Again I am alone, without a family. I wonder if this pattern will follow me all my life. But it is during this time that I bury myself in my art, concentrating on landscapes.

Pierre H. Matisse

32
IDENTITY

It takes two to speak the truth; one to speak, and another to hear.

HENRY DAVID THOREAU

I AM SIXTY-SEVEN YEARS OLD and still hoping to find my life partner. I subscribe to a few formal introduction matchmaking services, which result in thirty-five first dates. I know what I'm looking for in a wife and can spot red flags immediately. None of the women I meet are the right one.

What I don't know is that a woman named Jeanne is being strongly encouraged by a friend associated with one of the dating services to get in touch with me. It takes a while, but on July 25, 1995, she finally makes the call.

I have heard of love at first sight, but I know I love Jeanne at the sound of her voice, during our first phone conversation. I don't pull any punches, quickly letting her know that I am not interested in casual dating; I am looking for someone to share my life with. She tells me both her size and her age, thinking that one or the other fact will certainly deter me. I just tell her my size and age.

With that out of the way, we discuss our philosophies of life, our views on relationships, the qualities we are looking for in someone, the fact that we don't just want a companion—we want it all.

"I believe that there are really only two kinds of people in the world—givers and takers," Jeanne says. "Takers should never be given a marriage license—they should be given a business contract!"

I completely agree.

I am captivated by her honesty and openness. She is bright and engaging, with an opinion on almost any subject. Midway through our first conversation, Jeanne asks if we can take a short break so she can drive home. It turns out that the entire time we've been talking, she has been using a Simon personal communicator mobile phone in her parked car, overlooking the ocean. (To this day, Jeanne says that we were introduced by Simon.) I give her time to get settled, then call her back, and we continue our four-hour conversation. We share our hopes and dreams and move on to shared interests: music, books, God, family, travel, photography, movies, and museums.

Jeanne has worked in costuming and set design for Broadway productions and ballet in New York City and has been in the travel industry and with Universal Studios in New York for both film and TV. And if that isn't enough, she has done furniture design and fabrication with her father and brother, showcasing her creativity. I can't believe that she has built furniture too!

Jeanne is Native American mixed with Scottish and French blood—one cannot be more American than that. I say that I was born in Paris but now am an American citizen—nothing more. At five minutes to midnight, we say good night, after I ask Jeanne to join me for dinner the next evening. We agree to meet in front of my house, where she will leave her car, and we'll drive to dinner.

We go to a Chinese buffet, and Jeanne tastes her first mussels. How could that be! She had told me she loved oysters, so I naturally concluded that she must like mussels, too. Thankfully, she does. The restaurant isn't busy, so we have the place nearly to ourselves. As I head back to the table with our dessert, I look at her sitting there and think, *What a lovely woman she is.*

When we get back to my apartment, I invite her inside to see my "etchings," which are actually my paintings of Florida. Once again, we talk until midnight, a continuation of the conversation from the night before. I realize that we can be true to ourselves and be true to each other at the same time. In essence, she is a delight.

At the end of the evening, Jeanne asks if I would give her a hug. "Yes, of course," I reply, taking her in my arms and kissing her gently on the forehead. You could say our first date went well, because we marry on our second date—a week later. My proposal is simple and to the point: "Why don't you pack a bag, come for dinner, and spend the rest of your life?"

"What time do you want me to arrive?" Jeanne asks.

Later that evening, our vow to each other before God is simple: "I vow to spend eternity with you."

TWO DAYS LATER, I get cold feet. I am afraid of our age difference—I'm sixty-eight and Jeanne is forty-nine. What if I'm unable to care for her at some point? I don't want it to end, but I don't want Jeanne to make a mistake and be hurt either. She senses my deep anxiety and is ready to leave. But before she leaves, she says, "I love you. But I won't stay where I'm not wanted. If you can look me in the eyes and say you don't love me, I will leave right now."

"I can't say that because it's not true," I respond.

"Then it is settled. We are together for eternity," Jeanne replies.

I know I have met my soul mate, which Jeanne believes with all her heart has been God's plan all along.

When I meet Jeanne's family and we tell her parents that we are married, her mother says, "This can't be allowed. There was no ceremony, no family, and no reception."

As I panic, Jeanne joins her mother and they begin to plan a more formal ceremony and reception, choosing the date of September 23. We fondly refer to this as our second anniversary.

Over the next week, I meet all five of Jeanne's children. Her daughter

Laura says, "Mom met, fell in love with, and married this French guy. She was suddenly totally occupied before he was even on the family radar screen."

Obviously, I'm the French guy.

THAT SAME WEEK Camille Leroy jumps back into my life yet again, after three years of silence. Annie Leroy calls to tell me her husband has died. I respectfully console her in her loss, all the while feeling nothing, not even a faint sense of loss at the passing of this stranger.

A few days later, Annie calls back in a panic. Camille's lawyer, whom I met three years ago in France, has messed things up. The plan for Annie to inherit everything instead of splitting it with me has been foiled. The French authorities never finalized my "adoption," probably suspicious of an adoption request involving someone in his midsixties at the time—me. I am still Camille's legal son and receive a letter notifying me of my inheritance. Annie Leroy is stuck; she cannot settle the estate without my approval.

I haven't changed my mind about the inheritance, but I do not want to keep this a secret from Jeanne, even though now I have to explain this name and identity mess to her. *Will this change Jeanne's mind about our future together?*

We sit down, and I give her a quick version of my family history that has led to the frantic phone call from Annie. I can see the surprise on Jeanne's face, and then she says, "Pierre, this is your inheritance to give away. You do what you feel is right for you and Mrs. Leroy."

That is all I need to hear. I send more official papers to France so that the grieving widow can inherit all of her husband's estate. Even though I still have the Leroy name, I am finally finished with that part of my life.

I know that Jeanne fell in love with me without knowing any of my ties to the Matisse family, and yet I battle an underlying fear: Is this marriage going to work? I want it to work. I remember what Tata said to me the last time I saw her, more than fifty years ago. "Pierre, I can see that when you marry, you'll be good to your wife." Yes, Tata, I am trying to do that.

Months pass and then years, and our relationship grows stronger. We love each other every moment of every day, and we make sure to let each other know it. Love is like freedom—one must not take it for granted. One must work at it and protect it continually.

Each year we celebrate not a single wedding anniversary day—August 1—but an entire week, beginning on July 25. Even if we are in the same room, Jeanne picks up the phone and calls me, just like she did twenty-one years ago. We recreate the opening lines of that first conversation, until we start laughing together.

Jeanne is creative, too, which means she understands me well. And like me, she is also a dreamer who works hard. We have a lot in common but enough differences to keep life interesting. That's my girl. Jeanne thinks that I am Mister Wonderful four times over.

Retired and happy with Jeanne, I turn to my painting, photography, and inventions with a passion. Over the years, I have built my own computer and been at the helm of a remote-controlled sailboat that Jeanne bought me. Every time I look at it, I'm reminded of the toy boat I had when I lived with Tata. And I have realized my dream to soar in the sky. I have a pilot's license and love to fly over Florida's miles of white shoreline.

IN NOVEMBER 1995, Jeanne bursts into the house after visiting her oldest daughter, Wendy.

"Pierre, we have to talk whenever you can take a break."

"What, my darling?" I ask distractedly from my art studio, lost in my new composition.

"Honey, you are not going to believe this!" she continues. "Never question what you know in your heart about your true identity. Sit down, and let me tell you what's happened."

The word *identity* catches my attention, and now I am all ears. Seeing Jeanne's expression, I know that what she is about to tell me is important. To be honest, it makes me a bit nervous.

"I was helping Wendy with the plans for the family Thanksgiving dinner. Joe was on the computer, working on one of his college courses, and Spencer was reading a book next to him. Just then, Spencer looked up from his book and glanced at the computer screen to see what his dad was doing and got very excited."

"Daddy, it's Grandpa Pierre. It's Grandpa Pierre with a beard. Look, Nanny, it's Grandpa Pierre on the computer. I didn't know he had a beard!"

On the screen was a quotation underneath a photo of a man—Henri Matisse. A person that seven-year-old Spencer believed was me.

"We tried to explain that it wasn't you," Jeanne says, "but he wouldn't hear of it."

Spencer doesn't know that I am connected to the Matisse family. Actually, none of Jeanne's family does. "I quickly told them that Henri Matisse was your grandfather. Joe pulled up some of your grandfather's artwork to show us that he was an artist like you."

"And Grandpa Henri had a French accent, too," Wendy told Spencer, "just like Grandpa Pierre."

"Interesting," I say. Jeanne knows about the turmoil inside of me that I've carried all these years. She gives me a kiss and whispers, "It's late. Let's go to bed, and you can sleep on it."

That night I have a vivid dream that takes place on rue Lecuirot in Paris on the first of February 1928.

"NOT AGAIN!" In the dimly lit bedroom, Jean Matisse stops pacing back and forth. He squeezes his eyes shut as tightly as possible, but the dark cannot shut out the cries coming from Louise, who is in labor.

"Louise's mother died delivering her," Aunt Henriette had told him at some point before.

Died at childbirth. Died at childbirth. This phrase keeps pounding in Jean's head like a drumbeat, and he resumes his pacing.

He wonders how much longer he can stand hearing her cries of pain. If only he could do something.

"How much more can Louise endure?" he asks, distraught.

Mathilde, Louise's mother-in-law, and Henriette are busily trying to work around Jean's frantic pacing.

For a moment, Louise relaxes and lays her head back against the damp pillow. Poor Jean, she thinks with a tired smile.

"It won't be long now, Louise," Henriette says reassuringly. Louise and Jean hope her words are true. They long for this to be over, to finally hold their child in their arms.

Jean continues pacing. He hears another moan and circles the bed, bumping into Mathilde and swearing thunderously.

After much commotion, all quiets down. Then, out of the silence comes a soft cry. Then another, stronger this time, as the miracle moment arrives. Jean has tears in his eyes. He can only nod to himself when Mathilde announces, "It's a boy."

Louise is straining to see the baby being bathed. Both Mathilde and Henriette seem pleased. The baby looks so tiny, so red, and he keeps crying.

"Is he all right? Is something wrong?" Louise asks, her voice shaking.

"But of course—he's perfect, everything is fine," Mathilde says. She wraps the baby in a thick, soft blanket and brings him to Louise to hold for the first time. Louise smiles as she looks down at the tiny head, covered with fine, downy hair, its color similar to that of someone else she holds dear. She looks up suddenly.

"Jean? Is he . . . ?" Her question trails off.

"He's right outside. Mathilde chased him out after he stepped on her foot," Henriette laughingly explains.

"Jean, you can come back in now," she calls out. "Louise wants to see you."

"Ah, good! I want to see her, too," his voice booms back from the corridor.

"Thank you," Louise says to her aunt and Mathilde. "Go and get a cup of tea. I'll be just fine with Jean."

Jean's head peeks in as the door opens. At his questioning look, Mathilde nods and motions him back in.

"Just for a little while—she'll need to rest soon," she whispers in passing.

He practically runs over Mathilde again but then pauses at the door. He seems suspended in motion. There, in the soft yellow light, is Louise, damp hair clinging to the sides of her face, looking down at the child in her arms. Their child. He feels a chill down his spine and an amazed sense of awe, as if he'd never considered before what it was to create a life. He walks slowly, almost solemnly to her side.

"Isn't he beautiful?" she exclaims.

"The most beautiful thing I've ever seen. Have you decided on his name yet?" he asks, thinking *beautiful* seems too small a word to describe something so incredible.

"I like the name René, after our friend who first introduced us. Yes, René it is," she replies with a contented smile. "There, Jean, I have chosen the first name. Now, it's your turn."

Jean reaches out a hand cautiously and strokes the baby's tiny head, running his fingers, feather-soft, over the silky hair to the tiny ear, then around the cherub-like chin.

"Very well, let's see, hmmm . . . Well, his chin reminds me of both my brother and Papa. I suppose we could use either Pierre or Henri."

"Why not both? Three for the price of two, we can include your brother and your father and you, Jean *Henri* Gérard Armand Matisse," she suggests.

"Wait, how about Louis after your own name, my darling?"

"We'll use them all," she replied, giggling like a young schoolgirl.

Then she looks down at the little sleeping bundle and whispers, "René Pierre Louis Henri."

"René Pierre Louis Henri. So be it," concludes Jean.

He edges over a bit closer and moves his hand from the child to the woman, stroking her head and hair, then sits on the edge of the bed and puts an arm around her. His eyes wander back to this little miracle in her arms.

"Welcome to the world, my son," he whispers.

Louise nestles in, her child in her arms, her lover's arms around her. At this moment, she thinks that life is complete for her—she has never been so content.

A head peeks around the corner. It is Henriette. "Jean, I think it's time. . . "

Louise interrupts her aunt before she has a chance to finish.

"No, let him stay just a little while longer," Louise implores. She leans further into him, feeling his warmth surrounding her and their son. So perfect. Everything is so perfect.

As she drifts off to sleep, her sense of contentment is suddenly intruded upon as Mathilde enters, saying something important.

JEANNE IS SHAKING ME GENTLY. "Honey, wake up."

"What's the matter?" I ask groggily, somewhere between sleep and wakefulness.

"You were shouting in your sleep," Jeanne says.

I slowly get my bearings, and my mind clears. *How strange. I was dreaming about the day I was born.*

Why would I be thinking about my birth now? Jeanne holds me, and I tell her exactly what I just experienced. I feel relieved to no longer be alone, to have someone to be able to share not only my dreams with but my nightmares as well. Someone who cares for and comforts me.

As much as I try to forget the dream, it revisits me in fleeting moments. *René Pierre Louis Henri.* The names my mother and father gave me. When I was young, they would often tell me the story of my names at bedtime. They are beautiful names, carefully chosen after people they love.

How many times have I looked in the mirror and seen Jean Matisse's reflection? Ever since I was twelve, I've struggled with the question— René Pierre Louis Henri *who?* I go out for a walk on the beach and stay out for quite a while, trying to put my head in order.

Apart from the sounds of the surf and the gulls, everything is serene. Above me, Jupiter is a sparkling diamond, and my old friend, the magnificent Orion, is there. I'll have to introduce this extraordinary constellation to the grandkids, just like my father introduced the hunter with the starry belt to me when I was young. The deep, dark blue-green of the firmament is incredibly beautiful, just like the color of Jeanne's eyes.

The sky tells me, *Be true to yourself. What are you afraid of? Scandal? So what?*

I decide then and there that I am going to reclaim the name of the only father I have ever known and loved—Jean Matisse.

Would I do it if my name wasn't famous? Yes.

It is time to recover my identity. It is not too late for the truth. The time has come to be the man I am: René Pierre Louis Henri Matisse.

TWO NIGHTS LATER, when Jeanne and I walk on the beach, I have come to a decision. "Jeanne, I am going to take back my true family name. It's not about money or prestige or ego. I want to die with my family name, belonging to the only family I ever knew. It is as simple as that."

"Pierre, I will help you in whatever way I can. How do we start?" she asks.

The most time-consuming part is tracking down my early school records from France that will verify my given names. Packages come in over a period of months with different papers, and each time they arrive, I read them over several times. I have mixed emotions throughout this whole process because I am reconnecting with the family I had lost. There are moments of wonder and moments of grief. When I receive the copy of my school record from Lycée Michelet Vanves, I pull it out and stop. *It's Maman's handwriting.* I recognize it clearly. I recall when she and Tata had made the decision to send me to that school, and now they are helping me make the decision to take back my name. I imagine them smiling and nodding their approval.

When all of the necessary information arrives, I petition the US court for my name to be changed, and once the documentation is verified, I legally change my naturalization papers. Those records are then sent to Canada and France for my name to be changed to Matisse in all existing records, since I receive pensions from both of those countries. Slowly, the Leroy name, a weight I've carried all these years, disappears.

Jeanne knows that this is a great burden off my shoulders, but it isn't the only pain I have been carrying in my heart for all this time. I have not seen my four children for thirty years, and I have no idea how to fix that or where to find them. Jeanne gets to work again, contacting each one of them on my behalf.

IN 1998 JEANNE AND I drive to New England for a family reunion with my oldest son, Patrick. It is early evening when we arrive at his home, and the man who answers the door is about the same age as Jean Matisse was when I bid him good-bye for the last time—fifty years ago. Of course, my eyes are full of tears when I look at the man standing in front of me in the doorway, but this doesn't prevent me from seeing him clearly.

Who is standing there in front of me, tall and strong, but Jean Matisse, my father! I quickly come to my senses. No, it's my son Patrick, who has a

NOM et PRÉNOMS : *Matisse Pierre, René, Louis, Henri,*

Qualité : *EL*　　　　　　　　　n°

Date et lieu de naissance : *1er Février 1928 – Paris*

Adresse des parents : *M.- 86, Av. de Clamart Issy (S.)*

Profession : *Décorateur*

Correspondants :

Observations :

Entrée :	Sortie :
20 Janvier 1939	*13 JUIL 1939*

Mich 3441 18-10 37 5.000

193 8 –193 9	193 –193	193 –193	193 –194	194 –194
8e 2				
194 –194	194 –194	194 –194	194 –194	194 –194

CERTIFIE CONFORME

A L'ORIGINAL

Le Proviseur du

Lycée Michelet - 92170 VANVES

2 3 JUIN 1997

LYCÉE MICHELET
LE PROVISEUR
92170 VANVES

The school record with my name at the top in Maman's handwriting

LYCÉE MICHELET
5, rue Jullien
92170 VANVES
Tél : 46 42 61 50

striking resemblance to my father. I think I am seeing a ghost. My whole body begins to shake as I stand there, speechless. When I find my tongue, my first words to Pat are "You look so much like your grandfather." I can hardly believe this is my son, my Pat. The last time I saw him he was eighteen. As we hug each other tightly, Pat says, "Hi, Dad. I'm glad that you're here. I've been waiting for this day for a long time."

"You look so much like your grandfather," I repeat over and over, without thinking. I can't help myself. "You look so much like my father, your grandfather, it's uncanny."

The next day, I'm still saying it. I say it so many times during the week that Pat and his wife, Polly, and their kids—Pat, Danny, and Lindsay—crack up every time the words come out of my mouth. After this wonderful reunion with Patrick, Jeanne and I head to Maine to see Peter, my younger son, with his wife, Karen, and their two boys, Peter and Tyler. I also see my two daughters, Louise and Nellie, during the trip. On our way back to Florida, I can't help thinking, *God is so good.* I thank Him that I have some of my family back again, and my heart is filled to overflowing.

33

REVELATIONS

Three things will last forever—faith, hope, and
love—and the greatest of these is love.

1 CORINTHIANS 13:13, NLT

Success is not final, failure is not fatal: it is
the courage to continue that counts.

WINSTON CHURCHILL

I'M THINKING ABOUT PAPA. I saw him again this morning when I looked
in the mirror. What would he say or do right now if he were here? What
would he tell me? I have a pretty good idea. He would look at me as if
I were a boy again, smile encouragingly, and give me a big bear hug. Then
he would pull back to look in my eyes and say, "My boy, do things all the
way or don't bother doing them. Period."

I'm nearly ninety years old now—it seems impossible that this adventurous spirit I got from Papa continues to course through me. I am just
an old dreamer with a young heart.

As a child I was surrounded by creative family members and friends, some whose masterpieces now hang in museums all over the world. When I took back my family's name, I was freed to be myself—the son of Jean Matisse, the grandson of Henri Matisse, and an artist in my own right. I have been creating and exploring art through numerous mediums all my life and exhibiting my work for more than two decades across the United States and abroad. I take advantage of every opportunity to encourage children and adults to fall in love with art, especially through hands-on workshops. Sharing my passion for art is important. We must all support art education as a part of the curriculum at every level and in every form of education.

But as passionate as I am about art and as proud as I am of my family identity, I now realize that I spent a majority of my lifetime seeking someone else without actually knowing it. Someone who alone holds the missing piece that makes me whole.

I never went to church as a child. And yet, because I spent so much time outside when I was young, I did have a sense of God as the Creator. I can't say where that idea came from, except I always wondered, *How else could all of the beautiful, intricately designed and obviously engineered things on earth and in the universe have gotten here?*

During the war, it was easier to believe in the devil than in God because the devil was all around, doing his work right before our eyes. Where was God during that time? To me, God was busy doing Big Things, like fighting the Nazis in different ways and taking care of people who were injured or sick.

I wasn't a Big Thing, so I didn't really consider He had the time or the inclination to watch over me. I did follow our chauffeur Monsieur Jacques's advice about how to pray: "Always say thank you, no matter the answer." But otherwise, I didn't want to concern God with trivial things.

Still I did pray to God about the truly Big Things in my own life— such as when I needed courage to keep Monsieur Effel's dinghy afloat during the torrential storm and when I prayed for Madame Schmied as she rode off on her bicycle for Paris with those suitcases of food for her husband and child. These pleas for protection seemed right and just.

After my third marriage disintegrated, I didn't feel like I could ask God for another wife because I had already failed in three marriages.

I considered that a trivial request, like someone who is in a line of wounded people and has only a small cut while so many others are seriously bleeding.

And yet, God brought Jeanne and me together. When we got married, Jeanne made no secret that she was going to pray for me every day, that I would know God personally. She prayed for my health and well-being, and that I might honor God with my art through the talents He has given me. Jeanne talks to God like He is a real person sitting there with her, conversing with Him lovingly, just like she does with me. She says that even though God already knows every detail of our lives, He enjoys our company and He wants our prayers to be specific.

Having Jeanne's love and seeing myself through her heart has allowed me to view myself and others differently. I have certainly developed more patience—actually, we both have.

IN DECEMBER 2009, I was on a walk, trying to think of what to give Jeanne for Christmas. And then an idea came to me—I would illustrate a Bible! I was eager to get under way, so when I got home, I told Jeanne my idea and then asked, "Where do you think I should start?"

"Start at the beginning. God is the first and ultimate artist—start with Genesis," she replied.

First, I did my research. I pored over the first chapters of Genesis in the Bible that Jeanne gave me on our first wedding anniversary. I read and reread the description of the Creation story with my artist's heart open.

As I read, I began to have a more intimate relationship with God. It went beyond what I had known of Him during the quiet times in nature when I gazed at awe-inspiring, colorful panoramas on earth and the spectacular images in the night skies, or even the complex living organisms one can only see through a microscope.

Soon I had my story line and set out to create it in a cutout medium. As I began to draw each pattern, I was amazed when additions to my original planned images came to my mind's eye. I understood where the inspiration was coming from—God was leading and I was more than happy to follow. *He's a genius!* God is truly the Divine Creator and I am blessed to be allowed to retell this story.

God began putting images before my inner eyes rather than whispering in my ear. I began the project at Christmas, and I showed each piece to Jeanne as I finished it.

By early 2010, I was done. I took the eight pieces, laid them all out, and went through the story with Jeanne.

"They're wonderful," Jeanne said. "What is the next story you are going to do?"

"I don't know yet," I replied.

I had other projects under way, but in late December 2010, I went back to the Genesis suite and finished the last image—the seventh day—my interpretation of God resting. After being worshiped in church in the morning, God is on His boat *Sunday* fishing for lost souls. The water is full of them.

NEXT CAME ANOTHER God-inspired series of drawings called *The Gift* in early 2011. Unlike the process I used for *Genesis*, where I read the story and then created the art, the visions came first and I watched the story—God's heart tales—unfold before my eyes.

The second piece I did for *The Gift*—Jesus' crucifixion—was highly unusual for me because I had never created a sad image before. It also took me longer than usual because as I was creating the image, I was living it. That image of Jesus on the cross with His Father crying for His Son and both of them weeping for all of humanity, became an extremely personal epiphany for me. This helped me understand that Jesus is the key that opens the door to my true identity.

I finally understood that God and Christ had made this sacrifice for me, for my freedom—the gift of grace and the freedom to choose to love Him as He has chosen to love me. I prayed silently to accept Jesus Christ as my Savior and then later, when I was out for a walk, I prayed out loud. I titled the art "The Cost of Freedom."

The Gift is the story of a father and a son. Evil and death are overcome by the righteous sacrifice of God the Father and Christ, His innocent Son. Now I begin to understand: I have a heavenly Father who has been and will always be there for me, loving me and walking beside me. In my mind, I have gone from believing that I was insignificant and unworthy, to realizing I am a child of the living God who invites me to come into His loving presence.

As His forgiven—and restored—son, God and I now have Father-son conversations. I will never be alone or fatherless again. My heavenly Father is there sharing His insights, teaching and guiding me every day in every way.

I worked on *The Gift* for about seven months. When an artist is creating, time is irrelevant. You are oblivious to it because while you are creating, time simultaneously stands still and races forward at break-neck speed. You are so absorbed by what you are doing, you can even forget to eat.

Unlike *Genesis*, I did not show Jeanne any of the ten images until they were complete. This was between God and me. And when I finally finished, I was drained.

Art is an intellectual pursuit because you do a lot of thinking before anything happens. I can't help but think about God when I am creating because He is my inspiration. In some ways, I would say that creating art is my way of praying to God, something I have been doing all my life without even knowing that the two are connected and He was always there. Now, God has become personal, and my relationship with Jesus Christ has brought me both total freedom and inspiration.

IN SEPTEMBER 2011, Jeanne told me she wasn't feeling well, but we were scheduled to go on a four-week Mediterranean cruise for art collectors, and I was one of several artists being featured. Jeanne and I didn't have much time to ourselves on that trip. When we returned, she was feeling much worse. Not only was she experiencing great pain from whatever was going on internally, but she had wrenched her back too. It was impossible for her to find a comfortable position when she would lie in bed. During these months, I prayed all the time—for her and with her.

On January 23, 2012, Jeanne was transported to the hospital by ambulance, and they ran numerous tests, but the doctors could not pin-point what was wrong. Jeanne returned home, still in agony.

Although we rarely watch television, it became a diversion from the pain for Jeanne. One day she was channel surfing and landed on an episode of *Duck Dynasty*. The Robertson men were doing something silly that made Jeanne laugh, and she was surprised that at the end of the show the family prayed together around the dinner table.

She told me about the show, and I immediately got all of the episodes available on DVD. The Robertsons' humor, their love of family, and the godly sentiment displayed were perfect medicine for Jeanne and me. We became big fans, tuning in each week to see what kind of trouble Willie and his brothers were going to get into next.

By mid-June our friend Dr. Sam Marathe learned about Jeanne's condition and offered to help. He quickly solved the mystery of what was causing the pain and arranged suitable treatment.

In July, Jeanne had major surgery to remove a very large tumor. No wonder she had been suffering all that time.

AT CHRISTMAS WE WERE counting our blessings, the biggest one being that Jeanne was alive! True to her generous nature, she wanted to send thank-you gifts to the Robertsons and to the a cappella group Straight No Chaser, whose music had also kept her spirits high when she was laid up and in so much pain. She wasn't successful connecting with Straight No Chaser, which made her even more determined to contact the Robertsons.

Jeanne made a call to what she thought was Duck Commander in early 2013, but it turned out to be a different duck call maker. He had worked for Duck Commander before launching his own business so he gave Jeanne the last number he had for them.

"If that doesn't work," he said, "you can call the WFR Church, where Alan Robertson is the pastor. They would be able to help you." After the first number didn't work, Jeanne called the church and finally got the correct number.

Neither Willie nor Korie Robertson was available at Duck Commander, so Jeanne called Korie's father, John Howard. John was away for the week, but after hearing the reason for Jeanne's call, his secretary assured Jeanne that she would make sure John got the message. John called on his first day back, thanks to his secretary sticking a Post-it message to his shirt when he came in and walked past her desk.

When Jeanne asked me to pick up the phone, John kept calling me Mister Matisse, thinking that I wanted to be formally addressed because I was European. But I corrected him.

"No, please, call me Pierre. I am just a redneck from Paris!" (My definition of a redneck is a down-home Southern gentleman, and I think I fit the criteria.) We talked through the logistics of shipping artwork to the family, since I was in thank-you mode for how they had helped Jeanne.

That started our relationships with the entire Robertson and Howard families, which has grown from there. Over the years, there have been lots of conversations, other gifts, and letters between me and Mia, Jase and Missy Robertson's daughter, when she was going through her surgeries for cleft palate. In 2014, we watched and cheered for Willie and Korie's daughter, Sadie, during her amazing *Dancing with the Stars* journey.

Then came 2015, and in one of those interesting arrangements by God, Jeanne and I were invited to Louisiana for a week. I was featured in an episode of the show, giving an art lesson to members of the family and joining in other activities on the set. One night, Jeanne and I were at Willie and Korie's house for dinner with the extended Robertson family. I felt right at home among them, perhaps because of my own past adventures with colorful characters, combined with the family's welcoming Southern hospitality.

I enjoyed getting to know the adults, but my favorite part was interacting with all the kids. There wasn't time to go duck hunting on this trip, but I loved Willie's home cooking.

After dinner, Willie, John, and I were having a great conversation. Our discussion rolled around to God, Jesus Christ, and the meaning of baptism, and Willie asked me *the* question.

"Do you believe in Jesus Christ as your Savior?"

"I do," I replied.

"Have you ever been baptized?" was Willie's next question. Then, with Willie and John's encouragement, I took this step of faith. I was among fellow rednecks, so it had to be a redneck baptism right then and there. But where should we have it? We first headed to John's house to use the outdoor pool, but it was late February, and the water was too cold. So we moved the baptism inside to the master bathroom of John and his wife, Chrys.

While the bathtub was filling with water, there were some awkward moments as I was led to a room and given someone else's clothing to change into. Jeanne couldn't stop smiling—her prayers for all of our years together were being answered before her eyes.

My heart was racing as I realized that my personal desire to be baptized was about to happen. Soon, I would be a card-carrying Christian.

As I put my foot in the bathtub, I quickly pulled it out, saying, "I thought I was going to get baptized, not boiled!" Everyone burst out laughing, but I wasn't kidding. The bathwater was scalding hot. Korie and Chrys quickly solved this, and once the water was cooled down, I got into the bathtub. Willie knelt beside it, and he put his hands behind my back to support me.

"I am going to back you down into the water. Okay?" Willie said.

Then he asked, "So you believe in Jesus Christ?"

"Yes, I do," I confirmed.

"Right now, we are going to symbolize this by baptizing you in this bathtub to show that all your sins have been washed away. You will come up a new Matisse! All right?"

Willie proceeded with the baptism, and at the end he brought me up out of the water and said, "There you go."

"*Fantastique!*" I said. "All right!"

I went underneath the water and in that action professed Jesus Christ as my Savior. I came up out of the water, amid lots of hoorays and clapping, already knowing in my heart and soul what Willie was confirming, "Your sins are forgiven. You are a new Matisse!" I'm a new creation.

I understand creations. Et voilà. This is a new beginning.

It took a while for me to realize the actual difference this love, forgiveness, and grace are making in my life. The new acceptance and closeness I experience with God, Jeanne, and other Christians has been amazing. Finally, I was ready to write to Willie to thank him and John for encouraging and facilitating my baptism.

Fall 2015

Dear Willie,

I'm sorry that it took me so long to write and thank you for my baptism. It has taken me all this time to realize the profound meaning that I am a truly baptized, completed Christian.

I agree with you about infant baptism. I always thought that baptizing a baby was a little bit odd. A baby is not aware of what is happening, doesn't make a conscious choice to do it, or even remember that he has been baptized. In my opinion, it makes perfect sense to wait until you are old enough to make this choice to accept Christ as an acknowledgment of your acceptance of God's and Christ's sacrifice and your pledge to love and serve them forever. Infant baptism seems more like a dedication done by the parents, which I totally agree with.

Jeanne and I will never forget this experience as well as the wonderful time we spent with your loving family.

In these last twenty years, I have experienced a growing relationship with God, as He reached out to me and, in His grace, He drew me closer to Him. It has been an amazing journey that I would like to share with you and Korie someday.

Willie, first and foremost, I would like to thank you for your willingness to be used by God in this important, life-changing step of my spiritual union with God.

You see, the key for me is Creation—in every sense of the word.

Through the process, I came to a clear realization of God's knowledge, His love, and His plan, which is offered to all of us— His desire to have a relationship with His children.

My parents were, if somewhat unconventional, good, loving parents. The duty of parents is to do their best, whatever that best is. All parents do their best, and honestly so did I. Yet still, I wish I would have done better.

Today as I write this, I know what my parents were missing—a personal relationship with God. Knowing that when we confess our sins, we are forgiven and reconciled to God, allows us to try to live as God would have us do. The very knowledge that God your Father is always there and available is the greatest gift any earthly father could give his child.

Willie, if only we could give the gift of this knowledge to every child and lost adult in the entire world.

Now I have THE TRUTH—that I have always had a heavenly Father and a heavenly family: God the Father, my Father, and Christ the Son, my Savior, who paid the price for my freedom from sin. And the Holy Spirit to guide me.

Now as I create, I do so with the knowledge that creating is a part of my spiritual DNA.

My kids are healthy, all working, honest citizens. They are wonderful parents with wonderful kids, some of whom are talented artists and musicians. They are all doing much better than I did. Thank You, God, I am so grateful for that.

I think a lot about these things as I walk on the beach or create a new piece of art.

I know I am a child of the living God. Now I am always in communication with my Creator, both night and day. I am totally sold out to God!

Jeanne and I continue to have big dreams and plans for the future. We would love to see the launch of a museum/school, a place where people would be given opportunities to connect with their Creator as they explore the boundless creativity inside them. Dreams never end, and some come true, according to His perfect will and timing! We live to serve Him and His kingdom. To God be the glory.

New adventures are just beginning.

The best is yet to come . . .

Yours in Christ,
Pierre H. Matisse

I AM THANKFUL for my heavenly Father because as I am getting to know Him more, I can see how God leads by love and teaches by example. These two characteristics were true of Papa as well.

Love is so important; you never can say *I love you* enough. Papa taught me about love by example. I turned to God after I truly understood a father's love for his child.

This was who I had really been searching for all along—my eternal Father, who shows His love to me in unique ways that resonate with my creative mind and heart.

A FEW MORNINGS after I write the first draft of the letter to Willie, I take a walk on the beach, reflecting on Mark 16:15-16: "And then [Jesus] told them, 'Go into all the world and preach the Good News to everyone. Anyone who believes and is baptized will be saved.'" Et voilà. I have a clear mandate from my Master and my future is assured.

For the last few months, I have been poring over old photos of my mother's ceramics, the ones my grandfather had sketched and think about my latest art project. I have decided to do my own rendition of those images, paying tribute to Maman and Grandfather in my own artistic way.

Though deep in thought, I hear something. I turn, and there is Grandfather Matisse in his wheelchair, gliding along on the beach. He hasn't visited me in a dream since I lived in Canada more than fifty years ago.

"Nice morning for a walk on the beach, wouldn't you say, Pierre?" he says, catching up with me.

I shake my head, attempting to clear my mind of this vision, but he is still there. Why am I finding this so hard to believe? Maybe because I had decided that the long-ago dream was the result of my back pain, my desperation, and my longing for my family.

"Yes," I reply.

He moves effortlessly beside me. "Well, I totally approve of your new location," he says, shading his eyes with his hand. "These warm, sunshine-laden skies are a paradise for a painter."

"I couldn't agree with you more," I answer, wondering if I am really talking to myself.

"I am glad to see you kept with it," he says, smiling, "although we artists really have no choice. Your work is coming along nicely."

"There is something I've always wanted to ask you," I say. "Remember the color lesson you gave me?"

"What color lesson?" he asks.

"When Maman sent me to your studio in Nice."

"Ah, yes. Go ahead."

"You confiscated all my paints, except for four tubes. What did you do with all those tubes of paint?"

"I sent them to Picasso as a gift," he says, chuckling.

We stop for a minute and silently gaze at the rolling surf.

"I understand you have a new project planned," Grandfather says. "Since I created the original sketches, I thought I might give you a few insights."

Then—poof—he is gone. Maybe this new project is bringing back both good and bad memories for me, and this is my mind's way of dealing with it, or maybe I've gotten too much sun.

Later that morning, I head into my studio. My head, my hand, and my heart are ready to do battle with the charcoal and create the drawings. I put on Gershwin, and the jazz notes, played by my pianist friend Rio Clemente, fill the room.

As the image begins to take shape, I hear, "Bravo! Now you've got it. Capture the essence, but make it your own." Grandfather is back.

A handsome mustached man in a top hat is smiling on the page, with an elegant lady on his arm. They are probably going to a grand ball.

"Very nice." Grandfather nods in approval.

Next, I draw a distinguished bearded gentleman on his way to the same party with his charming lady, both impeccably dressed. Number two is done.

As I set up for the third drawing, Grandfather comes closer for a better view. A statuesque lady holding two lamps is on her way to welcome her husband at the door as he arrives home. I'll set them aside and give them some time alone.

Soon three beautiful debutantes, dressed in turn-of-the-century finery, are peeking over their fans. Grandfather takes this drawing from me and gazes at it pensively, then places it with the others.

"Your mother was a true artist," he said.

On to drawing five.

Standing by a charming balcony, an enchanting lady is dreaming about love. There is a clock on the wall beneath her that reads nine o'clock sharp. Maybe she is waiting for her suitor to arrive. She will have to wait with the others as I set her aside.

Aha, a lovely lady is fanning herself in front of me. She is wearing a long dress with crinolines that add volume to the skirt, which is decorated with hearts. There are two beaux courting her—which one will she choose? They both accompany her to the stack of finished drawings.

"You are moving right along this morning," Grandfather remarks, adding, "Simple—with no hesitation."

Only one more character left. I've saved him for last because I feel a kinship to him these days.

A harlequin, full of *joie de vivre*, is dancing in front of me. This exuberant little fellow obviously likes jazz. Is he going to a masquerade ball? As he rushes away, he waves his scarf at me. The three debutantes are waiting for him, and he must go.

"Well done," I seem to hear the harlequin call out.

"Well done," Grandfather echoes him.

I am finished.

Grandfather has a twinkle in his eye and says with a good-natured chuckle, "Haven't you forgotten something, Pierre?"

"I only planned seven pieces in the suite."

He gives me a knowing smile. Of course. I pick up the charcoal and sign each piece *Pierre Henri Matisse*. My tribute to Maman and my grandfather is complete. (You can see photos of these seven drawings when you click on "Tribute" at www.themissingmatisse.com.)

Grandfather Matisse nods, then says, "So now you know the secret to the source of your inspiration. God is truly the source of all divine creative inspiration, something I learned late in life when I began designing the Vence Chapel."

Smiling, he continues, "That project was my greatest joy. It allowed me to work and serve God. Imagine the privilege of working with the heavenly Master. What a wonderment! What joy." And then he fades away.

A week later, I start sketching spontaneously, without any particular direction. Suddenly, I have an unexpected visitor on my page—a warrior. An angel warrior, the archangel Michael. Just like it happened with *The Gift*, an image takes shape before the story.

Will there be more angels to come? Possibly. Certain pieces are divinely inspired, and others are not, and I understand the difference. Every day I work as an artist, but I only take commission work from God.

In some ways, this book may be considered one of those commissions from Him. For years, I have felt inspired to write my story. I knew I needed to fill in the details of my life for posterity. There have been moments when it has been painful to revisit the haunting memories, while at other times I have been liberated as I put down the words.

As I've said, Jean Matisse, the only father I've ever known, taught me about love by example. Because of that, I've chosen to continue my fight to honor his memory and the love he gave me by whatever means I have available to me. I am still hopeful that a DNA test will prove whether or not he is my biological father.

No matter what the evidence may reveal, I have a heavenly Father and an assurance deep in my soul of my spiritual DNA.

The best is yet to come . . .

Acknowledgments

THIS MEMOIR has been a journey back in time, and I would like to thank all those who have helped along the way to make it possible:

Eddie Adams ✳ Dr. Thomas Beaver ✳ Susan Stauffer Beckman
Larry Freirich ✳ Laura Holland ✳ Cody Holland
John and Chrys Howard ✳ Scott and Sharon Leahy
Daniel Leroy ✳ Willie and Korie Robertson
Bernie Roseaur ✳ Linda Spagnoli ✳ Judie Stack.
And Shirley Rose, our la femme à tout faire.

And for our team of new friends at Tyndale House Publishers:

Jan Long Harris ✳ Bonne Steffen ✳ Dean Renninger
Sharon Leavitt ✳ Jillian Schlossberg ✳ Nancy Clausen
Cassidy Gage ✳ Margie Watterson ✳ Sarah Kelley

"The labourer is worthy of his reward."
I TIMOTHY 5:18, KJV

Endnotes

xi **My father, Jean Matisse, is a sculptor** Jean Matisse was the oldest son of Henri Matisse. He followed his father's artistic lead by becoming a sculptor, although he never achieved the acclaim that Grandfather Matisse did. During World War II, he was an active participant in the French resistance against the Nazis and, as you've read, included me on some of those adventures.

xi **my mother, Louise Milhau Matisse** My mother was a painter, a ceramist, and decorator who graduated from the École Nationale Supérieure des Beaux-Arts in Paris, and from a very young age I assisted her in whatever way I could. She was always in demand, busy with commissioned work, even during the war.

xii **my grandfather—Henri Matisse—the master of color** The artist I knew as my grandfather was born to a seed merchant, but came from a long line of weavers who had been creating textiles for generations. After studying law, Grandfather, at age twenty, took up painting when his mother gave him a box of colors to pass the time during a long convalescence from appendicitis. He gave up law and moved to Paris to take up art full time. Grandfather's breakthrough as an artist came during the summers of 1904–1905, when he was staying and painting on the French Riviera, where the light compelled him to capture its intensity on the canvas with bright, bold colors that were emotionally explosive to the eyes. At Paris's fall salon in 1905, which showcased new artists, Grandfather's paintings were shocking, and he was labeled a *fauve* (wild beast). The sensationalism of fauvism lasted only a few years, and it didn't deter Grandfather from continuing to make a lasting statement with his creations. His body of work over a half-century included paintings, sculptures, drawings, lithographs, and cutouts, among other pieces.

6 **a family friend Monsieur Pablo Picasso** Grandfather Matisse first met Spanish-born artist Pablo Picasso in 1906 in Gertrude Stein's salon in Paris, and they became lifelong friends and artistic rivals. They exchanged art and inspired one another. One word that aptly describes Picasso is bohemian, albeit, he was a famous and prolific one when it came to producing art. Because of his fame, Picasso was untouchable to the Nazis even after they occupied France, and he remained in Paris while other artists fled. He was the co creator of cubism with Georges Braque, but Picasso never stopped experimenting, putting his own stylistic flair on anything—and everything—he tried.

8 **sculptor Aristide Maillol** Maillol began his career as a painter and tapestry designer, but when the intricate work of tapestry-making threatened his eyesight, he turned exclusively to sculpture. In his creations, Maillol balanced the real, human characteristics of his models with the eternal, stylized forms of Greek and Roman sculpture.

20 **howitzer, Big Bertha** Although most Parisians thought it was Big Bertha that was bombing the city during World War I, this famous Krupp gun's fixed target was Belgium. The long-range siege gun used against the City of Light was another Krupp weapon—the Paris Gun. It was capable of hurling a 210-pound shell up to eighty-one miles with an altitude of more than twenty-five miles, the first human-made object to reach the stratosphere.

28 *Monsieur Picasso's mural Guernica* Guernica is a town in the Basque area of Spain, which during the Spanish Civil War, was one of the bastions of the Republican-resistance movement against the Nationalists led by General Francisco Franco. On April 26, 1937, German warplanes bombed Guernica for about two hours. Hitler supported Franco and was using the conflict in Spain to test new weapons. Picasso had already been commissioned by the Spanish Republican government to do a piece for the 1937 Paris Exposition. When he learned what had happened to Guernica, he scrapped his original idea and in less than a month finished the antiwar mural. When the Nazis occupied France, they visited Picasso to take an inventory of his "degenerate" art. The Boche officer saw the huge mural and said, "You did that?" to which the artist answered, "No, you did."

39 *"He is Pierre Matisse, like me?"* My uncle Pierre, the younger son of Grandfather Matisse, started out as a painter but embarked on a new career in his early twenties as an art dealer in New York City. Once established, Pierre not only showcased his father's work and the works of family friends such as Picasso and Braque among many others, but also introduced Americans to prominent artists such as Joan Miró, Alberto Giacometti, Balthus, and Jean Dubuffet.

45 *People call this la drôle de guerre or the Funny War.* The English called it the Phony War, a seven-month period of time from September 1939 to April 1940. France and Great Britain had declared war against Germany on September 3, 1939, after Adolf Hitler invaded Poland, but no offensive action was taken against the Nazis during these months. In April 1940, Hitler's army occupied Norway and on May 10, invaded Holland, Belgium, and the Netherlands, with France in its crosshairs. That same day, Winston Churchill replaced Neville Chamberlin as England's prime minister, promising his country that they would never surrender to Nazi Germany.

55 *"In 1643, at the Battle of Rocroi during the Thirty Years' War, General Condé"* The general Tata was referring to was Louis II of Bourbon, a twenty-one-year-old duke who would later become the fourth prince of Condé. He led 23,000 men against the Spanish invaders at Rocroi, the first defeat on land of the Spanish army in more than a century.

86 *"Toulouse," Papa says, which means to Grandmother Amélie Matisse.* Amélie Parayre met Grandfather at a wedding in 1897, and even though he had no money of his own, her parents approved of the match, and they married in 1898. Amélie had a gift for designing and making hats for a fashionable clientele and opened her own hat shop a year and a half later with a partner, providing needed income. When Grandfather's work started being noticed, she began having fits of anxiety that took a toll on their marriage over the years, leading to their separation in March 1939.

87 *her inseparable daughter, Marguerite* Marguerite was Grandfather's daughter by one of his models before he met and married Amélie. Even though Amélie had trouble connecting with her own two sons, she loved Marguerite as her own child.

121 *artist Salvador Dali* Born in the Catalonian region of Spain, Dali became part of the Paris scene in 1929 with a one-man show. He initially was a leader of the surrealist movement, marked by his famous work featuring the melting watches, *The Persistence of Memory.* When the Nazis occupied Bordeaux in 1940, Dali and his wife, Gala, escaped to the United States, returning to Spain in 1948.

121 *One painter whose stories I enjoy is Maurice de Vlaminck* Another of the fauvism painters, along with Grandfather and André Derain, Vlaminck was a self-taught artist, who over his lifetime was a musician, actor, racing cyclist, illustrator, and novelist too.

121 *But my favorite family friend is Jean Effel* His real name was François Lejeune, but he went by his *nom de plume* Jean Effel. He was a caricaturist, illustrator, and journalist, celebrated for his illustrated series, *The Creation of the World.*

151 ***The Great and her daughter, Marguerite, will be arrested*** In April 1944, Marguerite Matisse Duthuit was arrested by the Nazis in northwestern France and sent to prison. She had been crisscrossing France by railroad, as a courier, and was picked up in Rennes. After being interrogated and tortured in prison, she was put on board a train headed to a concentration camp in Germany. As luck would have it, an air raid alert caused the train to make an unscheduled stop in open country. The French conductors opened the doors and said to their passengers, "Jump, and run for it!" Marguerite managed to get away, hiding out in the wooded countryside until France was liberated a few months later. Amélie Matisse's resistance activities were primarily done in Paris. Not long after Marguerite's arrest, the Gestapo had taken Marguerite's clothes and cleverly dressed a female Nazi conspirator in them. The imposter also had Marguerite's key to her mother's apartment which, when she let herself in, surprised Amélie and revealed evidence of her work for the underground. She spent six months in prison until Paris was liberated.

331 ***something I learned later in life when I began designing the Vence Chapel*** In 1941, Grandfather had undergone serious surgery and moved to Vence on the French Riviera from 1943 to 1949, during which time he employed a young nurse, Monique Bourgeois, who would later become a Dominican nun. Bourgeois had confided to Grandfather her wish to decorate a prayer room in their convent. Instead, Grandfather designed an entire chapel, working for four years on every detail involved—from the building, stained glass windows, ceramics, and even the priest's vestment. He considered it his masterpiece. In her book, *Matisse: The Chapel at Vence,* author Marie-Thérèse Pulvenis de Seligny quotes Grandfather during his time living in Vence. "I go every morning to say my prayers, pencil in hand; I stand in front of a pomegranate tree covered in blossom, each flower at a different stage, and I watch their transformation. Not in fact in any spirit of scientific enquiry, but filled with admiration for the work of God. Is this not a way of praying? And I act in such a way (although basically I do nothing myself as it is God who guides my hand) as to make the tenderness of my heart accessible to others."